MONTANA MODERNISTS

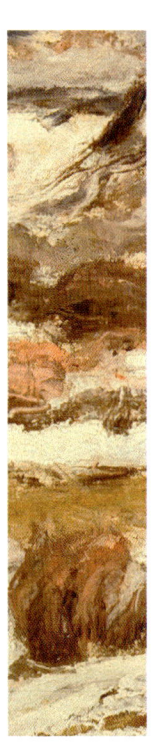
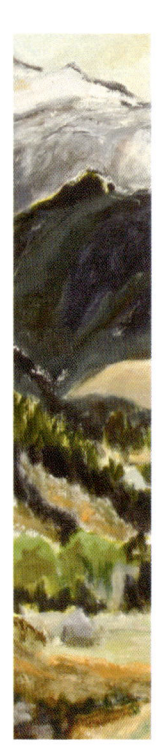
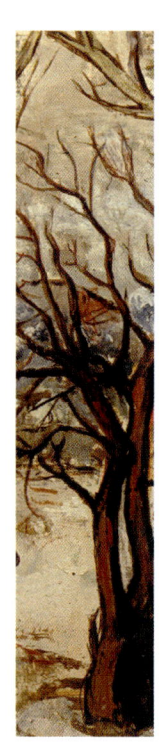
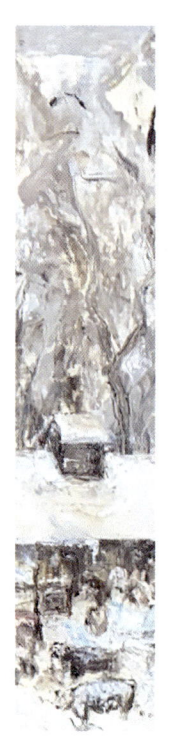
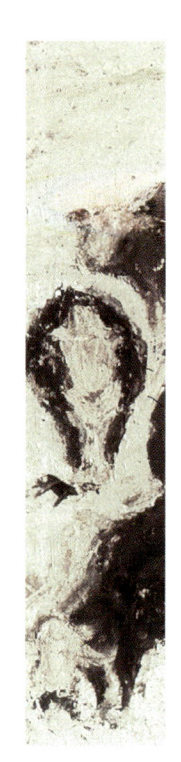
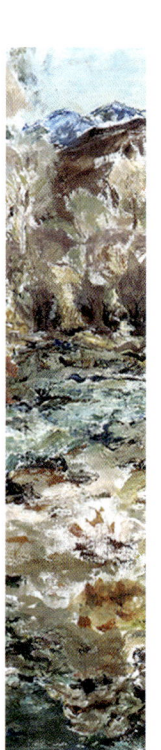

MONTANA MODERNISTS

Shifting Perceptions of Western Art

MICHELE CORRIEL

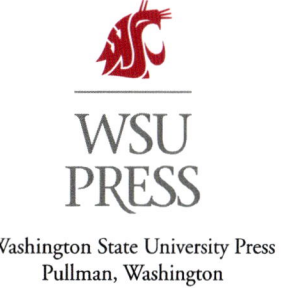

WSU
PRESS

Washington State University Press
Pullman, Washington

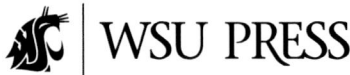

Washington State University Press
PO Box 645910
Pullman, Washington 99164-5910
Phone: 800-354-7360
Email: wsupress@wsu.edu
Website: wsupress.wsu.edu

Library of Congress Cataloging-in-Publication Data

Names: Corriel, Michele, author.
Title: Montana modernists : shifting perceptions of Western art / Michele
  Corriel.
Description: Pullman, Washington : Washington State University Press,
  [2022] | Revision of the author's thesis (doctoral)--Montana State
  University, 2019, under the title: Montana modernists : redefining
  Western art. | Includes bibliographical references and index.
Identifiers: LCCN 2022033511 | ISBN 9780874224191 (paperback)
Subjects: LCSH: Modernism (Art)--Montana. | Art and
  society--Montana--History--20th century. | Artists--Montana.
Classification: LCC N6530.M75 C67 2022 | DDC 709.786--dc23/eng/20220727
LC record available at https://lccn.loc.gov/2022033511

The author gratefully acknowledges Montana State University's College of Art and Architecture for its support of this publication and the invaluable assistance of the faculty and staff who helped along the way.

The Washington State University Pullman campus is located on the homelands of the Niimíipuu (Nez Perce) Tribe and the Palus people. We acknowledge their presence here since time immemorial and recognize their continuing connection to the land, to the water, and to their ancestors. WSU Press is committed to publishing works that foster a deeper understanding of the Pacific Northwest and the contributions of its Native peoples.

On the cover: *June Patterns*, by Gennie DeWeese
Cover design by TG Design.

DEDICATION

This work is dedicated to Terry Karson (1950–2017), whose footsteps I have followed all through this process. He was both a mentor and an inspiration. I only hope to have done his work justice

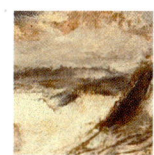

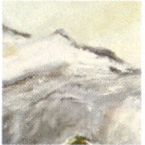

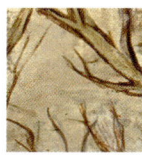

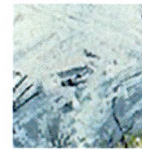

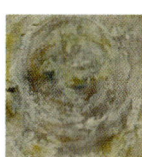

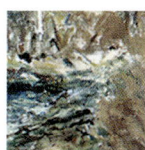

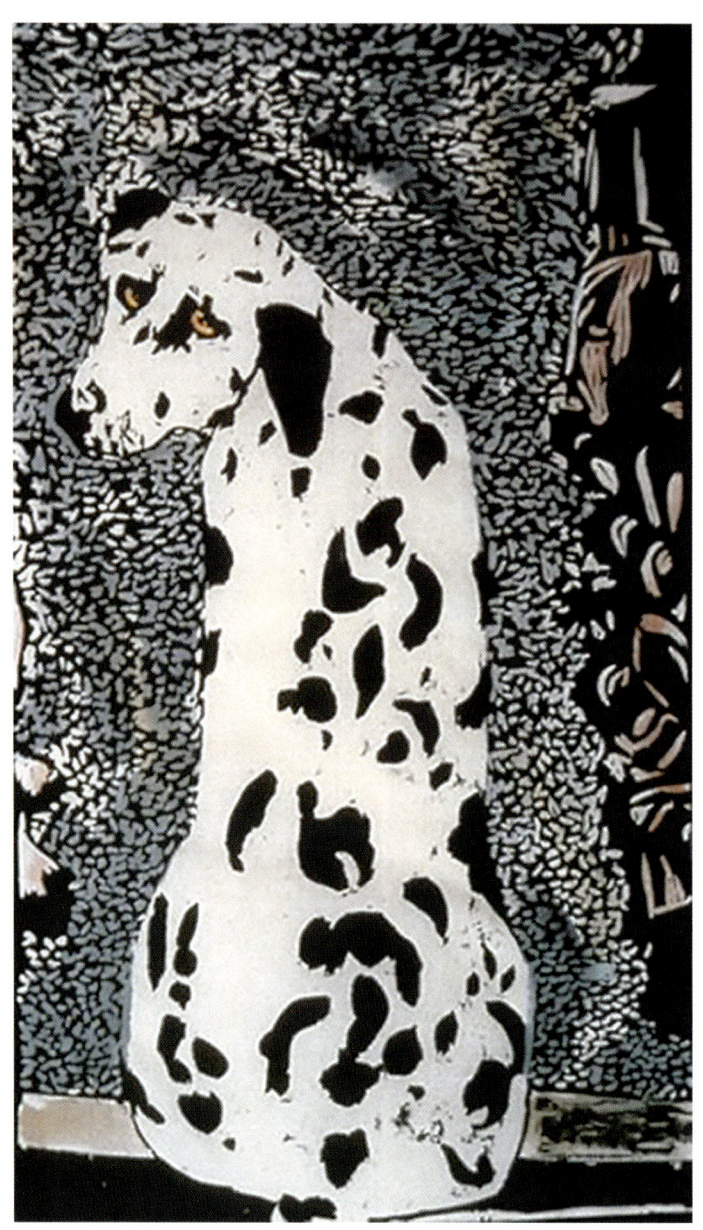

Gennie DeWeese, *Pepper With Doorway*
1994, Woodblock print with watercolor.
31 1/2 x 24 1/2 inches.

CONTENTS

ACKNOWLEDGMENTS   xi
PREFACE   xiii

INTRODUCTION: **MONTANA'S AVANT-GARDE**   1

SECTION ONE: **PLACE**   11
  A Sense of Place: Isabelle Johnson and Bill Stockton   11
  Isabelle and Bill: Working the Land through Their Art   12
  Bill Stockton's Portrayal of Place   28

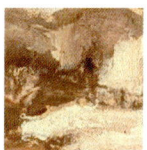

SECTION TWO: **TEACHING/ARTISTIC LINEAGE**   45
  Growing Artists   45
  Educational Lineage   46
  From Bauhaus to Abstraction   47
  Experiencing Art in the Classroom   55
  Frances and Jessie: Changing Perceptions   60
  The Human Gaze   64
  Making It Personal   71
  Frances Senska: From Her Roots and Back Again   73
  Making Precedes Matching   79
  From Bricks to Ceramic Arts: Archie Bray and Other Characters   83

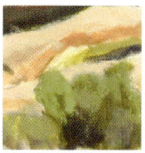

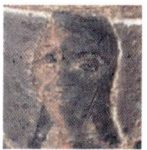

SECTION THREE: **COMMUNITY**   89
  Patronage, Art Movements, and the G.I. Bill   89
  The Democratization of Art   90
  Community: Strength in Numbers   92
  Politics and the Politics of Art   96
  Bob and Gennie   98
  Robert DeWeese: Responsibility Is the Ability to Respond   101
  Gennie DeWeese: I Paint What I See   117

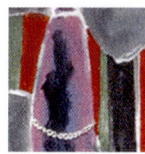

CONCLUSION: **REDEFINING WESTERN ART IN MONTANA**   133

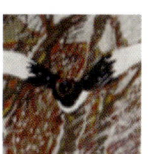

NOTES   139
BIBLIOGRAPHY   149
INDEX   157
ABOUT THE AUTHOR   163

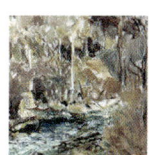

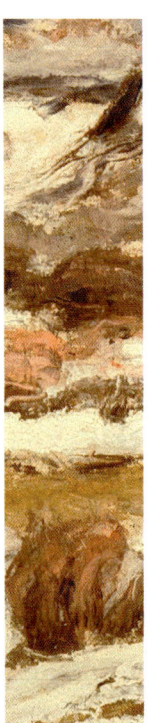
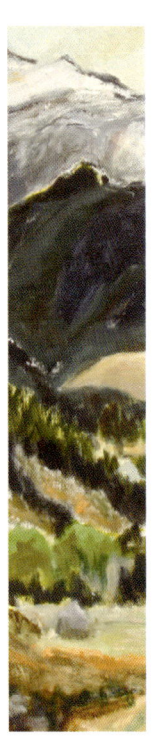
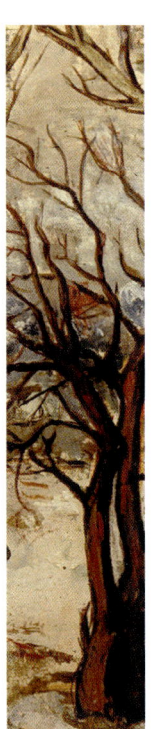
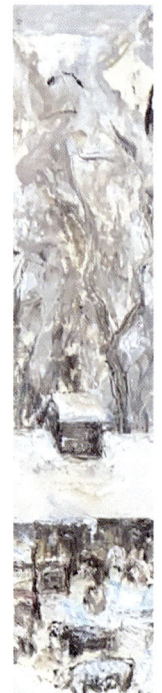
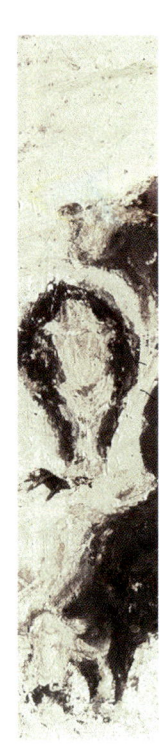
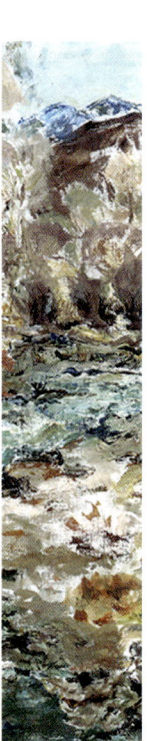

ART WORK

GENNIE DEWEESE

Aniline Dye Brush Drawing	128
Bare Trees	120
Clear Cut	126
Clover Year	122
June Patterns	129
Non-Objective Painting	51
Non-Objective Painting	x
Non-Objective Painting (Choral Composition)	119
Pepper in Doorway	vi
Spring by Karl's Bridge	131
Springtime in the Rockies	125
Winter Morning	130
Winter Willow Grove	121

ROBERT DEWEESE

Between Three Forks and Toston	106
Circus Ties	112
Collages	113
Figure Dancing	104
Flight (Red Boy)	108
Nine Ties, Seven Chains	111
Plains Sunset	114
Portland	105
VFW Studio Wall	109
Western Painting	102
Wolny's Hill (One Cloud)	115

ISABELLE JOHNSON

Autumn on the Stillwater	26
Calves, Winter	24
East Fiddler's Creek	19
Home Ranch	22
Red Willows in Winter Landscape	16
Trees, Winter	20

FRANCES SENSKA

Branch Bottle Weed Pot	78
Chicken Wine Set	76
Hungarian Partridges	60
Ring Necked Bottle	75
Surf Fishers (Pond Farm Vase)	79
YaBaBo Pot	74

BILL STOCKTON

Conversion of St. Paul (Saul on the Road to Damascus)	43
Dusk	39
Faded Roses	36
River Rocks	37
Rock Formations	42
Snow Formation	32
Start of Spring	34
Village in Winter	40

JESSIE WILBER

Birds and Trees	67
Cats in a Garden	66
Huns	62
Huns (on a pond)	68
Magpies in a Snowstorm	73
Owls	69
The Musicians	70
The River (Don't Dam It!)	69

MARGUERITE WILDENHAIN

Tall Footed Vase	81

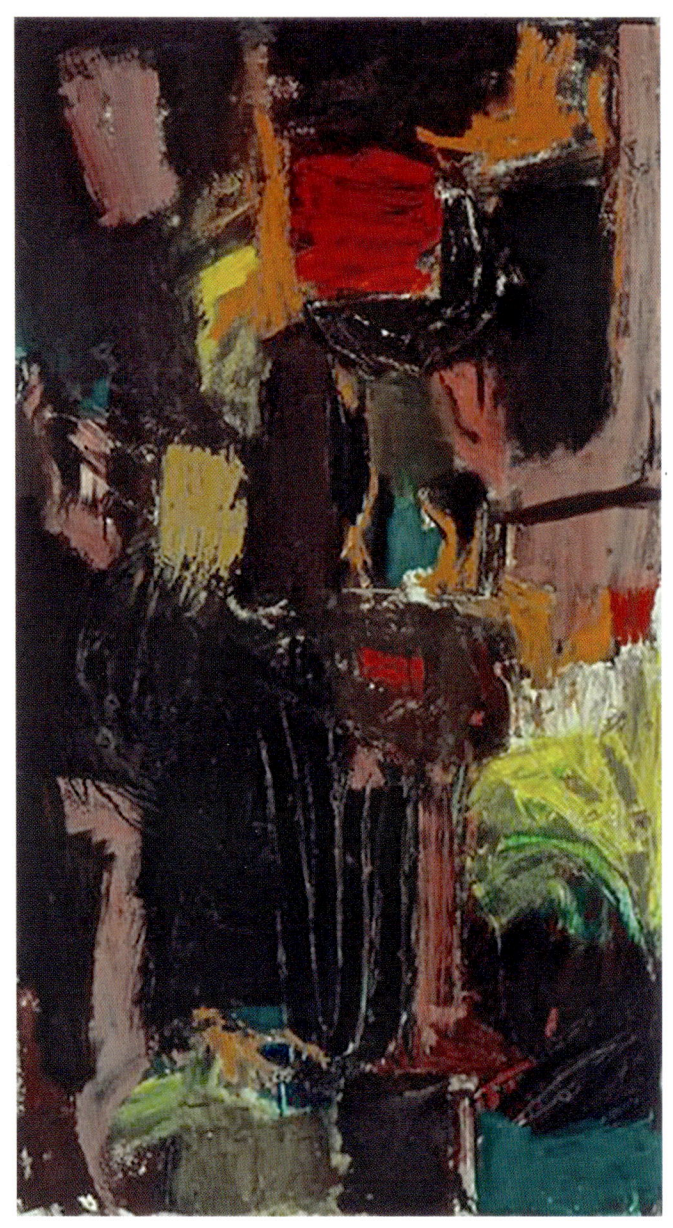

Gennie DeWeese, *Non-Objective Painting*, n.d.
Oil on masonite, 27 x 48 inches.

ACKNOWLEDGEMENTS

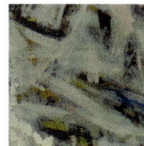

This book started before I wrote the first word. I wish to thank Harvey Hamburgh, who sat with me to talk the idea through; Mary Murphy, who guided my dissertation process; and the many students of these artists who generously took time out of their lives to share their experiences with me. Sara Mast kept me on track, adding insights and considerations. Josh and Tina DeWeese allowed me to go through their parents' papers, rummage through their boxes (and more boxes), and borrow catalogues; above all, they spent hours talking to me about these amazing artists who they knew and loved. It is through these people that I have come to love them as well. In addition, my undying gratitude goes to Gordon McConnell who helped me to navigate this journey.

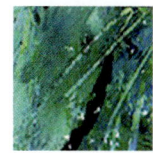

This book would not have been completed without the insight of Washington State University Press editor Linda Bathgate, who understood the historic significance of this work, and the generous help of Montana State University's College of Art and Architecture Dean Dr. Royce Smith, who encouraged me with his belief in this book.

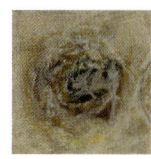

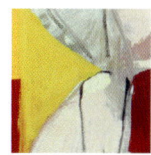

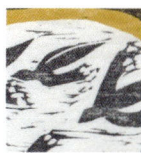

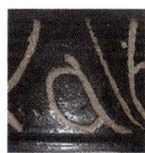

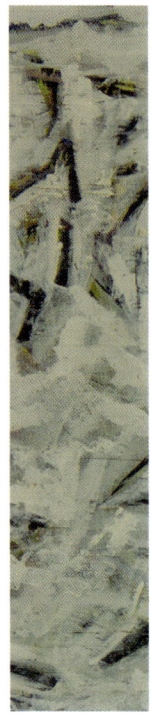

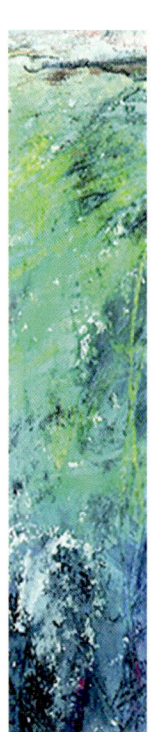
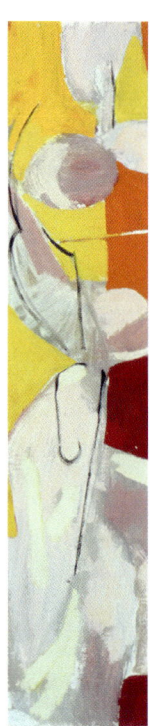
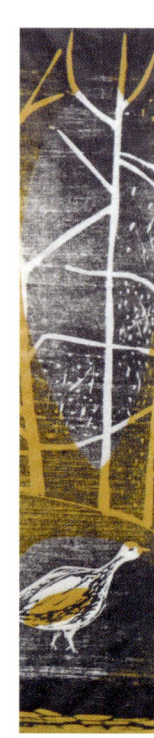
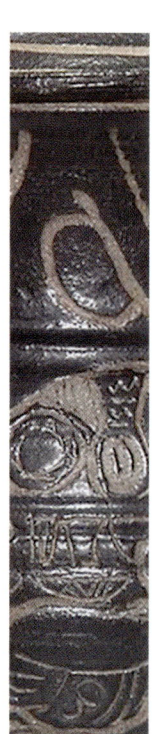

PREFACE

During my more than fifteen years of writing about art in Montana, the same six names came up again and again. Artists of varying aesthetics and disciplines repeatedly spoke of these people as mentors and friends. As I set forth to learn more about them, I discovered the untold story of art in postwar Montana.

Through my research into Isabelle Johnson, Bill Stockton, Jessie Wilber, Frances Senska, Robert DeWeese, and Gennie DeWeese, I developed a very deep, personal connection. Why was I drawn to these artists? Why did their work speak to me so directly? Their visions, which arose from lives lived in Montana, opened a door for me to explore a regional identity different from the usual stereotypes that come to mind when speaking of Montana.

In Wilber's prints of the things she loved—her cats sunning themselves in the garden or a covey of Hungarian partridges scuttling across her yard—I found the same intimate moments I had experienced. Gennie DeWeese's large oil stick landscapes painted in lush colors connected me to the views witnessed many times traveling across the state. In Robert DeWeese's sketches, I felt as if I were sitting in the room with him, seeing the same moments he observed, and my visceral response to his collages sent me back to my afternoons in the MoMA "conversing" with the Dadaists. I had not one bone of ranching in my body, yet Bill Stockton made me feel as if I had

just trudged across a muddy field or fought my way back home through a blizzard. Isabelle Johnson introduced me to her favorite hills and valleys on her Absarokee ranch, and Frances Senska won my heart with her hand-sized ceramic partridges. Through each of their visions, these artists allowed me to see Montana in a new way.

My sincere passion for these six artists and their art is expressed in my descriptions of their work. The interpretations of paintings and pots offered on the following pages are the result of my own research and reflection. I am grateful to each of them for their enduring concepts, which gave birth to what I call "Montana Modernism." Their work continues to give us new ways to see this unique place and its history through their eyes.

BRIEF ARTIST BIOGRAPHIES

ISABELLE JOHNSON (1901–1992): Born and raised on a ranch in Absarokee, Montana, she attended the University of Montana, where she graduated with a degree in history in 1922. She taught high school in Fromberg, Montana, for two years. She then went on to attend Los Angeles County Museum School at the University of Southern California, the Otis Art Institute, and Columbia University where she obtained a master's degree in history. She then enrolled at the Columbia University School of Painting and Sculpture to pursue further graduate work in art. While at Columbia she was selected by the artist

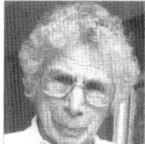
Isabelle Johnson

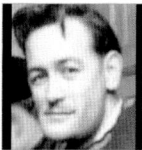
Bill Stockton

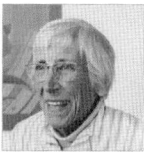
Jessie Wilber

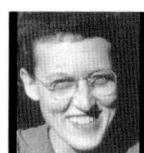
Frances Senska

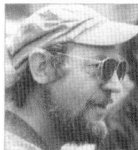
Robert DeWeese

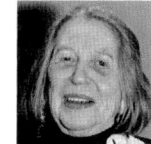
Gennie DeWeese

Henry Varnum Poor in 1946 to participate in the first class of the experimental Skowhegan School of Painting and Sculpture, in Maine. Intermittently, Johnson went back to Montana to teach art at the Billings High School when she needed money for tuition. After she finished her education, she took a year off to go to Europe and visit the works of the masters. Upon her return she taught art at Eastern Montana College from 1949 to 1961. In 1983 she was awarded the Governor's Award for the Arts.

BILL STOCKTON (1921–2002): Born in Winnett, Montana, Stockton moved to the family's ranch at Grass Range in his teens. He joined the army in World War II and was stationed at a hospital just outside of Paris, where he learned about sign painting. After the war he attended the Minneapolis School of Art and then went back to France in 1947 to attend the Academie de la Grande Chaumiere, in Paris. Upon returning to Montana with his French wife, Elvia Cirefice, he lived with her in Billings, but they eventually returned to the ranch in Grass Range. There, he raised sheep (for the most part) and painted. In 2003, a year after his death, he was awarded the Governor's Award for the Arts.

JESSIE SPAULDING WILBER (1912–1989): Born in Whitewater, Wisconsin, Wilber moved frequently as a child. Her family traveled from Illinois to Ohio, and from Oklahoma to Michigan before settling in Boulder, Colorado, when she was eight. She earned a B.A. and an M.A. at Colorado Teachers College, in Greeley, Colorado. She came to Montana State College, Bozeman, in 1941, and, in that same year, was awarded a contract to paint a Post Office mural in Kingman, Kansas. Wilber taught in the art department until 1972. In 1988 she won the Governor's Award for the Arts.

FRANCES SENSKA (1914–2009): Born in Cameroon, Africa, Senska moved to the United States in 1929 and attended the University High School in Iowa City, Iowa. She graduated from the University of Iowa with a B.A. and an M.A. in 1939. She taught at Grinnell College until 1942, when she joined the U.S. Navy and trained as a pilot. Senska took classes from Bauhaus artists László Moholy-Nagy and Marguerite Wildenhain. She also studied with Edith Heath at the California Labor School and Maija Grotell at the Cranbrook Academy of Art. She came to Montana State College in 1946, where she taught until 1973. There, she met Jessie Wilber, and the two became constant friends. In 1988 she was awarded the Governor's Award for the Arts.

ROBERT DEWEESE (1920–1990): Born in Troy, Ohio, he graduated from Ohio State University in 1942 with a B.S. in art. While at Ohio State University, he studied with artist Walter Kuhn and innovative art professor Hoyt Sherman. In 1942 he joined the U.S. Army and played flute in the U.S. Army Air Force Band, stationed in Hawaii. At the end of World War II, he married Gennie Adams, and he attended the University of Iowa, earning an M.F.A. in 1948. After graduation he taught art at Ohio State University, Columbus, and Texas Tech University, Lubbock. In 1949 he took a position at Montana State College, Bozeman, where he remained until his retirement in 1977. DeWeese was given the Governor's Award for the Arts, posthumously, in 1995.

GENNIE ADAMS DEWEESE (1921–2007): Born in Indianapolis, Indiana, she spent her first five years there before her family moved to St. Louis, then to Grosse Pointe, Michigan, and finally settled in Columbus, Ohio. In 1938, she enrolled at Ohio State University, where she studied with artist Walter Kuhn and innovative art professor Hoyt Sherman. There, she met and became friends with Robert DeWeese. In 1943 she received her teaching certificate from the University of Michigan. At the end of World War II, she moved to Detroit, where she worked as a substitute teacher and painted. When Robert DeWeese returned from the war, the two married. Gennie DeWeese accompanied Robert to Bozeman in 1949. They had five children. She kept up her art practice throughout her life, always demanding her own time in the studio. She taught at all levels of education, including as an adjunct at Montana State University in 1978. In 1995, after Robert DeWeese's death in 1990, Gennie DeWeese earned the Governor's Award for the Arts. That same year Gennie DeWeese was given an honorary doctorate in Fine Arts from Montana State University.

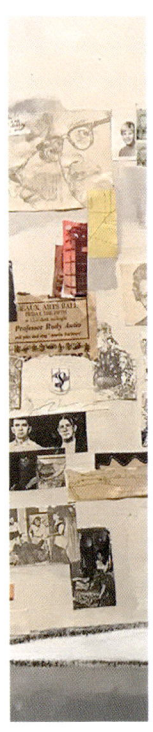
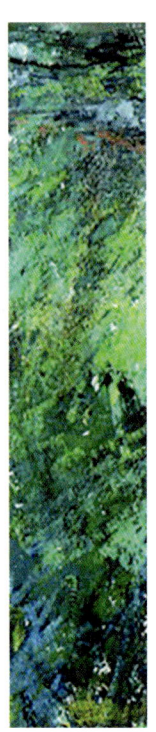
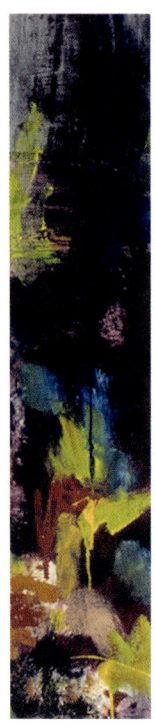
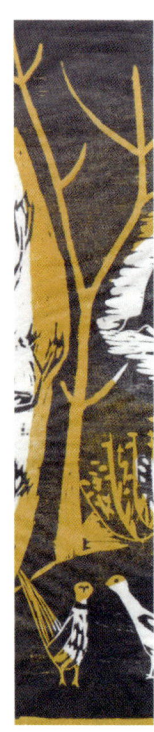
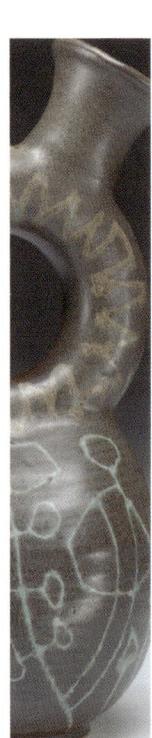

INTRODUCTION

MONTANA'S AVANT-GARDE

After World War II, Isabelle Johnson, Bill Stockton, Jessie Wilber, Frances Senska, Robert DeWeese, and Gennie DeWeese emerged as the first generation to bring Modernist art to Montana.

Other pockets of Modernism showed up throughout the state, including Val Knight (1905–1990), who experimented with encaustics and opened a cooperative gallery in Great Falls, and her mentor Jack Franjevic (1924–1992), who attended the Chicago Art Institute after WWII, then went on to teach at Grinnell College and finally at the College of Great Falls (now the University of Great Falls) for thirty years until his retirement.

Also in Great Falls, Sister Mary Trinitas (Rosalba Morin; 1908–1965) spent twenty-nine years as an art teacher at the College of Great Falls. Instrumental in the Montana Modernist movement, she helped Frances Senska build her first kiln and worked with Branson Stevenson as he tried various art forms. Her own art included metalwork, stained glass, ceramics, and woodwork. Henry Meloy (1902–1951) and his brother Pete Meloy (1908–1998), both from Townsend then Helena, contributed to Modernism in their own ways. Henry (Hank), a painter, taught art at Columbia University, in New York City, but would come back to Montana during the summers. Pete, a ceramicist, worked with Archie Bray

and Branson Stevenson in starting the Archie Bray Foundation, in Helena.

Helen McAuslan (1917–1970) studied at the Arts Students League and traveled the world before settling in Montana, where she became good friends with Gennie DeWeese. She is best known for her 1970 Kent State Shooting paintings. These artists are noted throughout the book and are worthy of further study, but they were not as visible or active in seeding Modernism in Montana as were Isabelle Johnson, Bill Stockton, Frances Senska, Jessie Wilber, Robert DeWeese, and Gennie DeWeese.

Keeping the focus of this book on these six artists was my decision, made after years of careful deliberation, research, and debate (with myself) as to who made up the core of the movement. Through their art, their teaching, and their camaraderie, these six artists invited Montanans to see themselves in a different light. By bringing a distinguished artistic lineage, combined with observations of their ideas of place, they created a community that ultimately opened its arms to Modernism, and, in so doing, brought a broader context to the Montanan identity. They spoke of themselves as "Montana's Avant-Garde" because they knew their art operated outside the mainstream.

Montana natives Isabelle Johnson and Bill Stockton, both ranchers and artists, portrayed their versions of place in a way that reframed

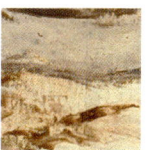
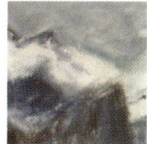
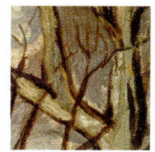
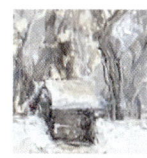
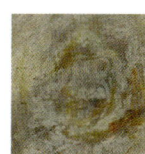
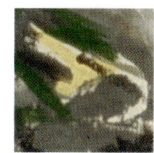

the narrative of Montana from that of the "Wild West" to a more intimate relationship inherent in day-to-day living. Artist and curator Gordon McConnell said, "I love Montana more because of Isabelle's paintings, seeing the landscape through her vision."[1] Frances Senska and Jessie Wilber inspired each other as they discovered their voices. Their presence as teachers, enhanced by their own work, invited students to become artists and artists to become teachers. Their influences can be seen in the art world today, passed down through generations. Robert and Gennie DeWeese showed by example what it meant to live life as an artist. Their home, nearly always filled with creative people, inspired decades of young artists to pursue the truth of their work on their own terms. Together, they offered an alternative to a state wrapped in an environment of Western art.

To understand the development of the Montana Modernists, it may help to define Modernism. For the Modernist, aesthetic issues have primacy over all else. In the case of painting, the abstract shapes animate the surface so that the entire painting is equally expressive. Modernism also asserts personal, individual expression over idealism and religion.

The first Modernist art movement, French Impressionism (1872–1892), was a reaction to a combination of new technology: the invention of photography (early 1800s) and the availability of portable paint tubes (1841). These inventions resulted in the artists seeking to express what they saw in ways that photography could not, and refillable portable tubes allowed them to paint plein-air. Their quest to convey the light coincided with the need to portray not only the physical attributes of their world but the societal differences between the classes. The manner in which these artists reflected their worldview impacted the way people viewed themselves—inclusive as a growing middle class. Art stopped being about historical figures, religion, and mythology. Instead, it began to question meaning beyond the subject matter, to bypass the subjects and focus on the limits of the medium.

Impressionism brought attention to the moment, the light, the air. A few years later, Post-Impressionist Paul Cezanne (1839–1906) used paint to examine the spaces between the objects, instead of the subject itself. Cezanne activated the entire canvas with the task of painting three-dimensional objects on a flat surface. In this way Modernism began to embody the search for new forms adequate to portray and express their era. At the time Cezanne painted his iconic apples (1873–1898), the Third Paris World's Fair opened in 1879, touting ice machines and electric lights. For Cezanne these inventions may have signaled a world where a closer examination of what seemed to be understood—a bowl of apples—may not actually be so easily known. By observing the apples in relation to the tablecloth, the folds in relation to the light, Cezanne gave his still life paintings a sculptural element, opening up a fresh avenue for the act of seeing and relating that act to a two-dimensional surface. In the 1950s, art critic Clement Greenberg, looking back at the beginnings of the art movement, defined Modernism in contrast to the artists who used "art to conceal art," which represented illusionistic painting. Modernists instead referred to the materiality of their work, to the paint, the flat surfaces, and the limits of the illusions of space.[2]

American Modernism includes the Abstract Expressionists, like Jackson Pollock (1912–1956), who, according to curator and art historian Kirk Varnedoe, showed the world the promise of modern art.[3] Art historian Meyer Schapiro noted that the change from pictorial art to abstract art could be likened to exchanging Mark Twain for Ezra Pound. In other words, it expressed an increase in intellectual and spiritual integrity, not something to be taken at face value. In his 1957 essay, "Modern Art," Schapiro said that the art of his time was modern not due to its contemporary setting but because it indicated a challenge of new possibilities; artists incorporated these new possibilities into their work—questioning unexplored perceptions, ideas, and experiences.

During the period in America after World War II, as soldiers became veterans, they searched for a way to express their experiences of fighting in a war within the context of peace. Atomic power, including the capacity for assured mutual destruction and a nuclear winter, preyed on many minds as schools taught children to hide under their desks in case of a nuclear attack. Couched in the Cold War terms of "communism," the idea of a government social safety net became dangerous during the McCarthyism of the 1950s. How would artists translate the fears and hopes they shared into art? Abstract Expressionism developed under these new conditions in a broad reaction to the basic elements of common experiences. Artists in the United States were asking not only what it meant to be human but also what it meant to be

American. Abstract Expressionism, a new arm of Modernism, symbolized an individual who realized a kind of freedom and deep engagement of the self within the work.[4]

Postwar Montanans, lacking art museums that could show them artwork firsthand, lived with a second-hand understanding of Modernist art. This may have influenced the resistance to a new aesthetic. Experientially, unless a person traveled to New York or Europe, they saw important paintings through print media in a magazine, on a postcard, in a book, or even amongst the pages of a calendar hanging on a wall. Viewing them in a personal space, holding the book, touching the pages, perhaps tracing outlines with a finger all make the images both more accessible and intimate. However, this experience deceives the viewer. Is it possible to have a truly intimate experience with a piece of artwork if it is viewed only as a copy, with all the inadequacies of reproduction? Lost is the actual experience of standing in front of a work of art.

In 1935 philosopher, cultural critic, and essayist Walter Benjamin put forward the idea that the mechanical reproduction of art devalues it, reducing the artwork's uniqueness as a singular work of art, claiming a loss of the "aura" of the original work.[5] In 1972 art critic John Berger raised the idea again that culture and technology influence how people see the world and, through that lens, view art. He posited that different cultures interpreted what they saw with the technologies available during their time. Berger points to the invention of the camera as a mechanism for changing the way in which people saw painted images:

Originally paintings were an integral part of the building for which they were designed. Sometimes in an early Renaissance church or chapel one has the feeling that the images on the wall are records of the building's interior life that together make up the building's memory—so much are they part of the particularity of the building.[6]

He goes on to posit the consequences of reproduction:

The uniqueness of every painting was once part of the uniqueness of the place where it resided...[I]t could never be seen in two places at the same time. When the camera reproduces a painting, it destroys the uniqueness of its image. As a result, its meaning changes. Or, more exactly, its meaning multiplies and fragments into many meanings.[7]

Berger implies that the easier it is to access these images, the more it becomes part of the commonality of the culture. Thus, the original meaning of the art changes from the intention of the artist to what it represents. With each copy its meaning degenerates. A painting meant to be a painting inherently changes when dispersed in multiples. As Bill Stockton put it when comparing Isabelle Johnson's work before her trip to Europe to study the masters with her work after her return to Montana,

[s]he had been influenced by reproductions, as were most of us here in Montana and elsewhere who had little access to study original paintings up close. Reproductions might well show the effect of the painting, but to get but a hint of the effects of how atmosphere and light are accomplished by underpainting and over-glazes...[A]fter this [trip] her paintings took on a different surface and her dark areas became more translucent.[8]

Stockton and Johnson, as well as the rest of the Montana Modernists, did see the original work of the Impressionists and the Post-Impressionists as they traveled to Europe or to various American cities. Johnson and Stockton's perspective, or way of seeing, stemmed in part from their personal point of view: chores and caring for livestock. For Frances Senska, Jessie Wilber, Gennie DeWeese, and Robert DeWeese, their point of view encompassed what they observed from their window and inside their homes. The land they interacted with each day, each season, with the minute variations and always-changing light, availed itself to their artist's eye and informed a personal statement that came through in paint and color, surface and texture, composition and form.

That they developed and redefined their art, perceived with a Modernist vision, into an environment exposed only to illustrative or mimetic artwork indicated that they felt the readiness of Montanans to accept this new visual language. Through the familiarity of print images, ideas of Modernism hovered in the minds of some around the state. People may have been familiar with Modernism, but, at that point, Montanans still did not see themselves expressed in it.

By the end of World War II, Montana had experienced a shift from a mostly rural, mining, and ranching state to a more city-centered economic platform. Veterans returned home, and many took advantage of the Servicemen's Readjustment Act of 1944, commonly known as the G.I. Bill, attending college in ground-breaking numbers. Many colleges, including Montana State College (MSC) in Bozeman, started full-fledged art departments for the first time (at MSC, the Art Department came under the umbrella of Home Economics), which developed a need for artists-teachers willing to move to the state. The Montana Modernists all taught art and exposed their students to unfamiliar genres. They taught at Montana State College and Eastern Montana College, and Bill Stockton taught art classes in Lewistown's Art Center. Their open-handed, generous pedagogy filtered into the lives of an exponentially growing number of artists, who were influenced not just by the art of their teachers, but by the egalitarian nature of the teacher–student relationship. Students, no longer treated as apprentices but as artists in their own right, shared their work and showed their art at the same events, hung side-by-side with their teachers. While this may not fall under the auspices of Modernism per se, it is applicable to the Montana Modernists. Due to the nature of these veteran-students and the closeness in age between students and teachers with similar backgrounds and experiences, a more equal treatment of students became part of the character of Montana pedagogy.

This wave of postwar artists needed to express themselves differently from the Western illustrative work that permeated the state at the time. Their experiences, their point of view, and the changing world they found themselves in required something more. As Robert DeWeese noted in a catalog essay, "The art students in 1949 were a completely different lot. They'd been in the war all over the world, and they were hungry for all of it."[9] It is not a leap to suggest that so many veterans who had seen the world, the war, the dropping of the atomic bomb, the devastation of Europe, and the reckoning with fascism needed a new way to communicate.

In Montana the regional experience and character of the land offered an opportunity to speak through the language of nature and the unique perspective of place.[10] According to geographer Yi-Fu Tuan, a place is knowable through daily experiences over time: "The feel of a place is registered in one's muscles and bones…Knowing a place…clearly takes time. It is a subconscious kind of knowing."[11] The Montana Modernists all showed a deep attachment to nature and to the particular places that enveloped their lives. They also understood that bringing Modernism to Montana meant they needed to take imagery already in art—the land—and translate that into a more expandable vocabulary that could include a broader context than that supplied by illustrative Western narratives, as told by men.

Community also played a large role in connecting artists across the state. Montana is 630 miles wide and 255 miles from north to south—a big state by any standard. In 1948 a group of artists, writers, poets, and other creatives banded together to publish a quarterly magazine under the auspices of the Montana Institute of the Arts. They met annually and convinced nearly everyone involved to contribute to their quarterly journal by writing about their work and sending in poetry or essays. Some submitted thoughts regarding the creative process; others wrote about their experiences in the art world. Through this organization and other smaller gatherings, Montana artists created a sense of belonging. They knew most would not break out as stars in the art world, but that did not matter as much as encouraging each other to tend to their individual self-expression. The support created a tight-knit and compassionate community that grew to embrace artists from all over the state. It was the strength of their commonly held values in artmaking that enabled this steadfast community to withstand the pressures of a basically non-existent art market.

The Montana Institute of the Arts helped to create that community, comprised of both students and other artists trying new things around Montana. As noted by former student, artist, and teacher Ray Campeau,

> Those were the people that were the glue that kept the arts alive in the state. There became a beauty [to it]—everybody in the arts was one big family. It was to the point where you went to a show—there were no art galleries in the state—so the Montana Institute of the Arts would put forth these shows. The leaders were the teachers, the people in higher education, they would exhibit too, not just the students, [everyone] became part of it. They'd give lectures, give demonstrations, share their beauty.[12]

Historically, the West provides the basis for numerous mythologies, creating villains and heroes as well as white hats and black hats spread through storytelling, memories, and art. Before World War II, Montana's art heroes consisted of those who told the best tales, namely men like Charles M. Russell, Edgar S. Paxton, and Joe DeYong. Other artists, like O. C. Seltzer, Joseph Meany, Will James, and Ralph DeCamp also factored in, adding their work to the overall aesthetic representation of Montana. Above all, their work captured a nostalgic West harkening back to the early frontier days of buffalo herds, cross-country cattle drives, wildlife, pioneers, and campfires under the open night sky.

In 1940 the Butte Public Library published a compilation of the artists living in the state. The library listed over 100 names; nearly all of them painted traditional Western scenes and scenery. None painted in an experimental or Modernist style, and the voices of women were but a whisper. As summed up by artist Dan Conway,

> [w]hen the annals of American art are conscientiously and honestly treated, Montana will stand high upon the role of fame, and there will be recorded on the historical pages the names of Edgar S. Paxson, Charles M. Russell, and Ralph E. DeCamp as a group of Montana painters who have not only done good work technically, but who have immortalized on canvas the Indian, the pioneer, the trapper, the ranchman, the cowboy, together with the fauna, the flora and the landscape peculiar to this section of the country....These three painters have had their homes in Montana, and they have proved themselves as much imbued with

Montana's atmospheric conditions and its topography.[13]

It is not hard to see the attraction to these artists, spokesmen for the wild frontier, even if the frontier may not have been as wild as they claimed at that time. Montana still sold itself as rugged, a place where sturdy individuals could make a name for themselves. As the societal nature of the West began to change, the art that championed a nostalgic West became a force against change. Briefly reviewing the careers of a couple of those artists delineates their hold over Montana art and sets the stage for the disruption brought by the Montana Modernists.

Charles M. Russell (1864–1926) ventured to the West from St. Louis, Missouri, where he worked on the open range, gaining his knowledge of the rugged life on horseback. He has been described as a "man out of time" because he consistently depicted a Montana that no longer existed. As the 2017 PBS documentary *C. M. Russell and the American West* states, "Charlie Russell described Montana at its best—the Frontier Dream." Russell assumed the role of preacher and progenitor for the myth of the West. Just as he was seduced by the idea of wildness, he eventually took on the role of seducer. "He lamented the West that was passed, then went on to convince us that the West, the mythic West, had been quite real," the documentary's narrator said. It was also noted that Russell's painting, *Waiting for a Chinook* (1887), put him on the map. After a brutal winter, Russell's small watercolor painting depicted a starving, rib-exposed steer barely standing in the white, white snow. Gray skies overhead loomed while wolves waited for an opportunity to take the steer. The title refers to the warm winds that come through in winter melting the snow and offering relief from an unrelenting season. "In the scope of a postcard, Russell had summed up the devastating winter of 1886–87, the end of the open-range cattle industry, and the commanding theme of all his work, 'The West That Has Passed,'" wrote Brian Dippie in his introduction to *Charles M. Russell: Word Painter*.[14]

Russell handed his torch to Joe DeYong (1894–1975), his first and only protégé. DeYong took on Russell's philosophy of promoting a "vanishing West" mythology. His paintings and drawings depict bucking broncs and rodeos. Russell's wife, Nancy, helped to promote his work and helped DeYong as much as she had helped Russell to gain renown. Both artists paid close attention to the finest details, being sure not to let the West of their memories die out. After Russell's death, DeYong made his way to Hollywood as a film consultant, establishing the basis for much of the "Western" tradition seen on screen and television.[15]

Financially, this romantic narrative of the West was reinforced through tourism's support for dude ranches in Montana, which relied heavily on the cowboy myth to sell a lifestyle to easterners looking to escape the urban setting for a few weeks' vacation. Beginning in the 1920s, quite a few of Montana's young people moved to cities both within and outside the state. Many of Montana's traditional jobs in coal, lumber, mining, and agriculture became stagnant or declined.[16]

Postwar Montana, compared to prewar Montana, dealt with a changing population, as areas that housed colleges increased between 29 percent in Bozeman and 36 percent in Billings. Areas populated by mining, like Butte, saw a drop in population of 11 percent.[17] One industry claimed an uptick: tourism. In 1926 the Montana Dude Ranchers' Association formed, with twenty-six ranches signing up that year. The number jumped to forty-seven dude ranches in 1927. By 1930 over 100 dude ranches had developed across the state, mostly around the mountains and valleys near Yellowstone National Park.[18] According to a study of Montana's economy at the time, "Rail-based tourism brought valuable dollars into the state, with tourists spending five hundred thousand dollars a year in Montana from 1900 through 1910."[19] Before World War II, tourism ranked fourth among the state's industries, ringing up $30 million statewide in 1941 alone. In 1946 notices went out to the tourist industry to get ready for a "flood" of tourists. In the first three months of that year, the tourist bureau reported an unprecedented wave of over 28,000 requests for Montana information. Max Dean, chairman of Montana's advertising committee, noted, "Montana is in competition with other of the western states for tourists. Montana's recreational advantages must be kept constantly before potential visitors, through the medium of advertising and publicity."[20] Branding the Montana experience started from the first group of dude ranches in the 1920s and continues today. The art of the Old West still promotes tourism.

Voices of the Montana Modernists were hard to hear over the roar of tourism dollars.[21]

Instead of adhering to the tropes already in place up until the 1940s, the Montana Modernists translated the experience of living in Montana through patterns, composition, and form. In other words, they tossed aside nostalgic imagery and instead related experiences to emotional and tactile responses that occurred in the moment: the notion of home and gardens, the feeling of a blizzard wiping out one's sense of direction, and the hard work of tending to livestock on a daily basis. They opened up a way for Montanans to see themselves as something other than a mere trope, and they invited women to the conversation for the first time. At the end of World War II, the Montana Modernists fought against the wave of nostalgic illustrative art by getting jobs at colleges, forming life-long relationships with like-minded people, and believing in and supporting each other.

It is no small matter that, out of these six artists, four of them are women. Donna Forbes, executive director of the Yellowstone Art Center (later the Yellowstone Art Museum) from 1974 to 1998 thought the women Modernists outnumbered the men because living in Montana makes women tough. "In Montana, you've got strong women. Nothing was too much for them," Forbes said, which may seem a bit simplistic but conveys Forbes' sense of the fierce independence she saw in the artists Isabelle Johnson, Jessie Wilber, Frances Senska, and Gennie DeWeese. Johnson, a rancher by birth and by nature, headstrong and independent, would not have let anyone tell her what to paint. Jessie Wilber came to Montana in 1941, by herself, to teach art and explore that place with a sense of wonder, a feeling that comes across in nearly every one of her pieces. Frances Senska moved to Montana after serving in the navy during the war. She brought with her a military exactness that paved the way for her students to find their own voices. Senska taught ceramics, but she learned ceramic art alongside her students. Both Wilber and Senska fought to get the Art Department out from under the auspices of the Women's Home Economics Department and to lose the "lady-hobbyist" label that many women artists suffered. Gennie DeWeese became a force of nature, a comrade in arms, and a singular voice that called out to young artists, especially young women artists. In midcentury America, just stepping out of the constrictive role of mother and wife took bravery and tenacity. To claim the status of an artist, a professional, as these women did, could be considered an act of gender rebellion. Taken as a whole, these women's bravery rose above the male-dominated culture. Thanks in no small part to these artists, Western art in Montana now includes female voices.

What holds these artists together is not their style, although all of them trace their lineage to Modernism, especially the work of Paul Cezanne, but rather their philosophy, their attention to the changing aesthetics buzzing throughout the country, and their discussions—political and academic—that would come across on the canvas and in the clay. The late nights, the conversations that lingered like so much smoke drifting across the room, bred a heady atmosphere. These art-

ists shared a philosophical aesthetic clearly at the forefront of Montana at that time. They believed in expressing the essential nature of place and winnowing objects down to the barest minimum needed to voice their perspectives. These artists pushed against Montana's mythical past to come away with a style of Modernism that offered Montanans a viable alternative way to recognize themselves and form their own identity. In order to be a Montanan, a person did not have to bushwhack in the wilderness or wrangle cattle on the open range. A Montanan could embrace an intellectual and academic freedom, love cats, or investigate the political landscape.

Place, education, and community—both individually and considered as a whole—contributed to developing a lasting impact on Montana and a way of seeing that had lasting effects on the struggle for an elastic yet authentic Montana narrative.

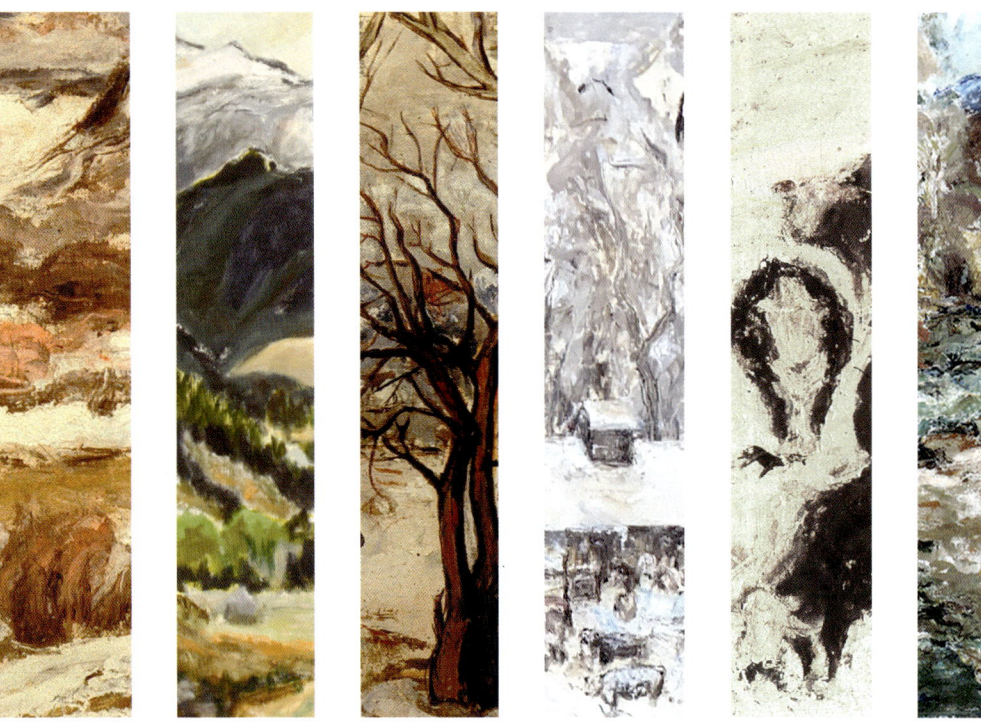

SECTION ONE: PLACE

The abundance of this place, the songs of its people and its birds, will be health and wisdom and indwelling light. This is no paradisal dream. Its hardship is its possibility.[1]

—Wendell Berry

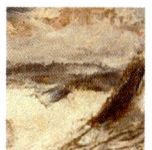

A SENSE OF PLACE:
ISABELLE JOHNSON AND BILL STOCKTON

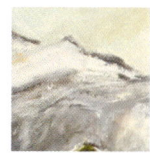

As anyone who ever stood in the shadow of a mountain or stared, exposed, against a windswept prairie knows, the land itself becomes a backdrop to everything; it crackles the sun-dried skin and pulls like old, muddied boots at pasture-flooded dreams. The power of place speaks not only to the present, but also to the past and the future. Place conjures and it chides. For artists, place can act as inspiration or as constriction. In the period just after World War II, Montana's landscape offered opportunity as well as isolation.

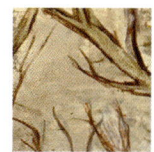

Here, the reference to place is not meant in a purely geographical sense, nor is it meant in a unifying, nationalistic way. Instead, this kind of locus speaks to time, space, and, as geographical philosopher Edward S. Casey states, "the formidable presence of place in our lives."[2] He posits that people are distinguished by place: "You are in them not as a puppet stuffed in a box—as would be true on a strict container view of place—but as living in them, indeed, *through* them…. To be somewhere is to be in place and there to be subject to its power, to be part of its action, acting on its scene."[3]

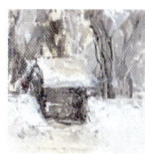

Looking at the landscape as a scenic text provides not only an understanding of a literal sense of place but also a deeper understanding of what that place means in terms of personal identity. While examining the cultural context within which an individual lives (in a geographic place), geographer Edmunds Valdemars Bunkse commented on that individual's "geographic life." It was a life dependent on place and landscape. He noted, "Landscape is distinct from ideas of nature, ecology, environment, space, place, and so on…They can represent a thoroughly humanistic idea and action, provided that all the senses can be engaged in discourses about and realities of landscape."[4] Granted, there is a thin line separating place and landscape in terms of a geographic location. To geographer Karl Benediktsson, the landscape as scenery has devolved into a trope, being too simplistic to actually carry meaning. He revisits the notion of the difference between how a tourist sees a landscape and the way a resident views it: "Even coach tourists can and sometimes do have quite profound experiences when confronted with unfamiliar and startling landscapes which they

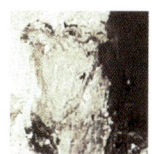

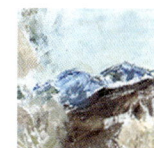

find moving." He notes the original meaning of the German word *Landschaft* as "territorial polity," which entailed certain rights and duties for those living within its bounds—a meaning that later took hold, especially in England (i.e., referring to a visual representation of a particular kind or "way of seeing"). Crossing the Atlantic, Benediktsson elaborates on the idea of wildness and how that seeps into the nature of landscape. He concludes, "An aesthetic experience is moreover made up of many strands of sense and emotion....[T]he aesthetic sense cannot be divorced from everyday life and practices."[5]

As was mentioned but is worth noting again, Yi-Fu Tuan acknowledges that place is knowable through daily experiences over time. This idea of daily experiences adds to the emotional and cultural landscape of Montana during the time of the first generation of Modernists. Unlike the tourists, those artists understood place on a daily basis, through the seasons, the tough times, and the joyous times.

ISABELLE AND BILL: WORKING THE LAND THROUGH THEIR ART

Isabelle Johnson (1901–1992) and Bill Stockton (1921–2002) were friends and colleagues with a shared sense of place, the knowledge of hard-earned calluses from working with the land, and something more. Rooted in the tangled gullies and stretching hills of central Montana, Stockton's work, imbued with fragility and stamina, speaks to the impending threats of winter and the anticipated orchestra of spring. Stockton's home,

a sheep ranch in Grass Range, Montana, marked his physical place on the land, but his art decodes his own experience in reflecting the power of place. Johnson was born and raised on a ranch in Absarokee, Montana, on her family's homestead; it sat along the Stillwater River, near the Beartooth Mountains, and became the context for her body of work. The geographical strength of her life matched the power of her paintings, centering on the landscape that shaped her. Donna Forbes, who knew both of them as friends and

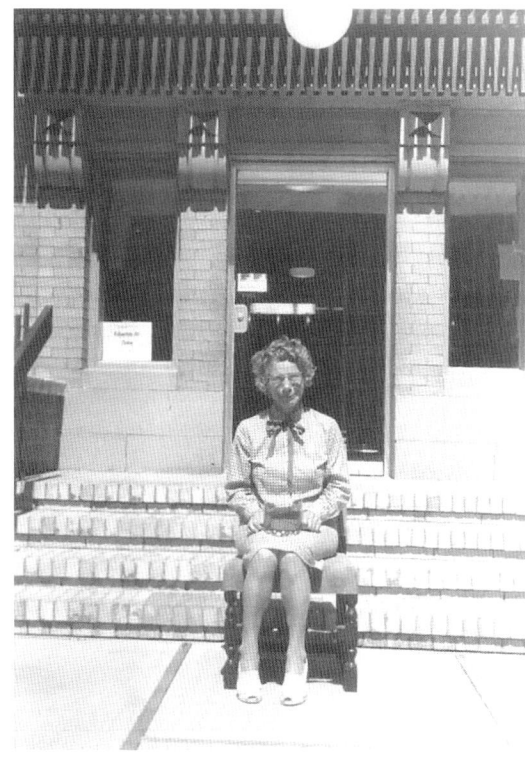

Isabelle Johnson outside the Yellowstone Art Museum, 1966

in her position as executive director of the Yellowstone Art Center/Museum, stated, "Bill had a wonderful art mind. He and Isabelle were very close. Bill and she were on another level." Forbes noted that Stockton would visit Johnson at Rocky Mountain College when she finished teaching for the day. "They would talk by the hour. They had a meeting of the minds about making art, who was doing important work and so on."[6]

Stockton notes that Johnson, like himself, was a rural person:

> Her life, or that part of it, which is really meaningful, is her limited world from the house to the barn to the river and an occasional jaunt up the coulee. I'm a rural person, and I know how important that is to her, because this is home...[S]o many [artists] will never consider that home and self are one and the same...There were artists who painted drunken cowboys of an 1890 vintage, and there are artists who are painting drunken cowboys of the 1971 vintage.[7]

Continuing to discuss what made Johnson's work powerful he said,

> There are artists that paint pretty little lakes bordered by pretty little Christmas trees, and there are artists who are only concerned with high, wide, and handsome Montana. And there is Isabelle. She is about the only artist I know who has really painted Montana, because she has exposed to us a way of life and the very things that attach human beings to the land.[8]

From the willowy outlines of Johnson's distant mountain silhouettes to Stockton's patterned impressions of his surroundings, art enabled them to translate the power of place. Both traveled to Europe to learn at the knee of the Modernists. Neither of them conceded to the commercial aspects of the art world. Their voices spoke in terms of the formal aspects of painting, which reflected their training. Both experimented with their own strand of Modernism that held fast to an intimate relationship with the land through abstract portrayals of nature, to which they gave concrete expression.

Isabelle Johnson, born at the turn of the twentieth century, grew up ranching with her two sisters and her brother, which meant hard work hauling rocks, cutting and baling hay, caring for sick animals or birthing cattle and sheep, taking livestock to the butcher, dehorning and branding steers, taking horses to pasture, shearing sheep, irrigating fields, mending fences, and repairing machinery. Her work ethic continued when Johnson graduated from the University of Montana in 1922 with a degree in history at a time when very few women earned bachelor's degrees. She taught history at Fromberg High School, in Fromberg, Montana, south of Billings, for two years before heading off to Columbia University for a master's degree in history. While at Columbia, Johnson took an art history course that pivoted her from history to art. She then enrolled at the Otis Art Institute in Los Angeles and even began working toward a doctoral degree in political science at the University of Southern California.[9] She had a deep love of learning and, before finding art, seemed to be attracted to disciplines explaining the past and how, perhaps, to influence the future.

With art she could discern her individual point of view about Montana and her beloved ranch in Stillwater, which seemed to draw her back time and time again.[10]

She said in an interview, "I got interested enough [in art] that I went on later and enrolled for one year at Otis Art Institute in Los Angeles. I'd go to school until I was broke then I'd come back to Billings and teach until I got enough money for more school—and then I'd repeat the process."[11] She took classes at the Colorado Springs Fine Art Center in 1938 and the next year studied at the Arts Students' League in New York under the tutelage of artist George Bridgeman, who taught anatomy and figure drawing. Johnson said of that time,

> I had my first lesson in art during that year. I was doing very well in drawing…. Bridgeman worked very mechanically, and I was drawing exactly as he was and doing exactly what he did, when one day he came in and went over my work and was very appraising.[12]

Then she heard someone behind her say, "It's no wonder he thinks she's good, she's not trying to learn to draw, she's trying to do like he does." That comment cut through her like a knife. "And I suddenly realized that [being an artist meant] you weren't working for somebody else, that it was something you developed yourself."[13]

From 1945 to 1946, she returned to Columbia University, attending the painting and sculpture school. While at Columbia, in 1948, a professor invited her to attend the Skowhegan School of Painting and Sculpture in Maine, the first year of the famous experimental art school. She accepted the invitation and, while at Skowhegan, she studied under the artist Henry Varnum Poor, who chose her as one of the twenty-five students in the country to attend Skowhegan. There, she found her own voice and established a significant style and aesthetic that would carry her forward. Johnson remembered an important moment at Skowhegan:

> [Painter] Karl Zerbe[14] asked why I didn't slice this way and that way and modernize my canvas. And so, I was having a real good time after he left, making all the lines that were in the Maine landscape into slices this way and that way and so forth down to the canvas, when for some unknown reason Mr. Poor appeared and he asked me why I was doing this, and I said because Karl Zerbe told me to. And he proceeded then with a lecture telling me that in any art, whether it was modern or any good art, there was no such thing as exaggeration.[15]

Poor told her that painters dramatized, simplified, maybe emphasized. Then he told her to study Cezanne:

> Cezanne followed completely the lines that were in nature, as did any of the great painters. And suddenly with that, he spent the whole afternoon with me, talking about various painters and the difference between real art and what you might call pseudo art, it was as though someone had pulled up a blind, and I suddenly knew I saw what I had thought I had seen many times and that was the difference between real art and that

which was seemingly art. And I think that did more for me than anything else in all the years that I spent studying or in school because I still have that really as my principal precept.[16]

Poor's own work concentrated on the natural world of landscapes. His lines and style, inspired by the French Post-Modernists, incorporated strong lines and graceful movement. The lineage from Poor to Johnson can be observed by comparing Johnson's portraits of her bare winter trees and Poor's *Willows and Mountains*. Even the color palette retains similarities with dark colors and deep earthy tones. Poor also advised Johnson to return to Montana, a place he said was a desert for art and a setting where her paintings would make Montana bloom.[17] Once she finished her formal schooling, Johnson took a year off to travel to Europe and study the masters. During an interview at the age of 70, Johnson noted that she did not feel comfortable calling herself an artist, "But I'll never forget that I'm trying to become one."[18]

She taught both art and art history at Eastern Montana College from 1949 until 1961, when she returned to her ranch on the Stillwater. During those years, some of which she spent as the department head, her students found courage in the relentlessness and inspiration of her example. Artist Ted Waddell credits Johnson for his painting career. "I met Isabelle Johnson in [my] first painting class and within three or four weeks of knowing her, I decided that I didn't want to be alive and not make art. I don't think there is any way to over-estimate the influence of Isabelle on all of us."[19] Johnson, in turn, cites Waddell as one her students of whom she felt most proud. Waddell held Johnson up as a model for women during a time when it may not have been considered appropriate for women to travel and to study abroad. Waddell added, "She not only did that, but she brought it back to us. Isabelle bridged a gap between the Impressionists and Charlie Russell and brought us into modern times. It's an amazing sort of circumstance when you think about it." Waddell, close to both Johnson and Stockton, noted their courage in painting during a time when there was, at best, a lack of attention paid to modern art. "She was fiercely independent yet wonderfully formal, and fiercely private. In all the years I'd known her I'd only been in her parlor once. The rest of the time we'd sit in her kitchen."[20]

In a 1952 essay Johnson wrote for the *Montana Institute of the Arts*, she started with a quotation from philosopher George Santayana: "The subject matter of art is life as it actually is; but the function of art is to make life better."[21] In the essay she speaks to the amateur artist and, in the course of this short article, her ability to inspire shines through:

> With constant drawing and painting, with keen observation of surroundings, the acquisitiveness born of increased knowledge, only form, design, beauty can result. If the desire is to paint realistically, the painter will simplify, clarify, invent new means of making his painting more real. If the desire is to express feeling, the feeling will be greater.

One could imagine her in a classroom studio accepting her students' abilities and yet pushing

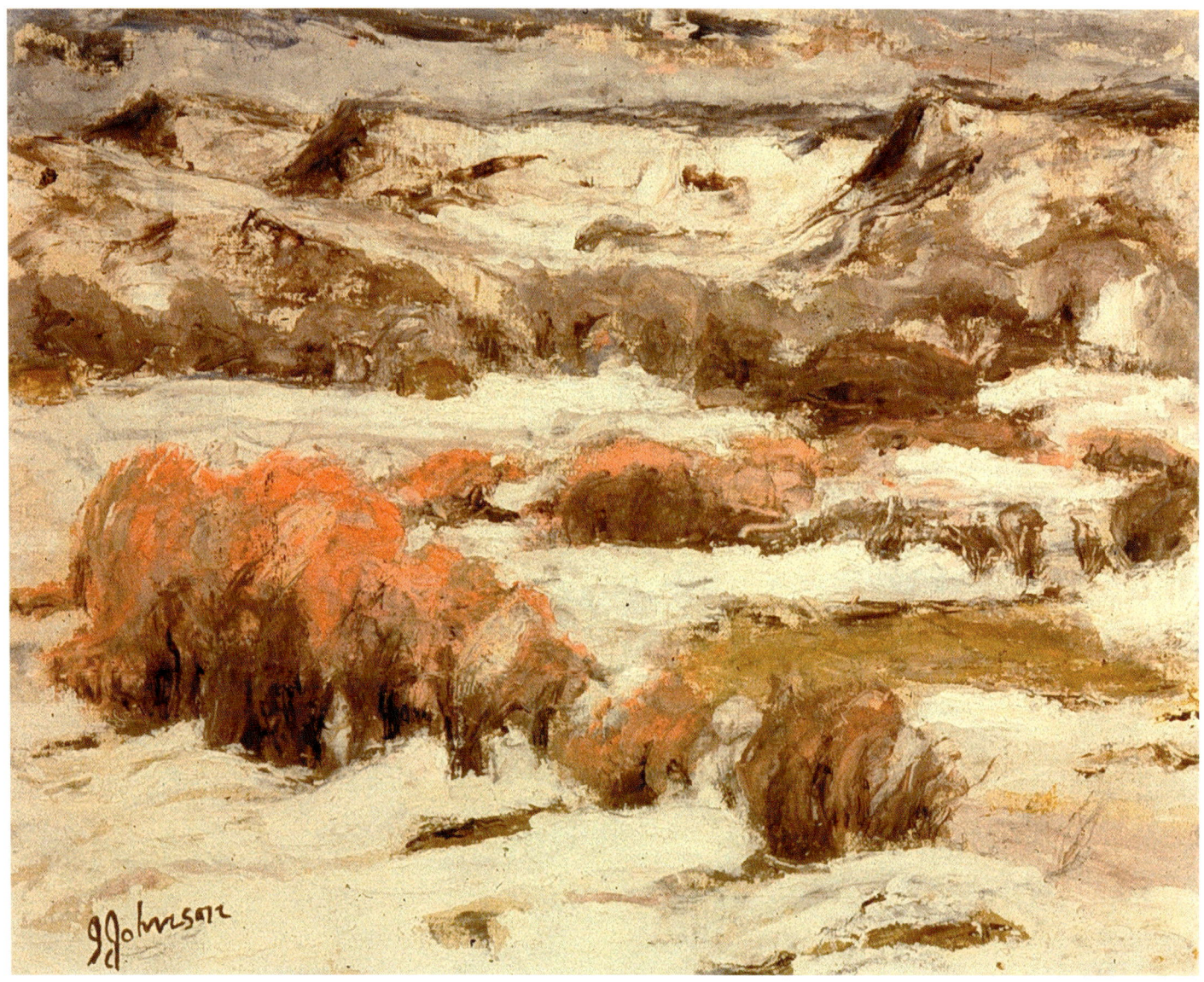

Isabelle Johnson, *Red Willows in Winter Landscape*, 1958, oil on canvas board, 15.75 x 19.75 inches.
Collection of the Yellowstone Art Museum; Gift of Isabelle Johnson Estate. Courtesy of the Yellowstone Art Museum.

them to their limits and beyond. "If the desire is to express relationships, dynamics, to symbolize, to abstract, to become more contemporary than the latest innovator, the door is open, and the amateur may pass through."[22]

Johnson considered the role of the artist as a way to connect with humanity. When asked what she learned by being an artist, Johnson answered:

> First of all you learn to see the way things really are instead of the way the photograph tells you they are because the photograph takes one view whereas the artist takes many views...I think all art is really primarily religious, not religious in the sense of Christianity necessarily, but that you have to rise above yourself and connect yourself with humanity as a whole if you're going to be successful or really do something as an artist.[23]

For her that meant to connect the viewer to her sense of place and what it meant to bond with the land in a meaningful way. This included her idea of the artist's multiple viewpoints and relationships within a painting stemming from the Cubists' perspective of portraying an object from all possible sides onto a flat surface. Cezanne, with his groundbreaking work depicting not only different perspectives but relating the spaces between the objects as well, influenced her work on many levels, especially in her use of sinewy lines that spoke to nature and, although decidedly not a Cubist, she did play with the idea of a personal perspective that did not necessarily reflect a mimetic illustration of place. For Johnson the lines in nature acted as a topography, guiding her in and around the foothills and creeks that expressed a wild and

infinite dedication to her interior sense of self meshing perfectly with her exterior surroundings. In her 1958 oil painting, *Red Willows in Winter Landscape* (page 16), a hint of denim blue works its way along the top of the piece, a thread of sky laid bare. Mountain tips obscured by snow-laden clouds frame the horizon. Deliberate, hard-edged cliffs stagger across the piece, black and smoothed by erosion. Along the foothills, a rolling tumble of grays shows the viewer the ox-bowed creek bottom, silvered in frost, buffered by snow. Although the title refers to *red* willows, their salmon-pink bodies bend in the inferred wind instead. Johnson's use of colors, like the violet shadows and ocher banks, expresses a season known for its colorless limits yet conveys a hidden abundance.

Founding Director of the Yellowstone Art Center (now Yellowstone Art Museum) Terry Melton wrote:

> She has never been diverted from her sense of place. To say that she was a well-schooled painter who ranched might have only a slight edge over a well-informed rancher who painted. Therein lies the real essence of Isabelle Johnson's work. Her drawings and paintings are essences of Absarokee, the home ranch and magnificent Stillwater country of southern Montana.[24]

Melton saw her pictures as the totalities of fragments of her beloved Stillwater County: "Smells of cattle, grassland, sheep and river; sounds of the North and the Chinook; documents expressive and factual of living, growing things, knowing all is tempered by the coming of winter of the land but never the winter of the spirit."[25] He wrote later that Johnson was so skilled in her seeing that she never had time to merely copy the landscape:

> For her, painting has become an organic growth out of the land. A genuine observer of nature, she has used objects only to lead her to the process of painting. A painter's painter, it's my guess that Isabelle thought no more than a moment about what to paint.[26]

When he thought further about the type of artist Johnson was and how to cast her work he wrote:

> Why should one make this attempt? Isabelle remained a painter of her own making, her own visionary, her own seer, her own self, and she was great enough to handle that extraordinary task. Her work is straightforward and independent of those pervasive (and oft-times attractive) influences, which beguile and turn heads of lesser painters.[27]

After Melton left Montana, he carried Johnson's artwork with him in his heart. During his service on the Oregon Arts Commission, he wrote a letter to the Smithsonian Institute enclosing the catalog from Johnson's retrospective show he curated. Melton wrote to the director, Dennis Gould, in 1971:

> Isabelle is a portion of that small slice of life which represents extremely competent people who have devoted more time to being competent than sounding public relations horns. She's a hellova painter. Montana has paid little attention to her because of their paranoia devoted to [Charles M.] Russell.[28]

Melton refers here to the overwhelming public dedication to everything Charlie Russell and Melton believed that this kind of dedication and limited appreciation had become detrimental to all genres. To Melton and Forbes, it felt like Montana's art-viewing public gave the Modernists like Johnson and Stockton short shrift.

Melton spoke about Johnson in a 1986 catalog essay: "In 1965 as director of the YAC, I purchased one of her small paintings for a new collection at that new institution. We had no funds for purchases; I cut back on other funds to buy it." He had hoped his purchase would provide a spark for the continuing purchase of work from important artists in the region. "Isabelle was by no means a new painter but was, as often the case, under-sung. Well before her exhibition at the art center she had established a personal, painterly style and has never strayed from it." In 1961 Johnson returned to her ranch for good. As Melton said, ranching was in her nature. He noted how she

> wrestled with many winters as well as celebrating those rare summers in the sweet grasslands of the north side of the Absarokee Mountains. The meadowlark calls, "Ab-sa-ro-ka" each morning, and the high country smells remind us that there are places to live beyond the gridlock.[29]

Forbes recalled that, in 1970, Mitch Wilder, director of the Amon Carter Museum of Art in Fort Worth, Texas, came to view Johnson's work. After staying for hours, he asked her to participate in an exhibition at the Amon Carter Museum. "Finally, recognition from a renowned expert.

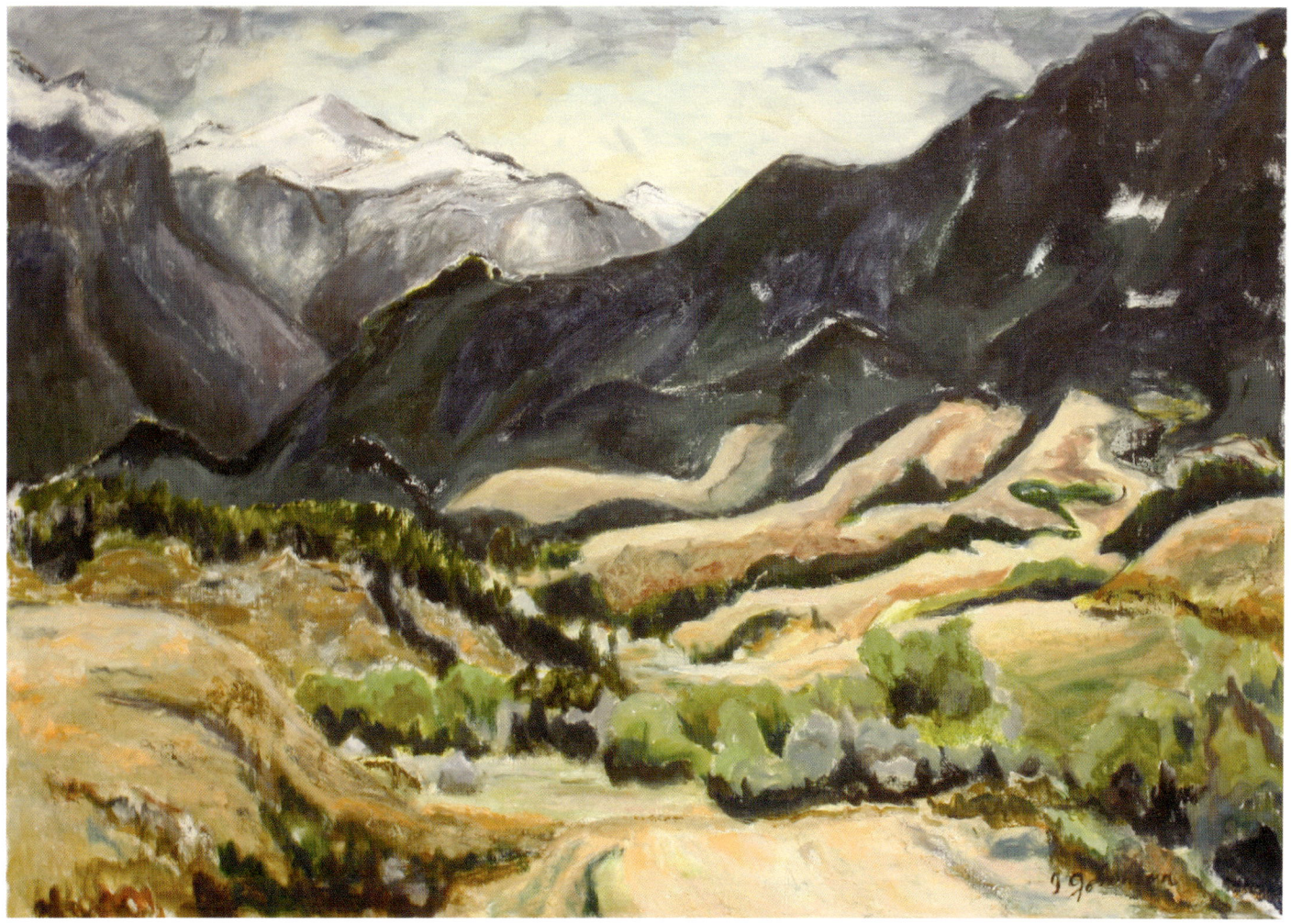

Isabelle Johnson, *East Fiddler's Creek*, 1967, oil on canvas, 36 x 46 inches. Collection of the Yellowstone Art Museum; Gift of Isabelle Johnson Estate. Courtesy of the Yellowstone Art Museum.

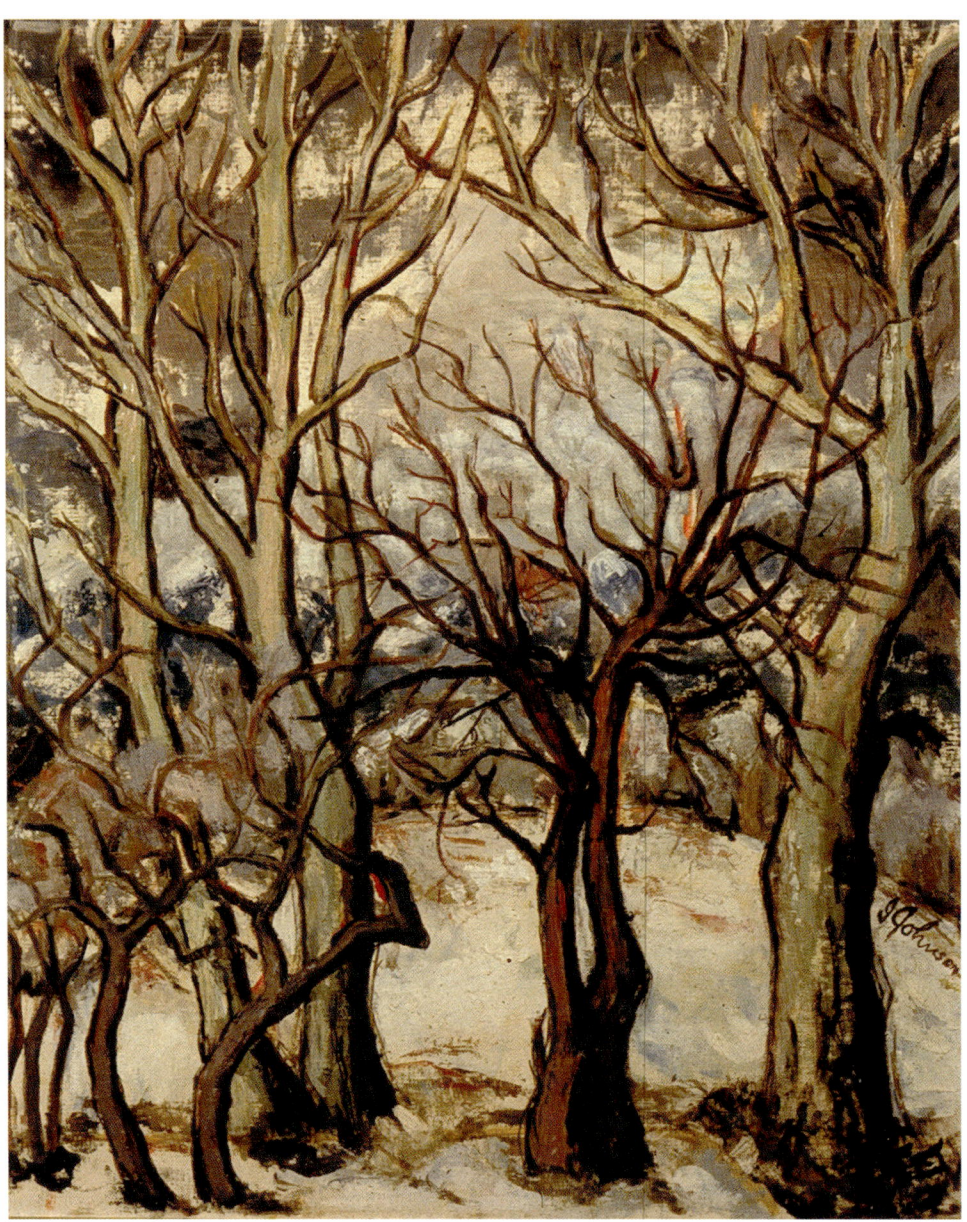

Isabelle Johnson, *Trees, Winter*, 1952,
oil on canvas board, 24 x 19.75 inches.
Collection of the Yellowstone Art Museum;
Gift of Isabelle Johnson Estate.
Courtesy of the Yellowstone Art Museum.

Validation. Isabelle was sixty-nine," Forbes said. Then she quoted Johnson's own words: "You are always becoming an artist."[30]

In her 1967 painting, *East Fiddler's Creek* (page 19), Johnson evokes her own biography in the contoured brushstrokes of the foothills. Uncomplicated lines communicate a wary but open trust. This painting conveys the constant scratch of sagebrush against denimed legs, the familiar cry of a rough-legged hawk as it dives into the tufted hairgrass for prey. Above all, her work displays a tonal undulation of browns with sparks of green and yellow. No depiction of the landscape can stand without the inclusion of sky, and, for this, Johnson hints at the storm in the distance.

Johnson found more inspiration from Cezanne than from Paxson or Russell. As Stockton once said, Paul Cezanne was her teacher and her influence. "As her teachers, Cezanne didn't explain how to apply paint, how to design or how to draw….NO….[H]e taught her only how to look with the eyes of a poet at the very things she loved. She learned on her own how to transfer that love into the images we see now."[31] As art historian and critic Meyer Schapiro said of Cezanne, "His still-life objects bring an awareness of the complexity of the phenomenal and the subtle interplay of perception and artifice in representation."[32]

Johnson continued to explore her own perceptions of the land by incorporating her own ideas about the complexity of Montana, her appreciation of the beauty, and the awareness of her experiences. Her ability to translate the lines

of nature into lines on the canvas provides an alternative to the raspy, quick draws of Charlie Russell. Johnson, a woman rancher, offered a new voice in the rugged landscape.

Not enmeshed in the traditional "cowboy" romance of place, Johnson wished only to portray her own sense of what it meant to live in Montana. This is most evident in Johnson's *Trees, Winter* (page 20), a 1952 oil painting depicting a tangle of cottonwoods vying for attention. Some trees bend in dancing grace, others stand with branches upward, echoing the trees Cezanne painted later in his career. Johnson gives her trees a heavy outline, as many of the Post-Impressionists did, to evoke feelings through form and line, space, and structure. Her use of broken color feels more like a quick sketched line than the fluid brushwork of Cezanne, but the connection to Post-Impressionism still exists. Former Yellowstone Art Museum curator and artist Gordon McConnell, who helped with accessioning her work for the museum, considered Johnson one of the first Modernist artists in the state. "She filtered her experiences of the ranch, the river, the mountains through her training and her study of the masters, above all, Cezanne. Johnson looked for the essentials of her subjects."[33] Melton also saw Cezanne's influence on Johnson's work, pushing and challenging the possibilities of her land as it was filtered through her personal vision and the way she saw the world. Melton said of Johnson's work, "[She] emphasized seeing, not merely looking, and never allowing one's work to be overtaken by the wiles of a facile hand or a false emotion."[34]

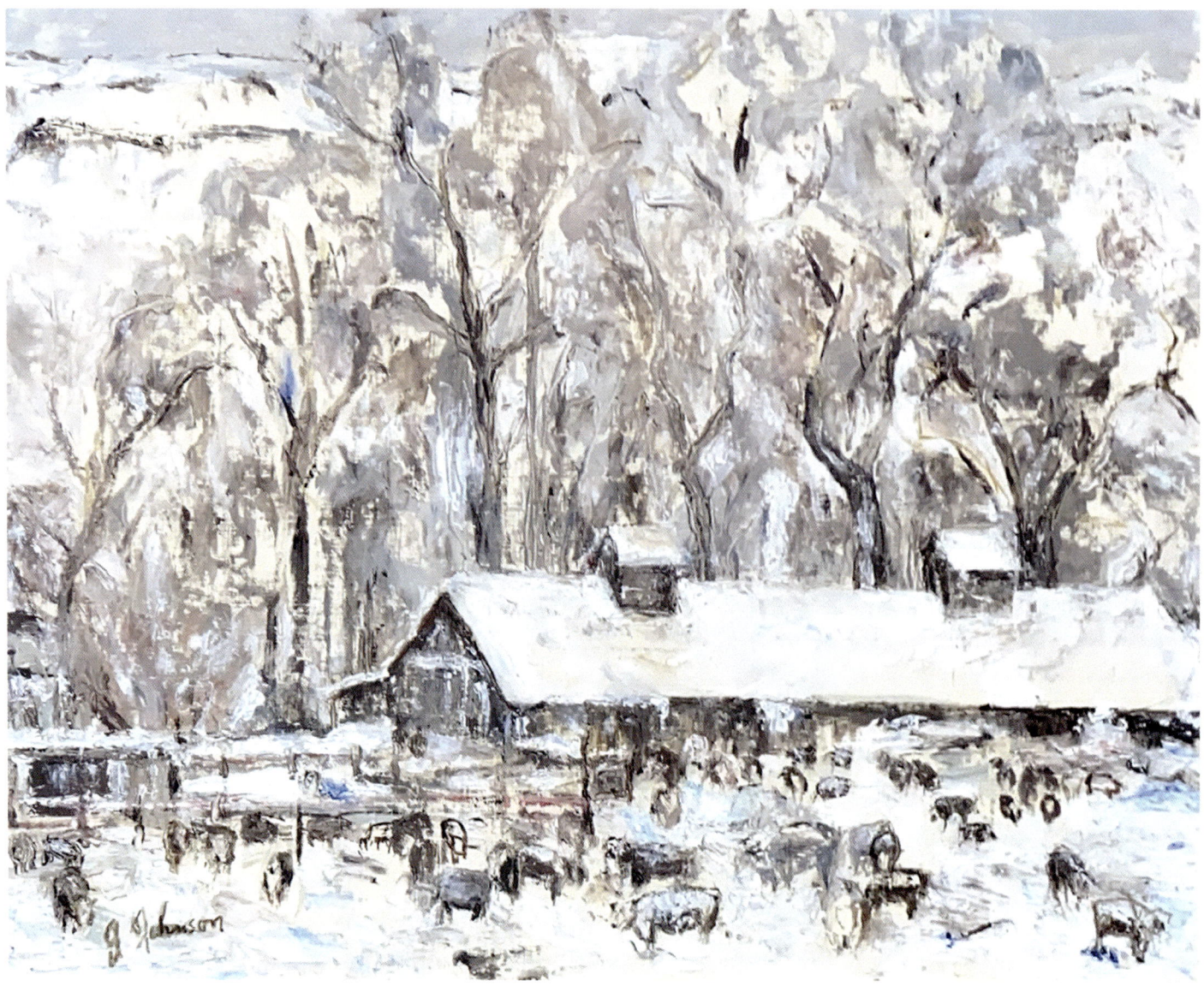

Isabelle Johnson, *Home Ranch*, 1955, oil on canvas board, 24 x 30 inches. Collection of the Yellowstone Art Museum; Gift of Isabelle Johnson Estate. Courtesy of the Yellowstone Art Museum.

Johnson explains the essence of her 1955 painting *Home Ranch* (page 22):

> It was in the winter and probably ten below zero or so. But the reason I did it in oil is that one summer when I didn't have very much to do I did a picture out the window of the sheep shed with the stock and the field. It wasn't very colorful, but a friend of ours came from Argentina and when he left, he picked the painting up and said, "I'm going to take this home with me and you have nothing to say about it."[35]

A few months later, he sent her a photograph of it framed, in his office:

> He worked for the embassy in Buenos Aires. And I thought, well, if that subject is good enough for an embassy office, it's good enough for me to paint. So when winter came, I started getting interested in the sheep shed and the cattle and so forth, and when it was really too cold to go outside and the cattle were fed and standing around still hungry looking, but satisfied and full, I started to work on what I call my home ranch series or sheep shed series, because I have three of these...it was in the winter when it was too cold to get out and work and that seems to be when I get the most inspiration and like to work the best.[36]

Many of Johnson's paintings depict winter; she has been noted as saying it was a time she liked to paint. Perhaps, as she was a rancher, the winter season came with the most downtime, which facilitated her ability to paint more often. In the 1950 oil painting *Calves, Winter* (page 24), John-son portrays nine white-faced calves deep in snow. All recognizable yet none distinct. Johnson's deep understanding of color and tone comes through in the vast array of stolen moments where she enables the viewer to see hints of spring through seemingly endless winter snow. Peeking out beneath the hooves, a sprinkling of vibrant early season grass in bright greens with a smudge of yellow can be detected. Her loose brushwork brings movement to the piece, as do the blurred faces that echo her colors adapted from the snow.

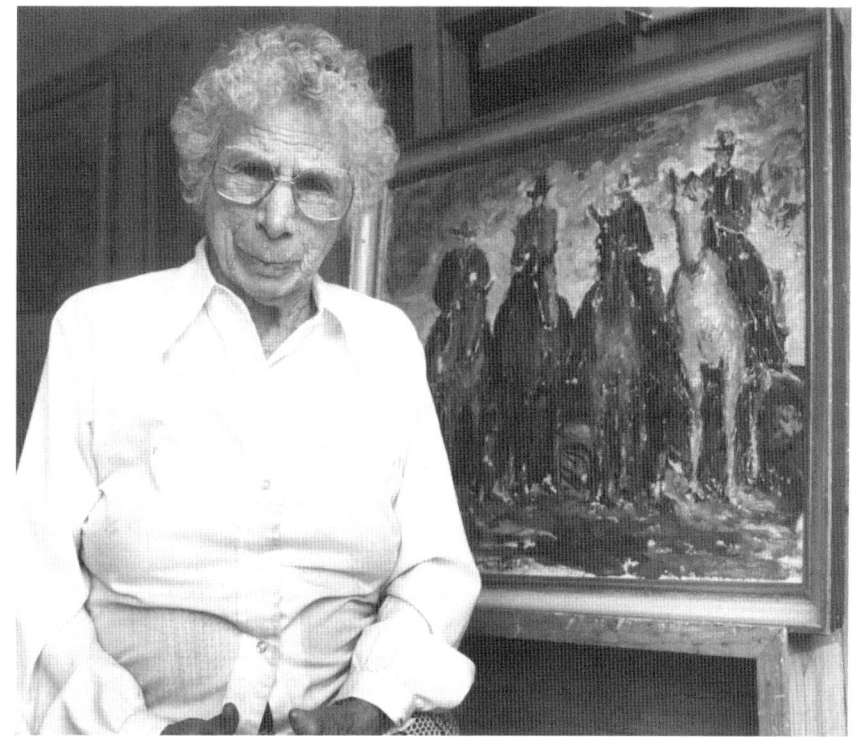

Isabelle Johnson in the 1980s.

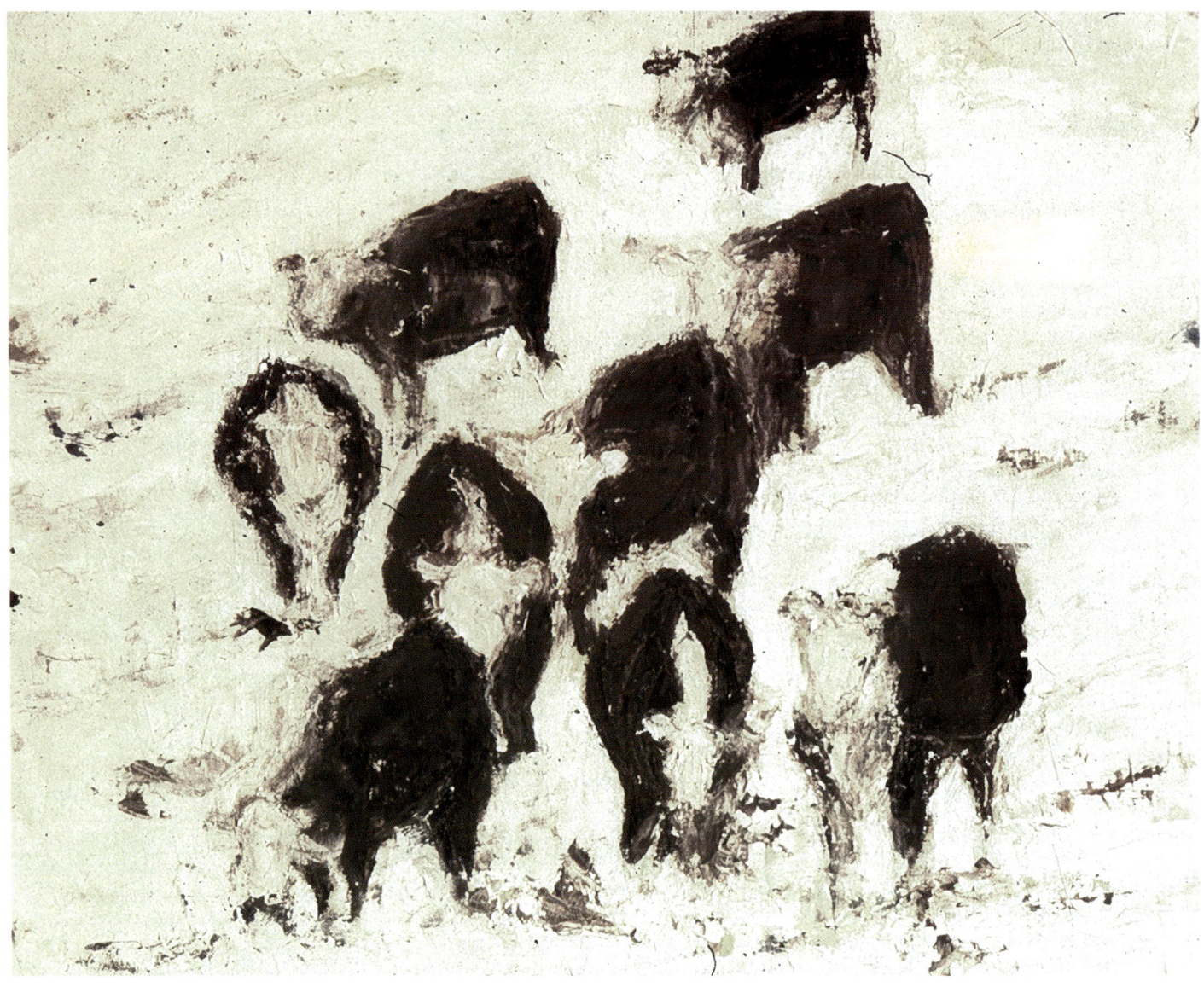

Isabelle Johnson, *Calves, Winter*, 1950, oil on canvas board, 15.5 x 19.5 inches. Collection of the Yellowstone Art Museum; Gift of Isabelle Johnson Estate. Courtesy of the Yellowstone Art Museum.

Many of her paintings, imbued with her love of winter, reflect a deep affection for that forced isolation apparent in her many-hued interpretations of snow. In fact she stated:

> It's winter I love the most. I don't know whether I like the muted colors that come with winter or I like the ice and things like that. I used to sit out when it was seventeen below zero and paint; I also liked the fact that if you were doing a watercolor, the paint froze, and I liked the effect it gave.[37]

After her years of teaching, she settled into her ranch life to paint full-time and, in 1983, she won the Governor's Award for Art. At this point in her life, she found no reason to leave the homestead, as everything important to her could be found in her surroundings. A lifelong student of nature and of livestock, she found inspiration lingering around every bend in the creek and in the shadows of every grove:

> Of course, most of paintings have to do here with the ranch. I think ever since I started painting, I have painted more at home than I have gone places to seek things to paint...because we've always had cattle; we've always had the river; we've always had trees; and we've always had mountains...so why go some place else when you've got everything right here?[38]

Upon Johnson's death she stipulated that three qualified people go through her work and decide which paintings and drawings should be accessioned by the Yellowstone Art Museum. Those people were Gordon McConnell, Bill Stockton,

and her closest friend, Donna Forbes. Forbes's relationship with Johnson paved the way for the Yellowstone Art Museum's acquisition of Johnson's entire studio collection, including 71 oil paintings, 240 watercolors, 317 drawings, and 40 sketchbooks. Stockton understood Johnson as a fellow artist; Forbes understood her as a painter and a friend. "I remember her hands. Tough, gnarled, arthritic. She was fond of looking at them."[39] Forbes saw the quintessence of Johnson's art embedded in those hands:

> They seemed to represent the embodiment of her art; the means of making that nervous line that marked on canvas or paper this place she loved so well....She saw this hard, rocky, handsome land with a painter's eye, and a rancher's sensibility.[40]

Isabelle had been warned while studying at Columbia that, if she returned to her home, there would be no one to understand the artist's struggle, no one to discuss those intriguing complexities found within a canvas. As Forbes said, "It was a lonely business, being a painter in Montana back in the 50s and 60s. She would have to be her own critic. Few rewards. Obscurity."[41]

Although she did not stray far from her ranch or travel much after 1961, she managed to create her own community through the visits of former students like Theodore Waddell and peers like Bill Stockton and Donna Forbes. She also kept up with colleagues through letters and postcards. In a letter to founding YAC director Terry Melton, she informed him of her comings and goings. "What makes you think I won't make the New York

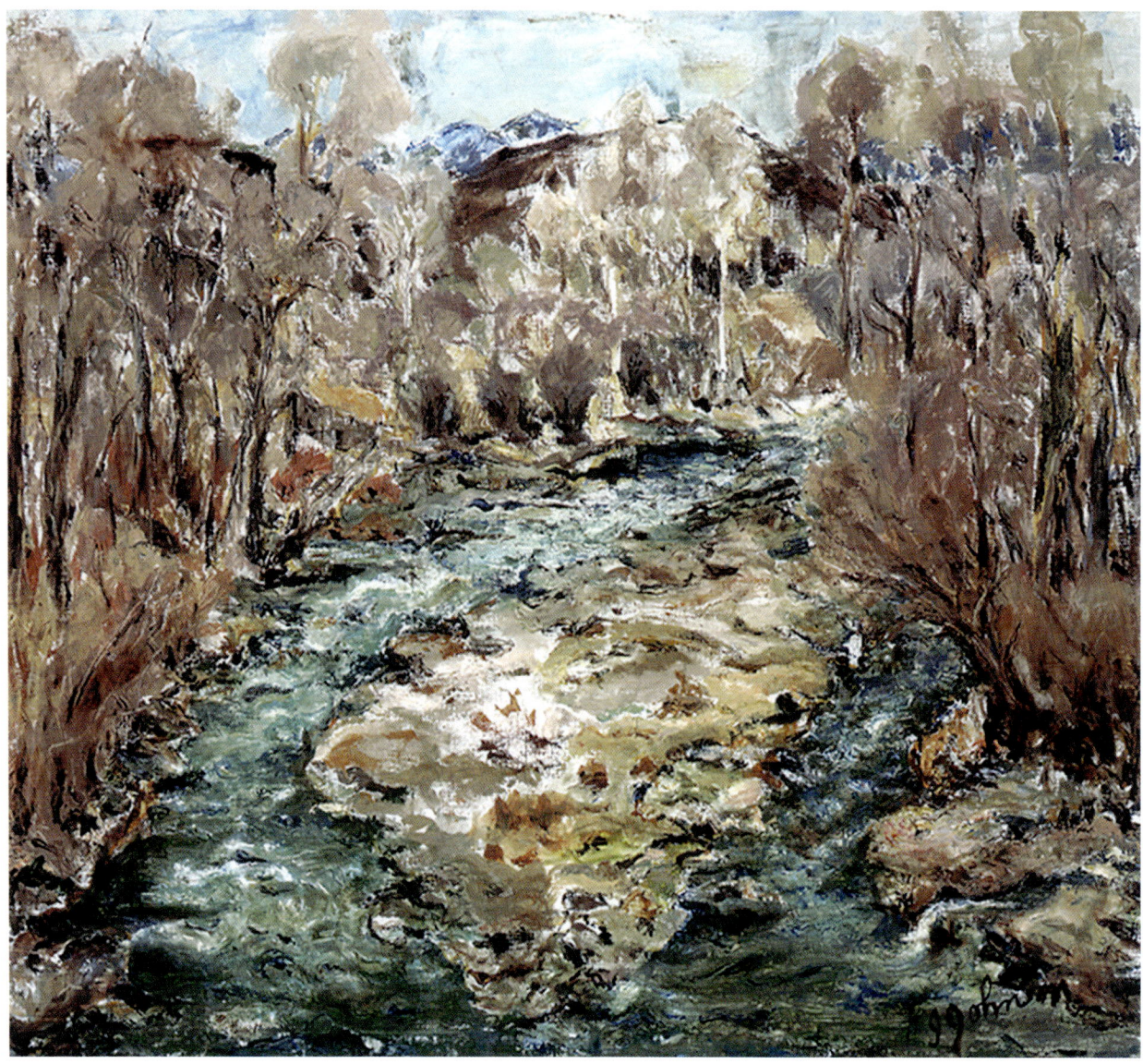

Isabelle Johnson, *Autumn on the Stillwater*, 1970, oil on linen, 38 x 42 inches. Collection of the Yellowstone Art Museum; Gift of Isabelle Johnson Estate. Courtesy of the Yellowstone Art Museum.

Scene?...I HAVE JUST BEGUN!" she wrote in 1971, at the age of seventy. "Hard to tell about the next ten years, I may degenerate to the level of the New York Scene—or—I may reach its heights." She went on to update Melton on Stockton, noting that he was too busy to make it to Great Falls for the annual Auction of Original Western Art Show:[42]

> He is too busy sounding off at the anti-coyote ecologists to attend openings.... [T]his summer there was a long article in the [Billings] Gazette about the saving of the coyote. A very sentimental and silly article written by someone who was unknowing of the animal (the coyote is my favorite wild animal, etc.).[43]

She went on to say that Stockton responded, "by packing two of his lambs killed by the coyote the night before the paper came out [and] he...mailed them, postage collect, to the *Gazette*."[44]

After Johnson's death, Stockton spoke about their relationship and his admiration for her work:

> Her paintings of the Stillwater River and the Beartooth Mountains and my paintings of my rock hillsides and brush coulees and images of our neighbors—we shared them—being Montanans and that was what it was all about, really. As an artist, Isabelle insisted on growth, not only for her students but for herself. She proved this in the 1950s.[45]

He admired her audacity in traveling to Europe at that point in her life, not as a tourist but as a student of art:

> She went as an artist, still searching, still curious, still learning. I remember when she returned, she mentioned to me that she had learned that Cezanne, her master, actually painted in layers of thin paint. Most of us have not sufficient humility to learn in our later years and this might be why Isabelle is a great artist.[46]

Former Yellowstone Art Museum Curator Gordon McConnell described her as crusty, authoritative, firm in her convictions, and able to justify any of her judgements very eloquently. His respect for her work grew the longer he knew her and the more he visited her ranch on the Stillwater River:

> She truly captures the experience of being in that country, the grandeur, and the enveloping quality of it, in a way that a more realistic painter absolutely could not do. Her work is so tied to the place, and she interprets the place on a high level of artistic expression. She was a true artist who changed my perceptions—I love Montana more because of her paintings, seeing the landscape through her vision.[47]

One of her later paintings done in 1970, *Autumn on the Stillwater* (page 26), envelops the viewer in the fauna of life as if they were standing on a bridge overlooking the dynamic Stillwater River. The muted fall tones frame the piece, but the thick application of oil paint textures a surface pulsing with movement. The composition, although likely thought through, feels spontaneous. The river's edge, rustling with color, speaks to Johnson's relationship with place. McConnell notes that Johnson, like Paul Cezanne, looked for the essentials of her subjects: "She strove not to over-describe. Her work is direct, strongly composed and harmonious, free of predigested rules and clichés."[48]

The value Johnson accorded to place extended beyond art to history and community. In addition to her contributions to education, after her retirement, Johnson helped compile essays for *They Gazed on the Beartooths*, a history of Stillwater County. She bequeathed her family photographs, personal letters, journals, and art studio furniture—along with a generous endowment—to support the Museum of the Beartooths in Columbus, Montana. Upon Johnson's death in 1992, the family's ranch was given to Montana State University and currently houses Tippet Rise, an outdoor sculpture park and performance space.

Johnson took the lessons of Cezanne, of color and form, of line, and an almost three-dimensional language and composition that connected her to her beloved Stillwater County. The creeks and valleys she knew and loved became a foundation for understanding herself through place. Throughout her life she sought to understand the nature of art and the history of place, and, in her own way, created a body of work rooted in Montana. The land might have appeared the same in the postwar period as it did before World War II, but she had changed, matured, and become more confident in her work. In the end, the way she depicted her cattle, her sheep, and her home became embedded with the light of Modernism.

BILL STOCKTON'S PORTRAYAL OF PLACE

Bill Stockton's paintings speak to place in a raspy hard-edged tone that catches on the prickly Rus-sian thistle of home in Grass Range. His own experiences blend to portray central Montana's hard edge and soft underbelly. Just before Stockton's birth in 1921, his father died and left his mother with a homestead in Winnett, Montana, as well as three daughters and a baby on the way. He was born in Minneapolis, where Stockton's mother moved to be with her sister for the baby's birth. Shortly afterward they returned to Winnett. During the early years of the Depression, Stockton's mother lost the homestead in Winnett, and they moved to Grass Range when Stockton was about thirteen.[49] According to Stockton's son, Gilles, Bill's mother met "a guy named Davies, a well driller. My grandmother always had cows, even though she lost her homestead. She and Davies entered some kind of relationship and together they moved to Grass Range, but he died from cancer immediately afterward." Upon his death Davies left Stockton's mother the property, which then became the Stockton family ranch. "I asked my dad what kind of guy Davies was, and he said he was a really great guy." Right after the move to Grass Range in 1934, Stockton's sister, older by one year, went blind and died. "That period had a lot of tragedy, the weather, the move, his sister, and Davies's death. It really colored his childhood."[50]

While in grade school, Stockton tried to get out of attending school any way he could, including by skinning skunks in the mornings before class. "I knew that young boys smelled bad naturally but add to that the smell of a skunk and the teacher wouldn't allow you in the classroom. I used this technique of skipping school several times. I had that figured out."[51] Still, Stockton graduated from high school in either 1938 or 1939. Sometime after graduation Stockton worked in Yellowstone National Park, where he met other young people from around the country, put on skits, and got introduced to the arts in a way that, according to Gilles, seeded his natural artistic tendencies. When he returned from Yellowstone, his interest in art was piqued. Before getting the opportunity to follow his interest in art, World War II broke out and he joined the army. Traveling from Salt Lake City to California as a military policeman guarding the troop trains, he sketched the African-American porters in exchange for the "good food."[52]

According to his wife, Elvia Stockton, Bill "was the luckiest solder in the whole American Army." Because he showed acuity with math, the Army thought he would serve best as a refrigerator repair mechanic and sent him to a school in Texas to learn the trade. When he arrived in Texas, the army never sent an instructor to teach refrigeration repair. "But it was on his papers, so when he got to France they said, 'Oh we need you in this hospital.'"[53] They asked Stockton what he could do, and he replied that he could paint signs. The luck came into play when, during the Battle of the Bulge, orders from Army headquarters demanded every able-bodied man be sent to the front. Stockton showed up to report for duty, but, because his papers still stated his position as a refrigerator repair man, he was told he was too important to the hospital and was ordered to remain in the town just outside of Paris.

Although he did not fight during the Battle of the Bulge, he did see the results:

They sent casualties from the Bulge, it's not what the average person thinks, a lot of those kids were from Florida and California, a lot of them never had seen snow, so there would be lines and lines of them out there on stretchers and their feet would be frozen. They amputated an awful lot of feet and legs.[54]

In the hospital Stockton worked as a sign painter, skills he learned from French and German sign painters. In a 1999 artist statement accompanying a traveling exhibit, he wrote, "It was [a sign painter] who taught me the right use of brushes, and how to apply paint. I use that knowledge to this day."[55]

The sign painters took him to a dinner party, where he met Elvia Cirefice, whose family's farm was just outside of Paris. "It was the first time I saw her. The second time I saw her was at a dance at the hospital. We got married at that hospital."[56] They married on June 30, 1945.

Gilles Stockton noted that his mother grew up between the farm and the city of Paris:

They had a house with a garden in the Ville Guif, it looks like it's called Jew Town but it dates back to a name of [a] Roman Villa 4 A.D. It also was a center for Communist Politics....[S]he talked about the girls going to Catholic School, but they'd sneak into the communist school because they had better treats.[77]

Gilles Stockton noted that his mother was used to the struggle of feeding herself and her family throughout the war:

They had a garden, and chickens, so she wasn't a total greenhorn [when she came to

Grass Range]. On the other hand, there was a culture of self-sufficiency in the women of Grass Range that she had to learn, all the canning, the cream, all of the things farm women did and they had to do it by themselves.[58]

After the war, when Stockton was discharged from the army, he took Elvia and his one-year-old son, Gilles, to Billings, Montana, where he worked as a sign painter. Elvia remembered not wanting to leave France and her own family for Montana, but she wanted to be with Stockton. "I felt terrible, terrible, but I was really too full of Bill. He never promised me anything because he didn't have anything. He didn't have a notion about the French." She knew he was a student and he liked art, "And that's all I knew about him."[59]

In 1947 he enrolled in the Minneapolis School of Art on the G.I. Bill and, the next year, went back to Paris with Elvia and his one-year-old son to attend the Academie de la Grande Chaumiere, a school previously attended by Hans Hofmann during the 1910s and Alexander Calder in 1926. He studied the Cubists like Georges Braque and Pablo Picasso, but it was not until he returned to Montana that he found his milieu.

In 1949, after Stockton returned to Grass Range, an issue of *Life* magazine suggested that the American Abstract Expressionist Jackson Pollock could be the greatest painter of his lifetime. Pollock's style reframed the infinite and incomprehensible compositions of nature into an active conversation between the artist and the canvas, changing how Stockton viewed both art and the environment. In an artist statement, he said, "It would be a few years later [after art school] that

I would see the Jackson Pollock paintings for their worth; he was composing patterns instead of objects."[60] While looking around his ranch, he noticed the intimate details of ranch life and said:

It made me see things on that hillside out there that never dawned on me before, why the hell do I need to paint a panoramic? Why can't I paint the things that are very close to us? I started looking at the textures, the patterns, the tones....I started to paint

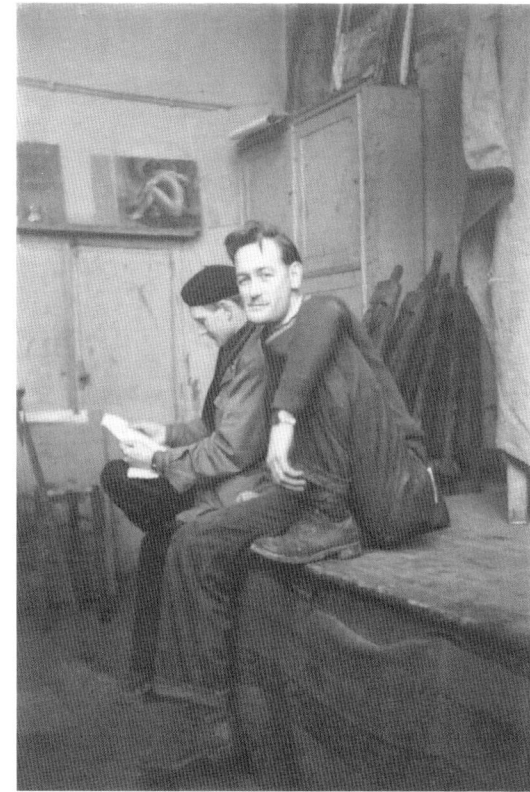

Bill Stockton in art school, Paris, 1948

that hillside, rearrange it, and compose it, put it in different rhythms.[61]

Underlying Stockton's work is a veil of a hard life scarred by living through the Great Depression, among other things. It was a time Stockton (and others who lived through it) called "The Dirty Thirties," referring to the dust storms. To Stockton the phrase became shorthand for the hard winters, the dry summers, and the death of his sister. These impactful and formative years laid down a foundation on which Stockton based a majority of his work and were the reason he never painted a clear, blue sky.

> I don't like blue skies. I go back to the [Great] Depression. The blue sky and the hot sun and the grasshoppers ate up everything. Even the worms came in and ate everything, then the Mormon crickets came in and they ate everything. Because of the hot sun we couldn't raise any crops, there's the Dirty Thirties on top of it. The Depression on top of it. All of it combined, I blamed it on the blue sky.[62]

His internalization of place embedded in his life lived in Grass Range comes across as the essence of his work, the tone of his paintings, and the compositions he envisioned. He noted that, because he lived in that terrain, walked out of his door to a horizon of hillsides, bushes, a few pine trees on the hill, snowstorms, and the bitter, dry weather of August, each day became a constant fascination to him. "These forms, I was born and raised in these forms, and thank god, Jackson Pollock came along and exposed me to them," he said.[63] It took him

a long time to understand that this was art, his art, his sense of place, and he could not help but paint it.

In the way of someone who knows every step of his property, every acre and every ewe, he stopped trying to convey the pictorial scene onto the canvas and instead relayed *what* he experienced, something he called the "uncommonness of life." As he wrote in the preface of his book, *Today I Baled Some Hay to Feed the Sheep the Coyotes Eat*:

> The snow is a foot deep; the wind continues to blow, and the sheep have given no sign that the weather will break soon. The storm is not unusual for April; it, like death, is part of the sheep business. Lambs... Lambs...Lambs...that is what it is all about: first, lives to be saved, then to be wasted. A paradox for a conscious carnivore—a natural procedure for the insensitive—I have so many memories of cold, miserable little lambs with stiff, clammy bodies—some so near death I had to hold a cigarette paper to their mouths to see if they were breathing...I have carried armloads of them into the house and warmed them by submerging them in basins of hot water. I have fed them for hours, drop by drop, before I could discern a slight movement in their prostrate bodies.[64]

Stockton's distinct voice calls out from Grass Range like the baleful coyotes he tirelessly kept from his sheep. His paintings divulge the sudden blooms of winter's snow, the boot-sucking mud of defrosting springs, and the dry, brittle grasses of blinding summers, where blue skies meant nothing but cracked soil in want of rain. It was Pollock's philosophy of portraying the patterns of his daily life, the rocks, the field, the weather, and the ground itself that enabled Stockton's work to evolve and embrace the abstractness of nature.

As in *Snow Formation* (1955; below), the angles of driving snow appear across the piece like a battleground with flying, jagged swipes of color. A blue background spans the painting without a clue to the horizon line, foreground, or background. Like a ground blizzard, *Snow Formation* steals the certitude of safety, of surefootedness. Wild brushstrokes slash black, grey, and white, while the blue underpainting speaks to the below-cold drifts, oblivious to any life it may smother.

Grass Range sits right in the middle of Montana. In 2020 it had a head count of 105 people and a population in steady decline since 1920.[65] For Stockton that meant few neighbors and even fewer artists with whom to share his ideas and his work. He notes in his artist's statement from 1999 that his wife, Elvia, "knows more about art than, sometimes, even I would believe,"[66] which may have indicated just how much Elvia was involved in Stockton's art world.

Stockton wrote a 1966 letter to Johnson sending his regrets about not making it to Johnson's opening at the Yellowstone Art Center, but he did get to see her show. "It was certainly one of [the] best I had seen there. In fact, there were three or four I would like to own. It was such a

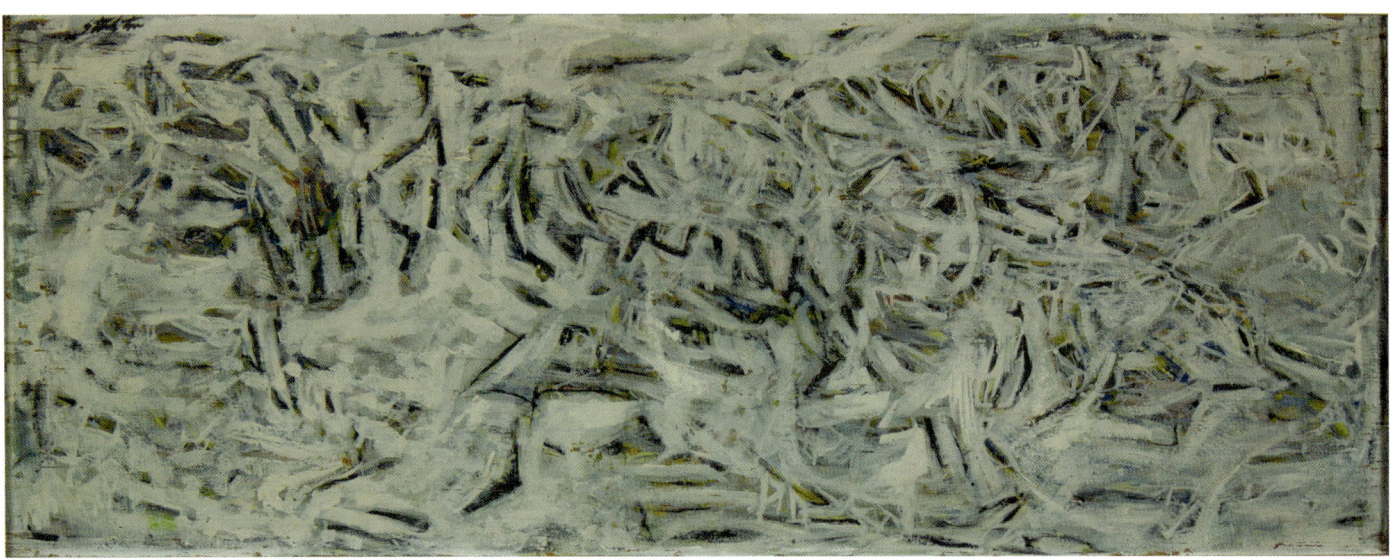

Bill Stockton, *Snow Formation*, 1955, oil on plywood, 18 x 48 inches. Courtesy of the Stockton Family.

relief to see someone paint with a little style." He noted, "I'm frankly very bored with all the arbitrary, pretty designs that the Center likes to call art." At the end of the letter, Elvia invited Johnson to dinner, ending it with, "We are anxious to hear from you."[67] Since they sent the letter together, it is most likely that Stockton shared his thoughts with Elvia and Elvia with him.

When Elvia Stockton relocated to Grass Range, she said:

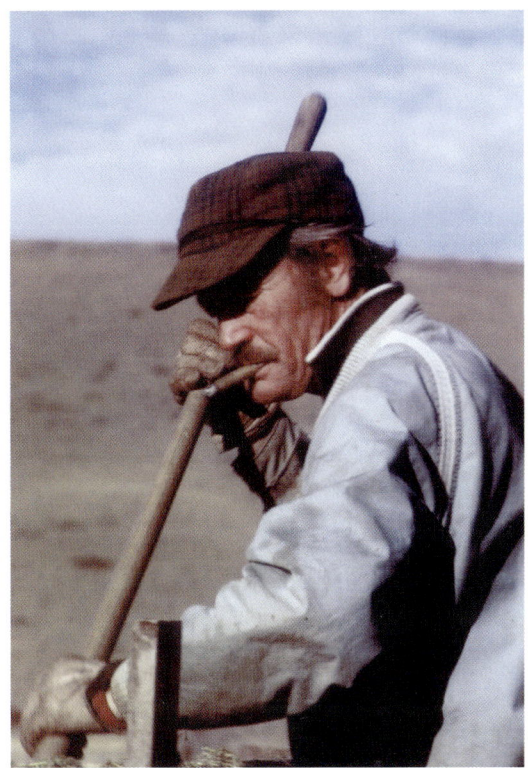

Bill Stockton feeding sheep on his ranch, 1972

It was a shock! There was really the shock! This place was just an old shack. [Stockton's mother] had a little house in town, but this place, I mean, Bill had told me that's the one thing where he didn't keep his promise. He said I would never be cold again. By Gosh, the winter of 1949-50 was the worst. I think it was forty-five below, and we had just a little old shack, and no water in the house. It was very cold.[68]

The hardships of Grass Range never became severe enough for Elvia Stockton to want to leave. "I liked physical work," she said. "We didn't have a cent to our name. We didn't have any livestock." The tough circumstances may have helped to form a closer relationship. Elvia said her husband never promised her riches or comfort:

He never told me that I would get this or that, never, so everything we done, we done together....I am not going to say that everything was rosy, rosy because the first ten years, anyway, really were very difficult. Bill was torn between all the work to be done at the ranch and his desire to paint.[69]

For both Elvia and Bill Stockton, there was not only the isolation of a small community but also an isolation of accessible culture, which may have added to the honest bareness of his work. The only contemporary museum in the state was the Yellowstone Art Center in Billings. In the winter, roads became hard to travel, although, when they could, the Stocktons would visit Bozeman, or the DeWeeses would visit Grass Range. While Terry Melton lived in Billings, Stockton would visit him on occasion. Melton remembered him as

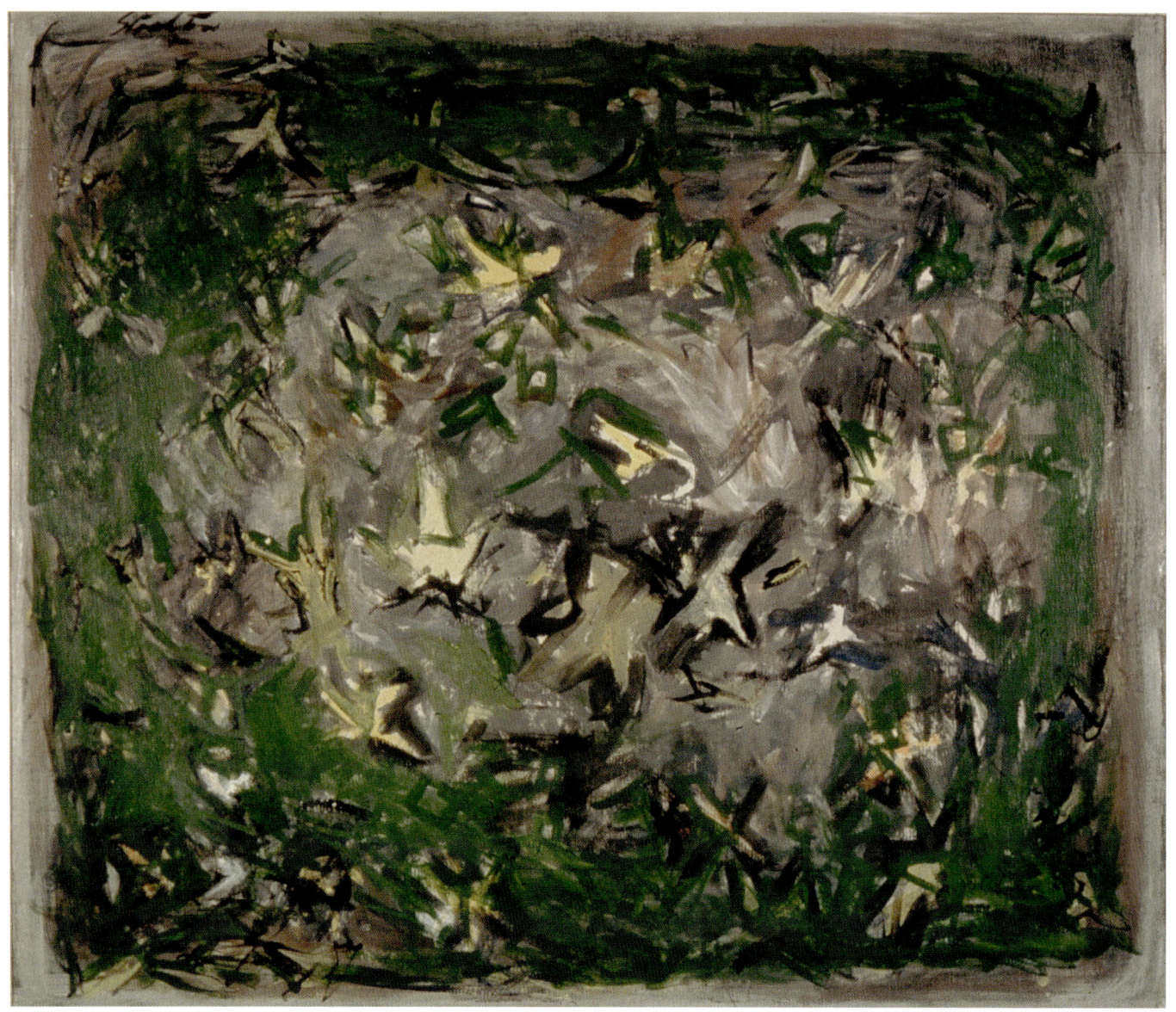

Bill Stockton, *Start of Spring*, 1957, casein on canvas, 21.75 x 25.75 inches. Courtesy of the Stockton Family.

an old friend and an authentic original. Bill was a painter, sculptor, rancher, curmudgeon of the highest order, sheep-raiser, pea-planter, and champion antagonist toward the US military ICBM silos being drilled into his prairie to the east of his hardscrabble ranch in Grass Range.[70]

Melton described Stockton's paintings as resembling the Abstract Expressionists, "but codified with his views of his prairie-ranch country. I really couldn't tell if his painting marks were Pollock drips or abstractions of prairie and riverside weeds and willows....Bill Stockton was a one-of-a-kind individual, a friend for all seasons, and a knockout painter."[71]

Through Stockton's abstracted observations of the seasons, the added joy of the end of winter can be seen in his 1957 painting *Start of Spring* (page 34). In this piece, Stockton's pure elation at the first nibs of grass, the swirl of the meadowlark's call to spring, and the complication of longer days, which meant more work, all fight for space on the canvas. Throughout, sounds of the season permeate the piece. By depicting the individual forms, Stockton conveys the feeling of the soft earth thawing through a tough frost. "I've always been fascinated by the ugliness of it, the hardness of it. That's me. I'm not dainty," he noted in a documentary video. "I suppose my lifestyle had something to do with my temperament and my mental processes. Why would I consider a bunch of dead Russian [thistle in a] coulee beautiful? I don't know why. It says something to me."[72] This reflects the way Stockton internalized his place in the world, not just in his backyard. The physical

isolation he felt comes through in the starkness of a limited palette and the frenzied motion of his brushstrokes.

McConnell noted Stockton's intellectual acuity regarding art: "Just observing life, being very present in his experiences, he loved the remoteness, being immersed in nature and struggling to make a living—which gives his work real power."[93]

In 1958 Stockton's work was accepted into four important shows, including *Art USA* in New York and the annual art shows in Denver and Spokane,[74] but it was a show in San Francisco that soured his attitude to the larger "art world." Leaving Grass Range with his wife, two sons, their dog, and the promise of a gallery show, he headed west. Once there he lost his confidence when, standing in the gallery, he heard someone say, "By God, people in Montana think they're artists?" Oddly enough, the show opened the door to invitations to New York City, Denver, and Spokane shows, but, for Stockton, it was too late; the dream was shattered. Looking back on that incident in 1994, Stockton said, "I came home and said to hell with it. I'm happy to become a Montana artist, a regional artist, and I'm happy the Yellowstone Art Museum has my stuff."[75] In Montana he felt his work could be understood as part of the language of a shared landscape.

Theodore Waddell, who knew him well, described Stockton as a "wonderful curmudgeon who could snatch defeat from the jaws of victory,"[76] summing up Stockton's shying away from a burgeoning international art career. After Stockton decided he wanted no part of the bigger art world but preferred to keep to the places

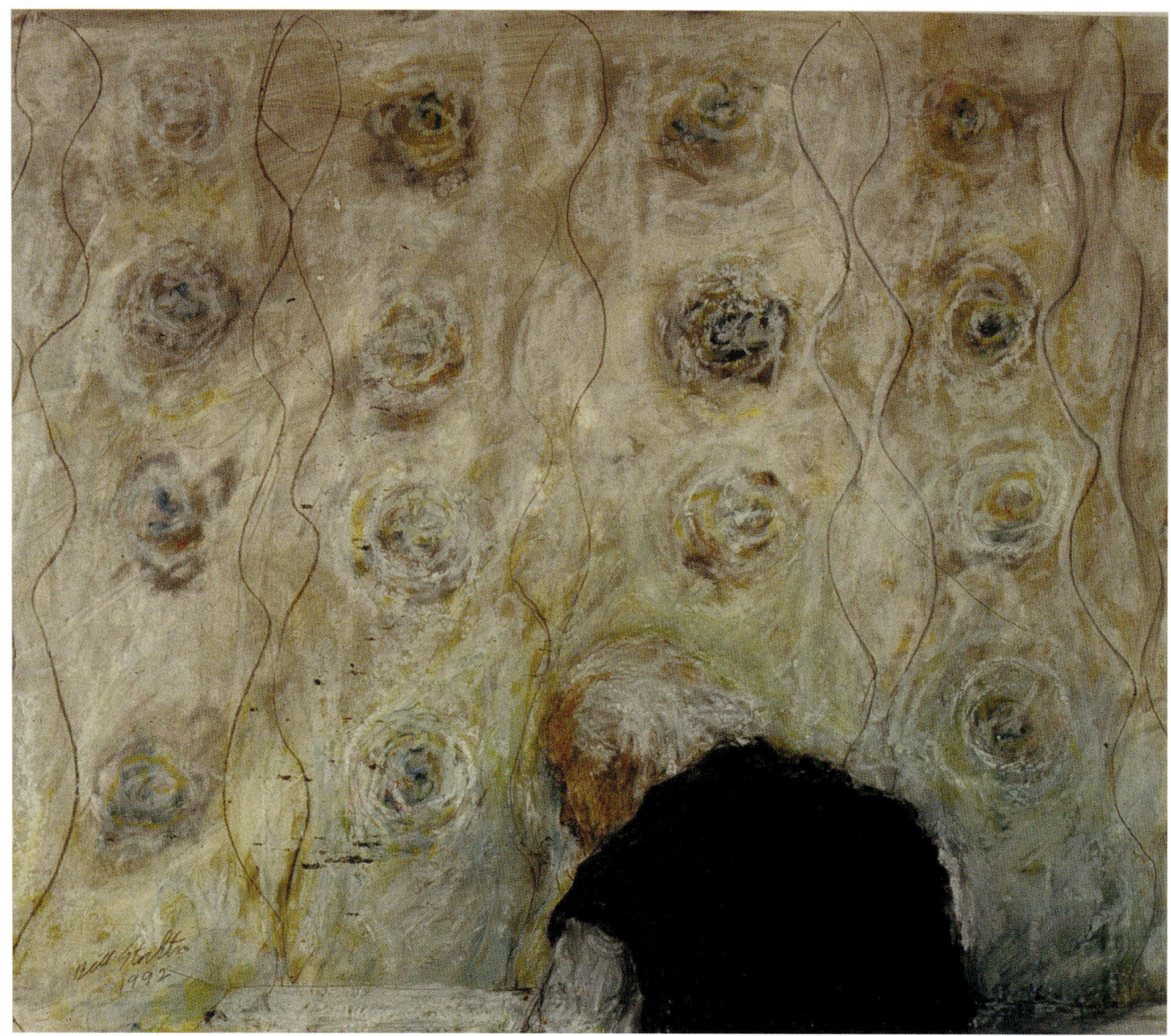

Bill Stockton, *Faded Roses*, 1992, livestock marker and graphite on paper, 22 x 28 inches. Courtesy of the Stockton Family.

he knew firsthand, his audience and potential collectors shrunk. For a time he was not sure he would survive, making a living off his sheep alone. By 1961 Stockton, fed up with the art world, wrote, "I realize that easel painting was the artist's greatest downfall. If he were lucky, it gave him a place among the middle class, it also offered the middle class the expensive, snobbish hobby of collecting."[77] In saying this he also spoke to the state of art collecting, by this time spread from the elite to the middle class. Then, in 1993, art patron Miriam Sample arranged for the purchase of seventy-seven of his paintings to be held in the permanent collection at the Yellowstone Art Museum in Billings, Montana.

When Miriam and Joe Sample sold their chain of television stations across Montana in 1984, they started their careers as philanthropists. Miriam Sample's project, the Meadowlark Fund, purchased the work of Montana artists. At first she bought art strictly for the YAM, but she later expanded to museums across the state and bought for the Buffalo Bill Center of the West, in Cody, Wyoming, which developed a contemporary collection based in part on the Yellowstone Art Museum's permanent Montana Collection.

According to Gordon McConnell, Yellowstone Art Museum curator at the time, "Miriam wanted to help Montana artists and Bill was the one she most bonded with, she felt like he was living in squalor, had a bad back and a broken-down bed. Her heart went out to him." She paid him $10,000 a year for ten years for the works she acquired. McConnell recalled that Stockton had built a kind of root cellar in the backyard where he buried his paintings. "We

were all just worried to death they would be ruined. His early work was as good as anyone was doing in the country at the time."[78]

For Stockton the sale to the Yellowstone Art Museum became another turning point in his career. With a major museum purchase, Stockton could stop hiding his paintings in the metal vault he kept under his bed or in the underground root cellar. He knew the best of his paintings, or what he called the "keepers," remained in safe hands.[79]

In his 1956 oil on plywood painting *River Rocks* (below), there is a likeness of the subject but

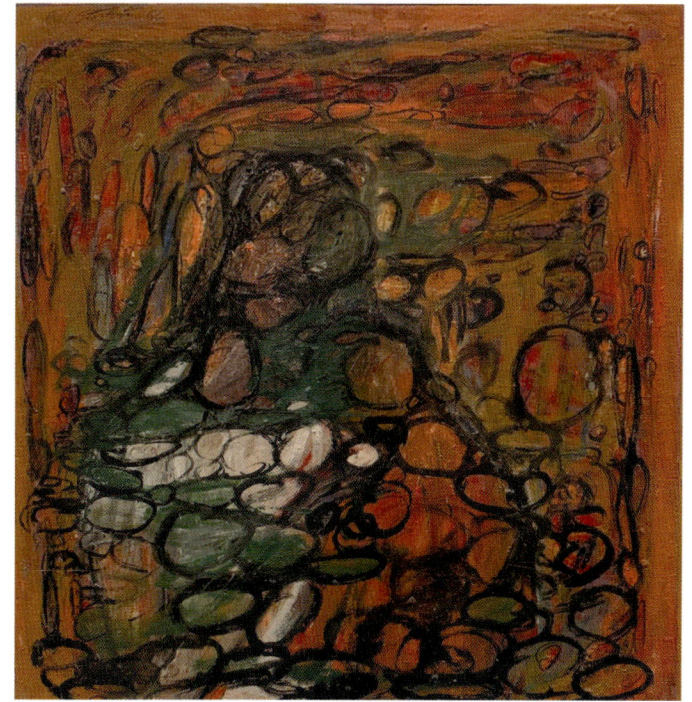

Bill Stockton, *River Rocks*, 1956, oil on plywood.
Courtesy of the Yellowstone Art Museum and used by permission of Gilles Stockton.

an insistence of the object of the painting itself. Each circle, an idealization of the river rocks, is not really a depiction of rocks per se. We can see right through them; the outlines are there to remind us of a river bottom flooded with rounded and polished rocks, but the colors—both vibrant and muddied—convey an honest portrayal of the underbelly of the river. The black outlines are reminiscent of the works of Post-Impressionists like Matisse and Cezanne, which draw our eye to each individual area of the painting, activating the entire canvas.

Another aspect of Stockton's work concerns his emotional past and is revealed in his wallpaper series. The series speaks to the role of memory in creating the formidable markers of life that resonate within the artist through his work. It is a kind of interior sense of place, one that feels more intimate than his pattern-impressions of the land.

One such piece from his wallpaper series, *Faded Roses* (page 36), painted in 1992, consists of the repeating pattern of ghosted flowers, disappearing petal by petal into the yellowed and uneven background. Although the pattern gives the viewer the impression that each repeated rose appears identical, the maker's hand clearly stands out. Like so many days gone by, differences gradually dissipate. Deviations from each rose denote not only a wistful regret but also the countdown of the calendar. Included in this piece is Stockton's own bent figure, with a downward glance as seen from behind. His white hair and aging face, delicately defined, echo the self-portraits of Rembrandt. He includes himself because this wallpaper reflects his own memory of growing up

in small houses, in small towns, where the bare cobbled walls offered little distraction from the hard farm life in central Montana. Stockton said, "In an attempt to bring some art into our crummy little houses [my mother would] look in Sears and Roebuck and buy some wallpaper. And then they'd try to paste it. It came with instructions, but you really need a professional, they [made] a hell of a mess." For Stockton, the wallpaper represented a way to think about home and hearth, and an avenue by which to access the individual's struggle for beauty under even the most dire of circumstances. There is a certain strength in the recollection of a place when that place cradles hard memories and deep-seated emotions:[80]

> And those damn things, roses or some kind of flower, things never matched, they never got it quite right, they even show up sometimes in an abandoned old farmhouse and you still see wallpaper stuck to it. That's my memory of wallpaper—it's a repeat design. It slid here and it slid there, even Cezanne would drop one end of a table top to give it motion, they did that and created something.[81]

In his work with oil, water colors, tempera, and oil stick cattle markers, Stockton's interest in the surface and texture of the piece, no matter the medium, beautifully complicates his art. Observing each aspect of his ranch, from the coulees to the hillsides, from the sheep he tended to the interior of his home, he never forgot the formal aspects of his art. For him it was about creating tension through "the push and pull of color, line, texture, and form," as Hans Hofmann taught. "Opposing directions… it takes your eye one way and then the other,"

Stockton said, talking about the way he thought about composition. "I got very fascinated with the brush, more than the rocks. What I had to learn in painting was to create the surface."[82]

In *Dusk* (below), painted in 1984, his surface confronts the viewer with a thick and wild demeanor. Color fairly dances with the drawing down of light. Blues, greens, and yellows each swirl and shove as a single orange line across the top of the painting implies the horizon dipping toward evening. His use of graphite pencil enables him to detail the thicket amongst abstracted shadows of deep blue and black. The forms interact with a singularity that allows the viewer to participate with the painting. The rich hues and almost dreamlike colors demonstrate Stockton's ability to show depth and composition without giving in to traditional forms.

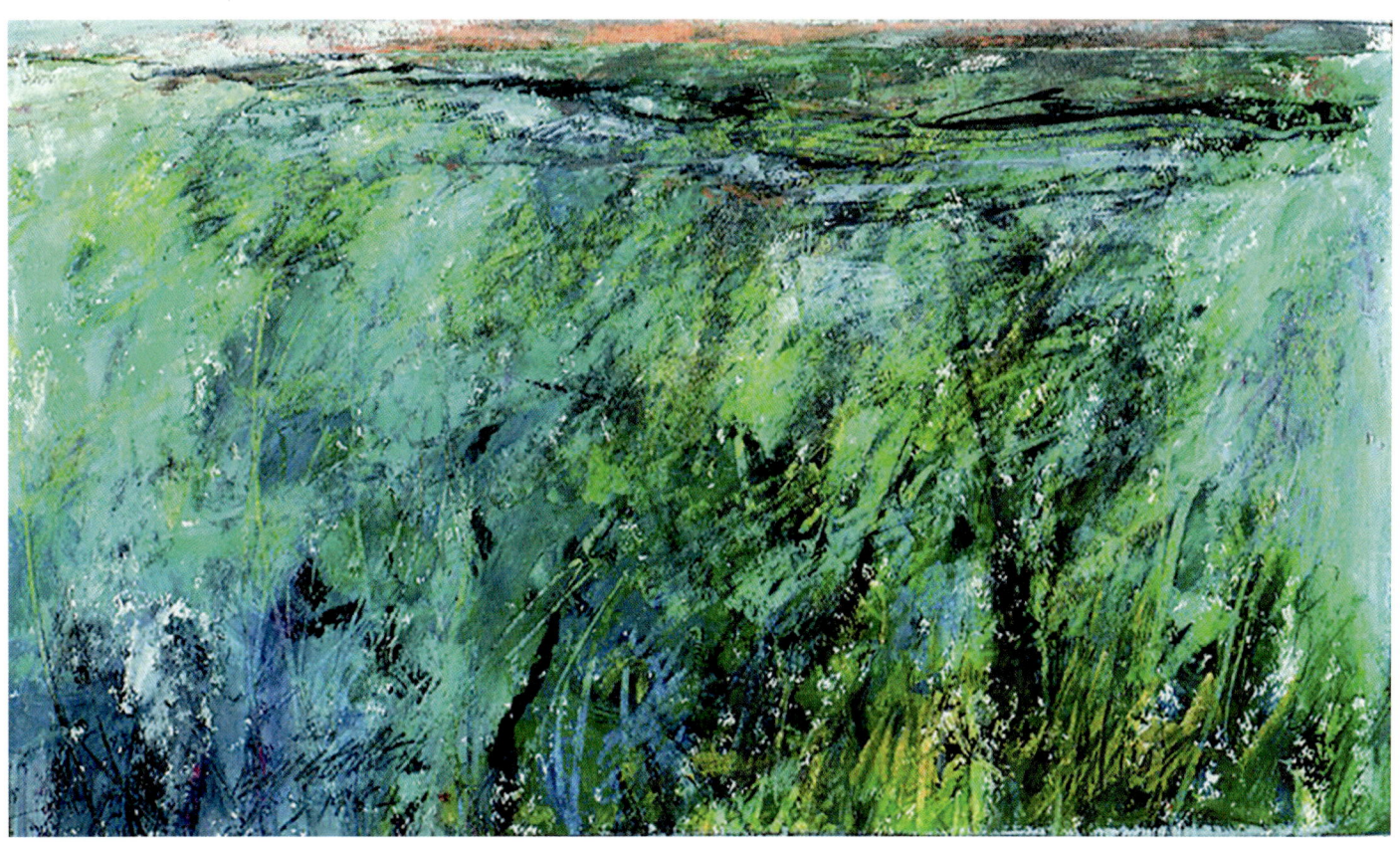

Bill Stockton, *Dusk*, 1984, livestock marker and graphite on paper, 9.25 x 17 inches. Courtesy of the Stockton Family.

In Stockton's 1983 *Village in Winter* (below), the isolation contributes to the tension in the painting, concentrated on a few windswept trees with hardly a leaf between them. Though the work is titled *Village in Winter*, the village is barely visible. The painting consists of a group-ing of rocks, a swell of earth, and a few out-buildings capturing the center of the canvas. The bluish white sky blends almost completely with the ash-like rendering of a snow-covered land. Swirling brushstrokes conjure frigid tem-peratures. This painting reveals Stockton's own

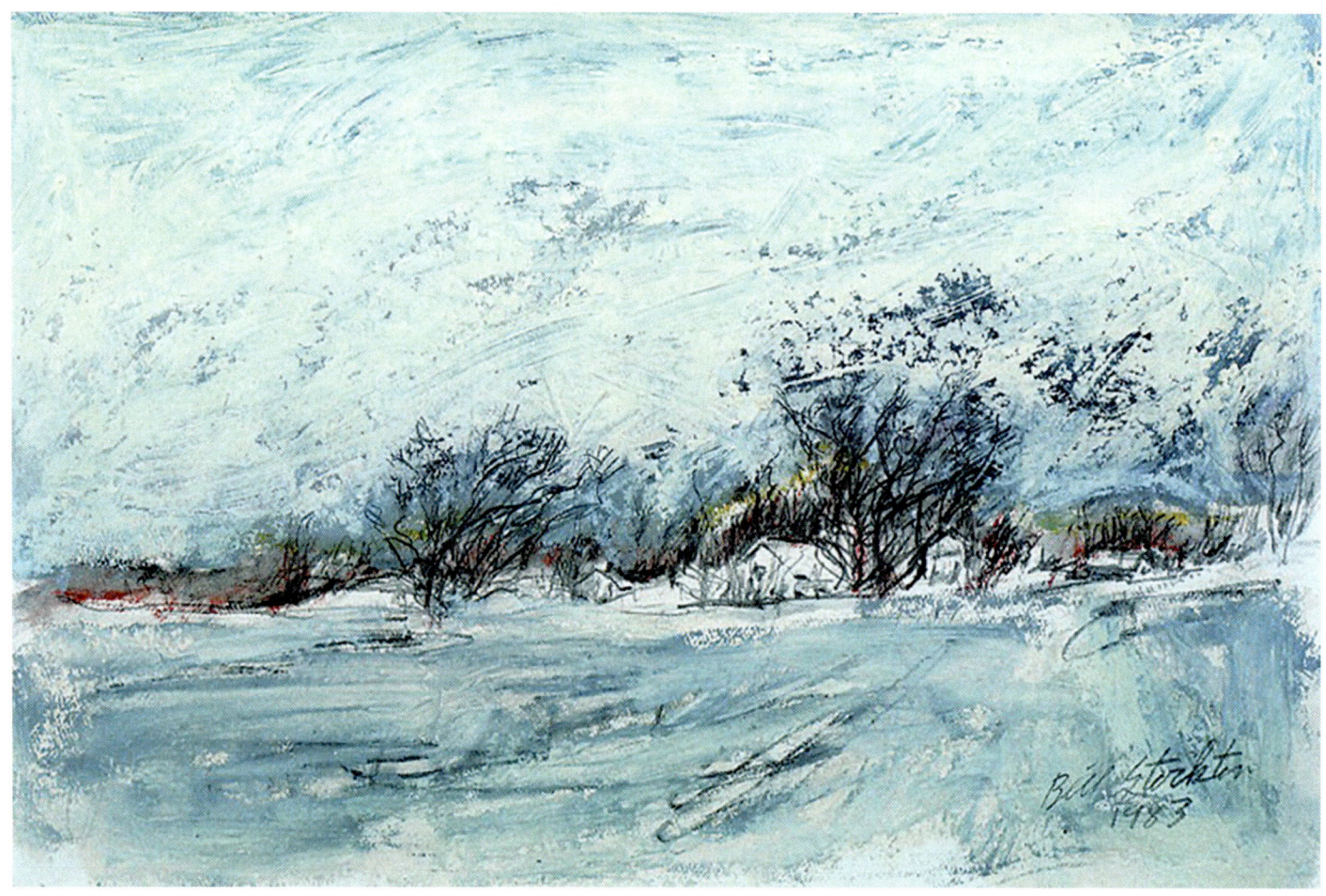

Bill Stockton, *Village in Winter*, 1983, livestock marker, graphite, oil pastel on paper, 10 x 16 inches. Courtesy of the Stockton Family.

experiential language as told through landscape as well as location. The bareness of the Montana prairie caught in the enveloping weather. Stockton's intimate relationship with chores comes through in an unfiltered and unromanticized expectation of the day.

Stockton did not keep to the medium of painting. He felted, made furniture, and sculpted—with a soldering gun and used iron nails he found. In his 1968 sculpture *The Conversion of St. Paul* (page 43), Stockton finds a way to talk about suffering and torment in the guise of the conversion of St Paul. This is the moment when Saul, on the road to Damascus, is stricken with God's light. Through his simple materials, nails and solder, Stockton is able to convey the fragility of life and the flash of enlightenment. Saul, whose job it was to persecute Christians, was on the road to Damascus when he was blinded by the light for three days. He experienced three days of darkness. Stockton's tender portrayal of Saul before he becomes St. Paul is very personal. He catches this single moment in time and enables the viewer to know what that might have felt like. One cannot help but make the association of nails with the figure of Christ, and so the meaning goes deeper with reflection. While the nail sculptures may not seem to speak to place, in fact, how else do we build our homes if not with nails? Stockton reminds us about the details of life, the days of labor, and the feeling of place, however we wish to define it.

Bill Stockton won the Governor's Award for Visual Arts posthumously in 2003, a year after he died of lung cancer at the age of 81. His notion of place became part of Montana's artistic history. He was quoted in the Governor's Award program as having said:

> I can get interested in almost anything: welded sculpture, hand-made felt, old photographs, stuff pasted to an abandoned farmhouse, and realistic portraits of my neighbors. But my main interest has been and always will be the harsh, abstract, semi-wilderness qualities of central Montana. Why? Because I was born and raised here, I guess.[83]

Donna Forbes observed that isolation became part of Stockton's process as well as his work. "He grew up in Grass Range, dirt poor. He took art classes in Paris, that's when he found his voice. But isolation is important to him and you can see it in his work."[84] She thought that it may be due to both his and Isabelle Johnson's shared sense of place, an acknowledgment of their Montana beginnings, and a need to put that on canvas.

Although twenty years apart in age, Johnson and Stockton both experienced a particular sense of their relationship to the land and sought to express that personal perspective through a Modernist lens. Both traveled to Europe, went to art schools in larger urban areas—Johnson in New York City at the Art Students' League and Columbia and later in Maine at the experimental Skowhegan school, and Stockton in Minneapolis and then Paris—then both returned to Montana with a new way to talk about who they were as artists and how they defined that.

Johnson and Stockton eschewed the commercially viable romantic scenarios of Montana

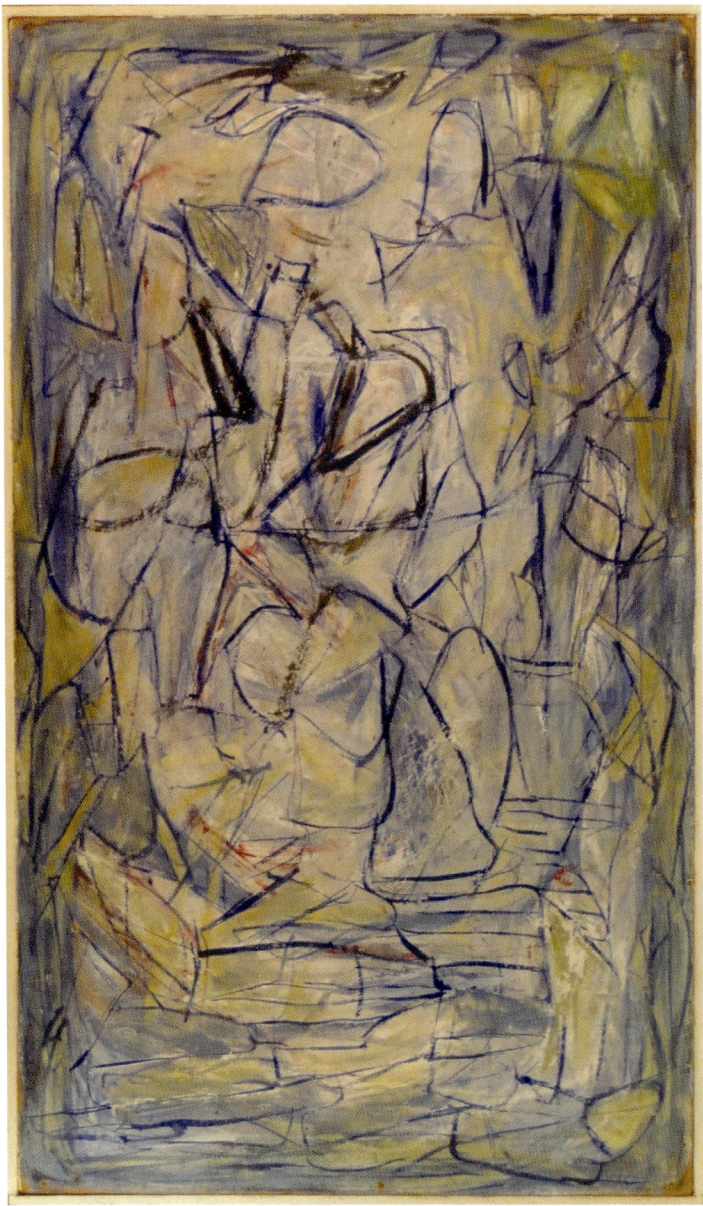

Bill Stockton, *Rock Formations*, circa 1950s, medium and dimensions unknown.
Used by permission of the Stockton Family

for something else. For them place as portrayed through their art embraced something more substantial, something they could stand behind. They were both ranchers, and their deep connection to and understanding of the land and animals brought them together and gave them a voice as strong as March winds across the prairie. As Donna Forbes stated of Johnson, "She was a rancher and tough as nails. Essentially her ranch and this Montana land here was her inspiration."[85]

Stockton and Johnson did not paint replicas of majestic mountains. They painted what they saw, exactly as they saw it, acknowledging the grandeur and the harsh conditions under which they toiled daily with equal measure. They brought their formal training to a place unfamiliar with the modern art world and, working on the vanguard of Montana's art scene, expanded the vocabulary of the day. In so doing they influenced many artists to come. Their shared perspective on where they lived and how they lived defined their art. It was a language that invited the viewer to understand place in the same intimate way they lived it. Bill Stockton and Isabelle Johnson offered up a landscape complex and gritty, helping others to understand their place, and in some way allowed viewers to make it theirs.

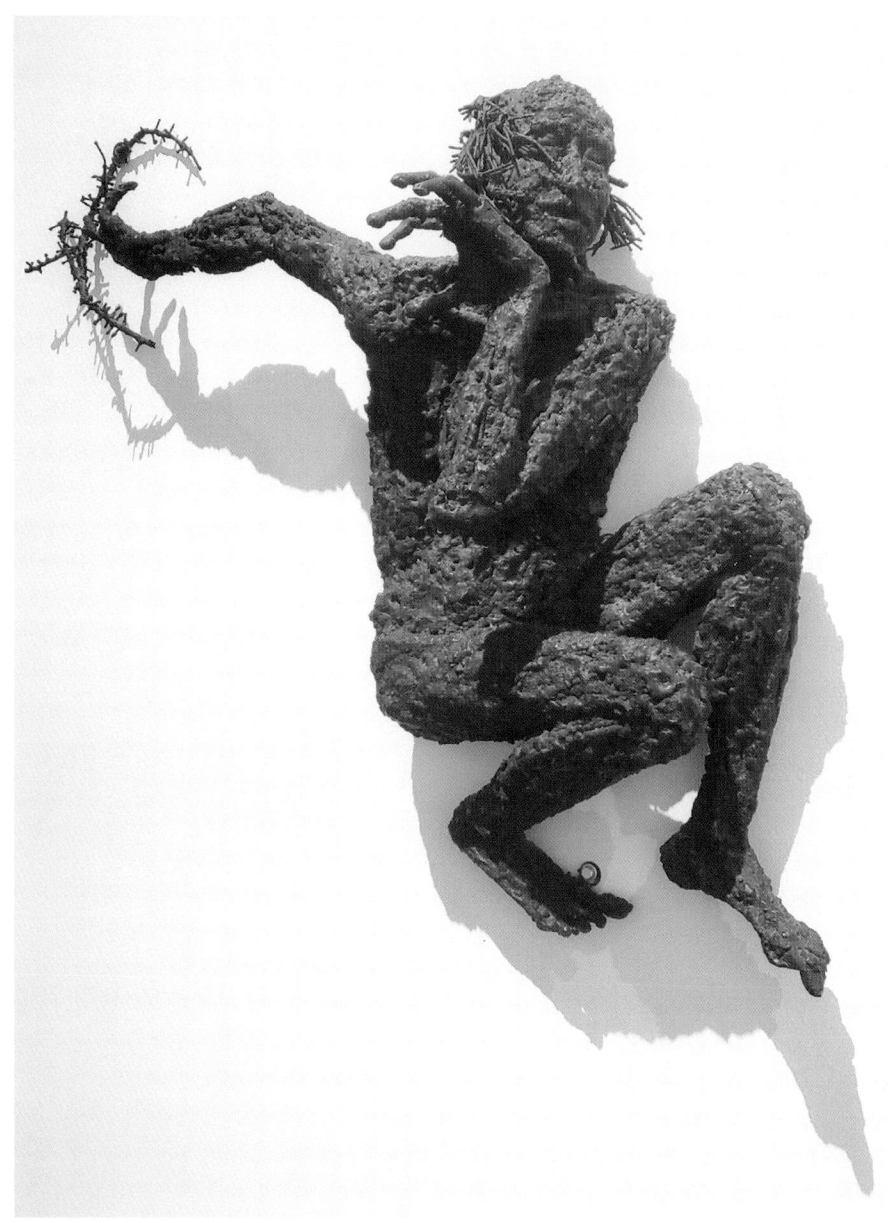

Bill Stockton, *Conversion of St. Paul* (*Saul on the Road to Damascus*), 1968, welded nails, 33 x 37 x 11 inches.
Donated by Lyla Dyer in loving memory of William Henry Eagle (1939–1962). Used by permission of Gilles Stockton.

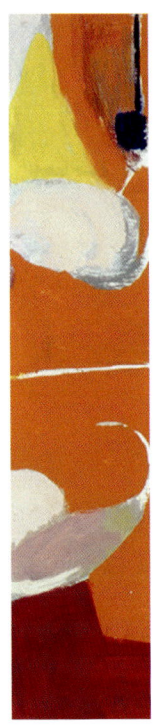
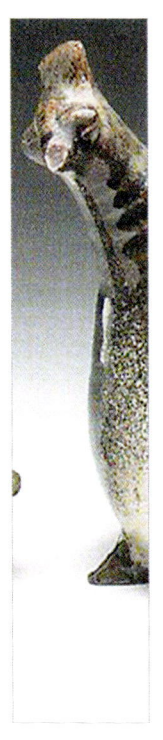
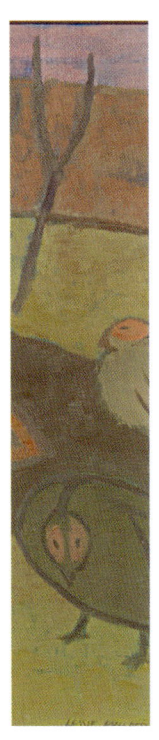
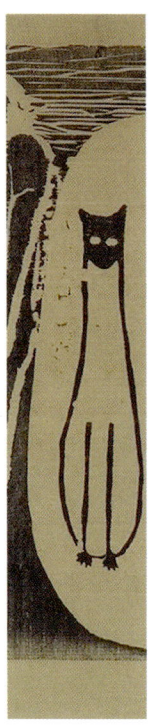
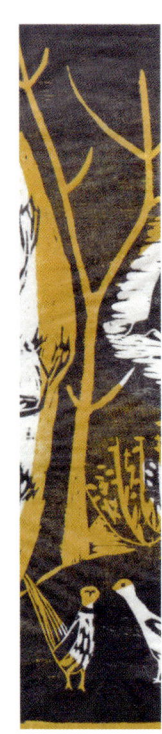
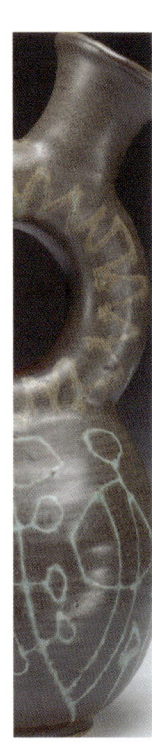

SECTION TWO: TEACHING/ ARTISTIC LINEAGE

Providing leadership by teachers and support of developing artists is a national duty, an insurance of spiritual solidarity. What we do for art, we do for ourselves and for our children and the future.[1]

—Hans Hofmann

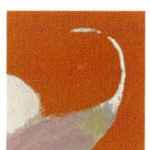

GROWING ARTISTS

Growing an artist is less like grafting than it is like planting seeds. When grafting trees, the aim is to reproduce the fruit grown exactly. When planting seeds variety and happenstance become part of the process. The first generation of Montana Modernists did not seek out students who would copy their techniques and concepts. Instead, the Montana Modernists' students grew into their own styles, creating the next generation of artists who passed on their knowledge, a knowledge culled from the generations before them.

Historically, artists worked with apprentices who watched and learned at the elbow of the master. A major shift in the student–teacher relationship happened in the postwar years due in part to the teachings of John Dewey and his methodology of teaching art as an experience rather than in a lecture setting. The art teachers at Montana State College adhered to Dewey's pedagogical principles and altered the traditional hierarchy of the classroom.

Frances Senska often said that the way she held her hands was the same way her teacher held them, and this is reflected in the way her own student, Peter Voulkos, held his hands. It feels more direct in ceramics due to the imprint of hands-on clay that follows from its maker to its beholder, from the artist to the person picking up the vase, the cup, or the bowl. However, the same can be said for printmaking, sculpture, and painting, in terms of technique and aesthetics. Robert DeWeese's students learned how to see through his mentor Hoyt Sherman's interpretation of vision. Jessie Wilber encouraged her students to experiment, to try something, as her teacher Otis Dozier suggested to her, and they did. Isabelle Johnson's round-backed horses merged with her student Theodore Waddell's cattle in his hillside imagery.

Through the filter of place and the experiences of their own lives, these artists passed on a unique aspect of their work; in turn they influenced their students, whose work was informed by them. Among those who took the baton of the Montana Modernists and passed it forward are those who also took on the role of teaching. The

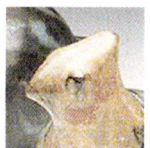

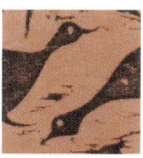

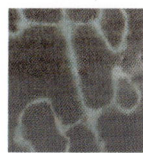

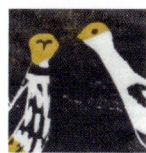

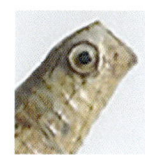

passing down of artistic legacy is as direct as the genetic inheritance of daughters and sons but as diverse as a high mountain field of wildflowers.

The list of artists whose work began with these six Montana Modernists is long, and its reach is far. (This short list is very incomplete but somewhat necessary to understand the depth and weft the first Montana Modernists had, and continue to have, for artists.) Pete Voulkos taught at the Otis Art Institute for five years and transferred to the University of California, Berkeley, to establish the Ceramics Department, where he worked until his retirement in 1985. Rudy Autio, together with Voulkos, was the first director of the Archie Bray Foundation and founded the ceramics program at the University of Montana in 1957. He continued teaching there for twenty-eight years. Ray Campeau, Butte-born and -bred, taught at Bozeman High School until his retirement and inspired many young artists. Sculptor James Reineking, a student of Robert DeWeese, became an internationally recognized minimalist sculptor, left Montana, and built a career in Germany. Pat Zentz, a student of Isabelle Johnson and friend of Bill Stockton, became a rancher and well-known sculptor who incorporates the environment and the language of science into his work. Theodore Waddell—painter, sculptor, and rancher—was deeply influenced by Bill Stockton and Isabelle Johnson. His work integrates the land and art, perception, and regard for place. Painter Jerry Rankin, a student of Senska, Wilber, and Robert DeWeese, constantly explores sound in his works. The DeWeese's son, Josh DeWeese, has carried on the legacy both directly by teaching art at Mon-

tana State University and through his directorship of the Archie Bray Foundation from 1992 through 2006. Although not a visual artist, Mary Overlie, an internationally acclaimed choreographer, credits her innovative modern/contemporary dance style to watching Gennie DeWeese paint.

It is through their teachings, their artistic lineage, and their lived lives that Modernism came to Montana, including the passed-down study of Post-Impressionist Paul Cezanne, the communal Bauhaus[2] philosophy, and the freedoms learned though Abstract Expressionism.

EDUCATIONAL LINEAGE

Hans Hofmann, one of the first artist-teachers in the Abstract Expressionist movement, described a legacy as a gift from the past to the future. Teachers who form future artists, like art-alchemists, take the raw talent and turn it into something greater than mere gold. By conferring their own experiences yet allowing for individualism and experimentation, the best teachers enable students to create their own rules and then figure out how to break those rules.

If we take a step back and examine educational lineage, the teaching philosophies of Isabelle Johnson, Bill Stockton, Robert and Gennie DeWeese, Frances Senska, and Jessie Wilber begin to gel. The Montana Modernists' educational lineage combines the Bauhaus aesthetics of László Moholy-Nagy and Marguerite Wildenhain, the teachings of abstractionists Hans Hofmann and Wassily Kandinsky, innovating artist-teacher Hoyt Sherman, and Texas mentor-artist Otis Dozier. Culled from these various disciplines and art philosophies is a common thread that can be traced back to Cezanne, "the father of us all," as noted by Pablo Picasso many times, due to his reckoning with the flat surface and his use of color to produce dimensionality.

With the exception of Bill Stockton, these Montana Modernists all taught art at the college level. Their work began in distinctly different disciplines, from Bauhaus and Abstract Expressionism, from abstraction and the science of seeing, yet they all thought of the classroom as a kind of laboratory where students were encouraged to embrace their curiosity. The big experiment, often used in reference to American democracy, found its place in the arts as well as in the classroom. Combined with the social aspect of a shared studio environment, the collegial attitude fostered a communal perspective.

FROM BAUHAUS TO ABSTRACTION

Frances Senska (1914–2009) attended **László Maholy-Nagy's** New Bauhaus school in Chicago in 1940. Then, in 1944, while still in the navy, Senska enrolled at the California Labor School with Modernist ceramicist Edith Heath. Senska also took classes at the Cranbrook Academy under the tutelage of Maija Grotell, often noted as the "Mother of American Ceramics," in the summer of 1946. Marguerite Wildenhain also heavily influenced Senska's style in art and teaching. Wildenhain's Farm Pond classes in California during in the summer of 1950 were the culmination of Senska's formation under Wildenhain's tutelage.

The Bauhaus Movement started in Germany (1919–1933) and moved to the United States under pressure from the growing Nazi regime. In 1937 Moholy-Nagy came to Chicago to be the director of the New Bauhaus: American School of Design, which reopened as the School of Design in 1939. It was later renamed the "Institute of Design" and is currently encompassed within the Illinois Institute of Technology. The following year, 1940, Senska became one of his students.

The main idea of Bauhaus combined fine art and function. Bauhaus ethics argued for taking the whole person into consideration. As the artist Maholy-Nagy said, "the healthy function of the man's body, his social performance and welfare, his nutrition, clothing and housing needs, his intellectual pursuits and emotional requirements, his recreation and leisure, should be the center of endeavors."[3] By integrating all conceivable aspects of the student, László Maholy-Nagy, along with Walter Gropius and Joseph Albers, envisioned an education of this magnitude producing "the genius" of the new technological age. Aside from learning methods for instilling aesthetics, they wanted students to experience the "organic and evolutionary" function of materials. The basic first-year course included technology, art, and science. The art component covered life drawing, color work, photography, mechanical drawing, lettering, modeling, and group poetry. "In all fields we would have the key to our age—seeing everything in relationship."[4]

When addressing the discipline of painting, Maholy-Nagy pointed first to Cezanne and then to the Cubists as beacons of forward motion in the arts. "Beginning in the last century a remarkable change took place in painting." Maholy-Nagy saw a new space-consciousness emerging. Movement, and capturing movement in art, held the interest of many artists, and Maholy-Nagy saw this in the emergence of Cubism. "Speeding on the roads and circling in the skies has given modern man the opportunity to see more than his renaissance predecessor. The man at the wheel sees persons and objects in quick succession, in permanent motion."[5] At this point Maholy-Nagy developed his core idea of a flexible perspective or a "vision in motion," which became a "vision of relationships," thus encompassing all the disciplines taught at the Institute of Design in Chicago.

As part of the curriculum, Maholy-Nagy included the analysis of contemporary painting, which presented several benefits to the student artist: By understanding new and perhaps unintelligible concepts, the student overcomes his or her fear of the unknown. Maholy-Nagy states that fear is destructive to the artistic process as it creates hostility and detracts from the pleasure of making art: "A school's duty is to sensitize the student to advanced thought and artistic expression."[6] Cubism, through the examination of Cezanne, played a large role in the new Bauhaus teachings of modern art. Maholy-Nagy stated, "Cubism, without being entirely conscious of its role, became a potent instrument in this process of indoctrination. Like Einstein in physics, and Freud in psychoanalysis, the cubist painters had tremendous impact. Their work introduced a whole new outlook."[7] Cubists like Pablo Picasso and Georges Braque came to the apex of the art

world in 1907–1922 as they explored ways to present the three-dimensional world on a two-dimensional surface. Paul Cezanne examined the spaces between objects, especially in his landscapes and still life paintings. For Maholy-Nagy, fascinated with movement, this idea of concentrating on the spaces between objects keyed in on his larger thesis of vision in motion. Cezanne studied how the eye tracked shadows and light in respect to other objects. Maholy-Nagy saw it as a space-time problem.

For Senska, participation in Maholy-Nagy's class meant taking various objects and trying to solve the problem of putting the objects together in a way that answered the time-space question. Senska had not yet discovered ceramics, but, once she did, she brought the idea of problem solving to the core of her practice. She kept meticulous records of her glazes, of what temperatures they fired at for the best results. The notion of problem-solving spread across the Montana State College's art department. Moholy-Nagy encouraged his students to try all kinds of materials and techniques, while teaching them that design is basically the act of problem-solving. "You weren't here to make art, but you're here to solve this design problem. If it turns out to be art, that's a dividend."[8]

Hans Hofmann taught at the Art Students' League in New York City from 1930 to 1933 before opening his own art school. Although none of the Montana Modernists took classes with him, his philosophy advanced quickly. For the Montana Modernists, Hans Hofmann's painting philosophy spread throughout the world of Modernism through his published lectures. A ripple effect from New York City to Grass Range, Montana, showed in the works of Bill Stockton, who often referred to Hofmann's "push and pull" theory of depth and perspective, as did Gennie DeWeese. Isabelle Johnson took classes at the Art Students' League in 1939, at a time when many of the Abstract Expressionists attended lectures there. In no way did Johnson's work reflect Abstract Expressionists, but her color combinations reflect an acute awareness of Hofmann's theories.

For each of the Montana Modernists, the social aspect of a shared studio environment meant all of these artist-teachers impacted each other's work. Each brought with them the lessons they had absorbed and filtered through their own work. In the tight-knit community of the art world in Montana, these lessons seeped from artist to artist, intentionally and unintentionally. Hofmann's theories of the picture plane, which refers to the actual surface of the painting as well as its illusion of depth, spread quickly as more and more artists picked up on his ideas. Art historian Michael Schreyach explained Hofmann's theory:

> Hofmann's distinction between literal flatness ("meaningless") and pictorial flatness ("the highest expression of life") is fundamental to his account of how material is made over into an expressive medium to convey the artist's meaning. For a painter, having the picture plane in mind as the basis of creation involves acknowledging the fact that the actually flat canvas is the condition that might enable the activity of marking and covering it with pigment to become a medium for expression, instead of a mere surface....We might say that flatness restored is mere flatness made meaningful by artistic intention.[9]

This awareness of the surface and commitment to discussing the flat nature of painting (and not trying to "fool" the viewer with a contrived perspective) comes across in much of Stockton's early abstract work and in Gennie DeWeese's non-objective paintings and flattened landscapes.

The other side of the picture-plane coin is depth, by which Hofmann means a creation of depth without sacrificing the picture's two-dimensionality. Here, he is trying to get a metaphysical notion of imagined depth rather than perspective depth as put forth in Renaissance paintings, one where the color stimulates tension on the surface. His famous "push-pull" color theory meant instilling a painting with active tension, with shifts back and forth, in and out of the picture plane. In Hofmann's eyes, Modernists' primary philosophy of acknowledging the flat surface of a painting goes beyond that flatness to recreate a surface engaged and reimagined. In other words Hofmann taught his students to overcome the limitations of flatness in order to transcend that two-dimensional container and delve into pure expression:

> Your paper is limited....Within its confines is the complete creative message. Everything you do is definitely related to the paper... The more the work progresses, the more it becomes defined or qualified. It increasingly limits itself. Your paper is a world in itself.... The work of art is firmly established as an independent object: this [is what] makes it

a picture. Outside of it is the outer world. Inside of it, the world of an artist.[10]

By embracing the flat surface, Modernist painters accepted the limitations of the painting. For Hofmann accepting the limitations of a two-dimensional format meant exposing the finiteness of being human.

He further explained the "push and pull" theory as movement and countermovement or force and counterforce:

> The picture surface answers every plastic animation automatically with an aesthetic equivalent in the opposite direction of the received impulse....A plastic animation into the depth is answered with a radar-like echo out of the depth and vice versa. Impulse and echo establish two-dimensionality with an added dynamic enlivenment of created breathing depth.[11]

The theory of push and pull was also described as a kind of plasticity, a spatial tension to create movement between points, pulsating the planes back and forth, which also engaged spatial relationships.

According to art historian Tina Dickey, "Hofmann himself observed this phenomenon as the moment when the surface works like a steam engine. Colors move in and out of depth like pistons." She quoted Hofmann's observation that a flat image felt empty of energy, empty of meaning: "You must have an inside to your picture—this is the creation of a cosmos. If you have no inside, it is only decorative."[12]

For Hofmann the difference between a painting with a spiritual aspect, and thus creating meaning, and something merely pretty was evidenced in the organic relationship between the formal elements of the marks and colors on the paper or canvas. Referencing Cezanne in one of his lectures, he conveyed the importance of noting the relationship between the objects, not just the objects portrayed themselves, "Cezanne understood color as a force of *push and pull.* In his pictures he created an enormous sense of volume, breathing, pulsating, expanding, contracting, through his use of color. In nature, light creates the color; in the picture, color creates the light," Hofmann said in talking about how color creates light through contrasts. "Teaching his students that color relationships develop through the act of painting, he encouraged them to discover the emotional nuances of color. He called it *experiential color.*"[13]

Gennie DeWeese illustrates this most clearly in her piece *Non-Objective Painting* (n.d.; page 51). Here, DeWeese speaks to both of these aesthetic philosophies by incorporating geometric forms and floral-like biomorphic shapes. Delicate lines stand out from the squared-up reds and oranges. While the yellow pushes the image to the forefront, the darker reds recede.

As a teacher, Hofmann realized the importance of his position in relation to encouraging younger artists:

> It is essential that the teacher himself have the power of quick sympathy and understanding of the unsure student. Such power should be developed like every other human

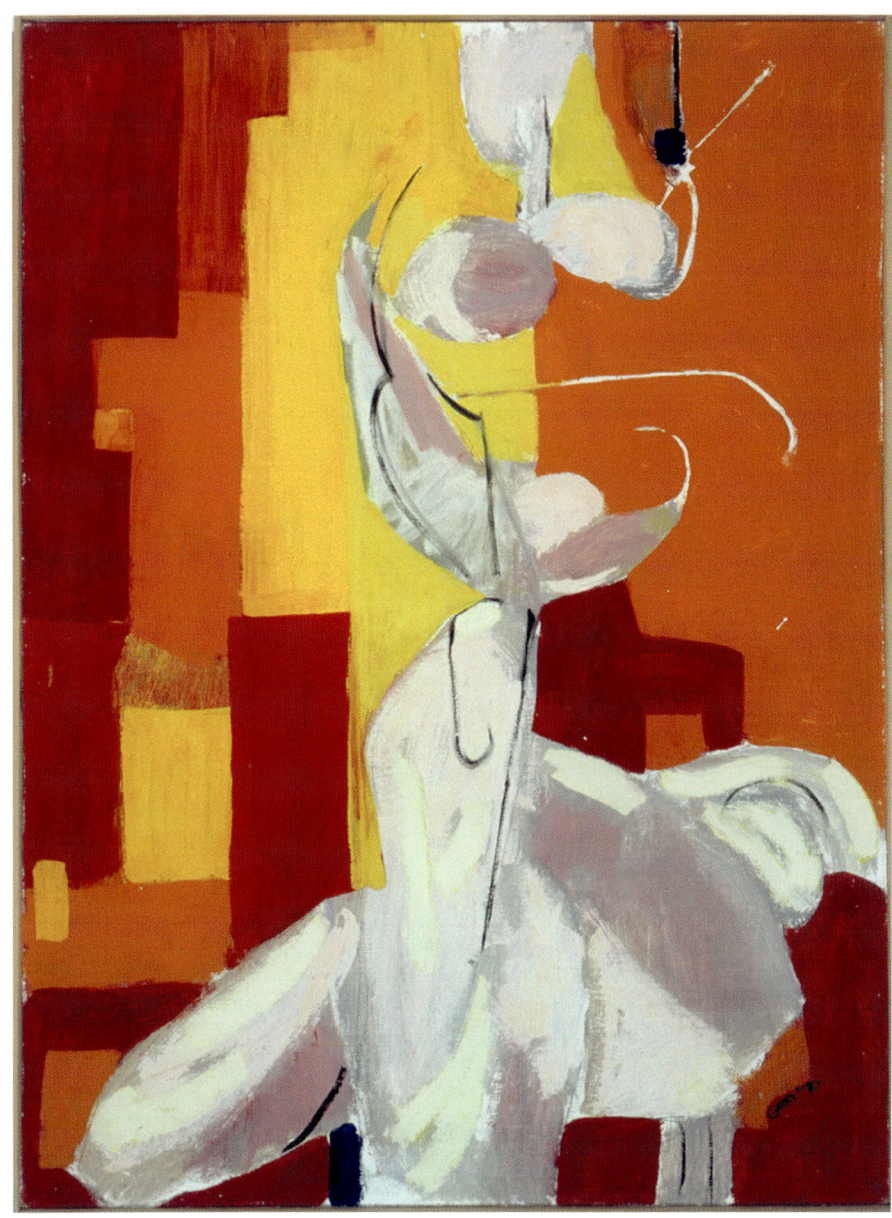

Gennie DeWeese,
Non-Objective Painting, n.d.,
oil on canvas, 48 x 36 inches.
Courtesy of the DeWeese Family.

attribute. The problem of art teaching is not limited to the problem of artistic development itself, but includes the problems of how to produce artists, comprehending teachers, art understanding in general, and art enjoyment in particular.[14]

Hoyt Sherman taught art at Ohio State University during the years Robert and Gennie DeWeese attended the school, from 1938 to 1942.[15] His new method for teaching drawing placed students in darkness while abstract patterns were projected onto a screen, flashing each image for a tenth of a second. With no verbal instructions, only music playing, the students drew the image they "saw" in the darkness of his Flash Lab. This idea of "Perceptual Unity" created a center of focus and trained his students not in how to draw, although drawing happened during the entire exercise, but in *how to see*. He trained his students in seeing the whole at a glance and, by drawing bold, broad patterns, delineating the whole field:

> Teaching people to see with perceptual unity is as much an unlearning process as it is a learning one. Most objects in our adult environment have become familiar through many associations. Rather than being seen for themselves, these objects serve merely as symbols for still other things with which our minds become occupied.[16]

Sherman claimed that people do not pay attention to objects in the background. "Training students so that they can become attentive to visual qualities and relationships is a matter of breaking these crusts of conventional reaction and introducing a fresh approach to the seeing act."[17]

Sherman believed that breaking the images into unfamiliar forms and then introducing objects such as chairs and wastepaper baskets later would help change the students' old visual language, enabling them to see landscapes or nudes without the old habits creeping into their work. The flashing aspect of the Flash Lab provided urgency as an important aspect Sherman tried to introduce in his students. By getting students prepared for a momentary image to appear, he began to instill "aggressive learning" as opposed to passive or inattentive seeing. As that attitude deepened, these newfound responses became habitual and enabled students to produce work "without loss of a dynamic quality."[18] Sherman also strove to bring out each student's individuality and felt that uniformity resulted in undesirable qualities. However, a teacher could go too far by *requiring* individuality:

> For a student to try to be different is, for him, to make as much of a mistake as he would make if he tried to get a product which met some standard of uniformity. The student's individuality should appear in his drawing as an incidental aspect of his work rather than as a conscious aim.[19]

Sherman noted that grades should be based on motivation rather than how well a teacher likes a student's end product.

Sherman devotes the last chapter of his book, *Drawing by Seeing*, to Cezanne. Not only could he use his theory of perceptual unity to analyze Cezanne's work in a new way, but he also felt that Cezanne modeled his theory perfectly. Painting, Sherman noted, used the eye and the brain together, "direct recognition of the fact that the process of seeing is embedded in the process of painting."[20] Seeing did not just mean observing. For Sherman seeing meant perceiving minute differences of perspective, of relations to space, and understanding the significance of a focal point. He used Cezanne to show the fundamentals of perception. "He sees a focal point; this point is determined by its position in a space relative to the observer; and it is not affected by color or brightness but is a function of position. Position is primary over color and brightness."[21]

During her time at Bauhaus, ceramic artist **Marguerite Wildenhain** (1896–1985) studied alongside painters Paul Klee and Wassily Kandinsky from 1919 to 1926, when she left to head up a ceramic workshop. She also worked closely with figurative sculptor Gerhard Marcks (her Form Master) and potter Max Krehan (her Crafts Master). In 1925 Wildenhain became the first woman to earn the Master Potter certification in Germany. Upon the Nazi regime's takeover, Wildenhain fled Germany and eventually ended up in California. There she established Pond Farm, on land owned by Gordon and Jane Herr, from 1949 to 1952. Pond Farm incorporated the egalitarian aspects of the Bauhaus art movement. Similar to Black Mountain College, founded by Joseph Albers (1933–1957), Pond Farm retained its teaching aspect while also incorporating communal ideals.[22] Wildenhain brought to Pond Farm the Bauhaus philosophy of uniting art with industry in order to create objects that possessed both the aesthetic of the artist and the function of utilitarian forms. In her teaching she sought to go

beyond mere technique and help develop a generation that "believes in the value of humanities, which will face the problems of our time honestly and without fear, with the deep will to understand other men and to learn to build a better future."[23]

This statement reflects the hardships she experienced under the Nazis, watching the stable, art-filled world of the Bauhaus in Germany fall apart around her. As a Jew, she left to escape the death camps; as an artist, her work remained forbidden. Her philosophy at Pond Farm approached the epitome of Utopianism in the face of McCarthyism and fought a residual anti-Semitic attitude in the United States. The atmosphere at Pond Farm provided a safe place for artists to experiment with clay. In the arts community, the inclination to found schools located outside of cities spurred the formation of several well-known art schools located in rural settings, including Black Mountain College in North Carolina and Cranbook Academy in Michigan, where Senska enrolled in 1946.

Wildenhain's lessons emphasized the ability of potters to be receptive to their curiosity, to explore, and to open themselves up to the possibilities of their process. Once a student learns the basics, then the student must "develop those forms that you would make if you had never seen a pot before, those that are your conception of what a pot should look like."[24] She understood the importance of knowing all the basics of building ceramic objects, but she also instilled the notion of expression in regard to the potters' artistic form. She eschewed a "know the rules before you break them" perspective. She asked her students to not be afraid to fail. Mistakes should be treated as opportunities to learn. Wildenhain's emphasis on the potter's understanding of the relationship between hand and form was key. "The experimental relation of the hand to the form is not essential only during the beginning period; it is in no sense merely a trial period that one must quickly get through," she said of her methodology:

> On the contrary, it is a very fundamental part of the whole potting process. The more the potter is able to carry into his maturity his initial alert sensitivity of the hand to the form, the better potter he is. For it is necessary for the creative potter to burst the limitations of tradition and the restrictions of convention to shatter the limitation of his own routine.[25]

For Jessie Wilber her cleft from Cubism came in 1949, when she spent her summer in Dallas, Texas, studying under the painter Otis Dozier. Dozier had been a guest instructor at Montana State College in 1946, where he and Wilber became acquainted. For Wilber, Dozier's abstract, loose brushwork with saturated colors left a deep impression on her. She credits him with luring her away from Cubism or any other kind of "ism."[26] Dozier himself searched to find his voice, but, once he did, he rose to the heights of Texas's and Colorado's regional artists acclaim. Dozier taught for seven years at Colorado Springs's Fine Arts Center as an assistant to Boardman Robinson, director of the Broadmoor Art Academy,[27] before returning to Dallas to teach at the Fine Arts Center. Dozier's early work reflects the hard, dark, natural lines used by Post-Impressionist artists like Cezanne. Growing up in North Texas, Dozier produced early work portraying the life of a tenant farmer picking cotton and portraits of old farmhouses with deep, seemingly bottomless fields ready for planting. Jerry Bywaters noted in an article about Dozier, "The earthy mysteries and dark tragedies of farm life were of logical concern to the younger artists—and have remained so to the mature artist."[28] In later years Dozier drew on surrealism as well as abstraction to portray his surroundings. He also took inspiration from experiential, personal observations, climbing 14,000-foot peaks in Colorado to understand the mountains from above or wandering from ghost towns to mining operations in order to delve into the native landscapes. By the time he taught at the Dallas Museum of Fine Art School in the 1960s, Dozier's paintings evolved to near-complete abstraction using complicated color palettes and imaginative symbols.

Paul Cezanne was important to all these teachers, although each used Cezanne to express a perspective or a viewpoint a bit different from the others. As noted by art historian and critic Meyer Schapiro in his 1959 essay, Cezanne felt "fresh and stimulating to young painters of our time."[29] What about Cezanne's work spoke to all these various aspects of art? Schapiro points to Cezanne's wide berth of color theory, drawing, expression, and elemental style. Looking at the first artist to understand the limits of and thus the multitude of solutions of the two-dimensional canvas one might have foreseen the Cubist movement to come. By peeling back the layers, artists could delve into one aspect at a time.

Hoyt Sherman latched onto the idea of observation and perception, while Hans Hofmann's work with the picture plane as a two-dimensional surface played into the referential work of Cezanne's Post-Impressionistic paintings. Bauhaus artists like Maholy-Nagy and even Marguerite Wildenhain looked to Cezanne as a space-conscious artist, the first to portray a kind of forward movement. Isabelle Johnson used Cezanne as a personal inspiration, studying his line and composition intensely. It was during her time at Skowhegan that she took Cezanne to heart in her pursuit of the lines of nature.

Montana Modernists trained in a variety of schools during their early years, prior to World War II, bringing their diverse visions and techniques with them when they came or returned to Montana. Through the combination of place and various methods of expressing new ideas, the Montana Modernists acquired their own classroom experiences and translated them for a generation of young artists seeking their own voices in the art world.

EXPERIENCING ART IN THE CLASSROOM

The Montana Modernists introduced the idea of equality in the classroom, upending the traditional status quo. As these artist-teachers opened up the door to an alternative way to be a Montana artist, to portray a more personal notion of what it meant to be a Montanan in the postwar society of the moment, their way of conducting classes became as important as what they taught in those classes.

Isabelle Johnson's teaching style, described in a 1963 essay, implores artists to forget how other people use color: "use the colors you feel in your mind's eye and your imagination. This canvas you are doing [is] not for husband, wife, or neighbor, but for yourself, so have courage to fail if necessary."[30] One of her students, painter Theodore Waddell notes, "She would take several of us to her house for hot chocolate and talk about art.... She was a figurative painter but she had this loose, graphic way of applying the paint that drew me to her."[31] Missoula painter Donna Loos, who studied with Johnson from 1960 to 1961 at Eastern Montana College, Billings, said one piece of advice she recalled from Johnson was:

> Go your way instead of following current fashion. She was willing to go out on a limb in a city and at a time when nobody else was thinking modern....[S]he felt it was a requirement of her job that she push us and lead us to look in other directions that were not traditional, and she did it without saying a mean word about Russell or any other traditional painter....[S]he opened up minds until we did it by ourselves.[32]

The Montana Modernist artists teaching at MSC in the late 1940s and 1950s—Frances Senska, Jessie Wilber, Robert DeWeese, and, occasionally, Gennie DeWeese[33]—approached their work and their teaching as reflected in the unified theory of education outlined by John Dewey, whose underlying philosophy was that teaching art is done best through the experience of art itself:

> The answers cannot be found unless we are willing to find the germs and roots in matters of experience that we do not currently regard as esthetic. Having discovered these

active seeds, we may follow the course of their growth into the highest forms of finished and refined art.[34]

These art professors took the notion of art as an experience, of learning by doing, and incorporated Dewey's democratically inspired classroom that consisted of students and teachers learning together.

Frances Senska's teaching style, patterned on that of her own teachers, Maholy-Nagy and Wildenhain, evolved into a hands-on, side-by-side environment. Senska's similar teaching style embodied the lessons of Wildenhain, without encouraging students to make pots that looked like hers. As noted by former student and artist Neil Jussila, Senska physically placed her hands on her students' hands to give them the right direction while sitting at the potter's wheel.[35] Two of her most famous students, Peter Voulkos and Rudy Autio, speak to her teaching style. Voulkos, whose iconic abstract and dynamic forms ushered in Abstract Expressionism in ceramics, and Autio's lyrical and figurative style, make it hard to believe their training derived from the same pair of hands. However, in an interview Senska did after receiving a lifetime membership to the National Committee on Education in the Ceramic Arts, she noted that someone approached her after seeing a student-made video she had shown instead of giving a speech. "You hold your hands just the way I do, but I learned from Peter Voulkos." To which Senska replied, "Well, it figures. He learned from me, and I learned from Marguerite Wildenhain. That's what education in the ceramic arts is all about. You learn from somebody who does it."[36]

Senska noted that she instructed in a style similar to Wildenhain's, giving instruction when needed without forcing any style on her students. She did recall telling Pete Voulkos that his work looked like something from "high school industrial arts, and I said, 'you know, it's been done. Come into the twentieth century.' He did!"[37]

When World War II broke out, Senska joined the United States Navy. While stationed in San Francisco, she took evening classes with ceramist Edith Heath at the California Labor School. From Heath she learned to throw clay on a potter's wheel. "Well, having discovered clay, I stayed with it," she said.[38] After the war, using her G.I. Bill benefits for education, Senska attended ceramic classes at the Cranbrook Academy of Art in Bloomfield Hills, Michigan, with Maija Grotell.

Jessie Wilber took the side-by-side philosophy to heart by drawing when her students drew, painting when her students painted, and, at the end of class, sharing her work along with the rest of her students without putting herself or her work above them, thus creating a safe and encouraging atmosphere for learning. Wilber's generosity of spirit gave her students the leeway to explore various materials regardless of the outcome. Ray Campeau, one of her early students, described Wilber's teaching method as the process of working beside her students, not in front of them. She would ask the students to set up their painting projects and then set her easel up in the classroom studio with them. Students and teacher painted or printed together, each working on their own pieces.[39] Wilber explained her process but never performed a "demonstration" for students to emulate her work. Instead, she asked each student to talk about their work, making each feel as important as the rest. "They [Senska and Wilber] never made anyone feel like they were less than them. They did things communally."[40] By not setting herself apart from her painting students, Wilber created a safe environment where students learned by doing and, at the same time, they learned how to respect each other's work as modeled by Wilber. Wilber herself found inspiration in her students:

> I learned more from them than they learned from me, or, at most, we were all getting hold of something that was at the heart of—to use a term in vogue at that time—the creative process. My students—some in small ways, some in major ways—gave me insights and confidence in my work and I no longer wanted to go out and study under another artist.[41]

Robert DeWeese took the other side of Dewey's coin, emphasizing the experience portion by exposing his students to art as much as possible. In 1960 Montana native and New York commodity broker Everton Gentry "George" Poindexter began donating his collection of Abstract Expressionist art to the Montana Historical Society's museum collection and the Yellowstone Art Center.[42] Eventually, he donated 382 works to the Yellowstone Art Center alone.[43] The Poindexter Collection, a curated selection of Abstract Expressionist paintings, including work by Willem de Kooning, Robert DeNiro Sr., Jackson Pollock, Richard Diebenkorn, Earl Kerkam, Franz Kline, and Jack Tworkov, among others, encompassed

the largest Abstract Expressionist art collection west of the Mississippi at that time.[44]

When Robert DeWeese heard about the Poindexter Collection and the nature and quality of the Abstract Expressionist art in the state, he drove to Helena and borrowed a few pieces from the Montana Historical Society. George Poindexter donated his collection to give educational institutions access to them, and DeWeese took that idea literally.[45] DeWeese did not think to bring the students to the art but instead brought the art to the students. For weeks, Willem de Kooning's *Woman*, 1948, as well as several other paintings from the collection, hung in the Student Union Building at Montana State College, available for anyone to see.

For Neil Jussila, an art student in the 1960s, the Poindexter Collection changed everything. It changed the way he thought about art and the way he connected to his own artistic expression. For DeWeese, it was a way, the only way, to communicate what was going on in New York City's art scene to his students. As Jussila remembered:

> [Robert DeWeese] had received an invitation from the Montana Historical Society—they had served notification that they had an exhibit, the Poindexter Exhibit. He got a state truck or something because the paintings were pretty big and took two or three students with him to Helena and picked up as many of those paintings as they could, and they brought them back to Bozeman.[46]

Jussila said the students helped install paintings from the Poindexter Collection in the lounge of the Student Union Building. DeWeese brought a copy of George Poindexter's essay and had the department secretary transcribe it and mimeograph it; then, he distributed it to all the students in his classes:

> He talked about the paintings, and we went over and looked at the exhibit and talked about abstract expressionism. The upshot—it was during my sophomore year in 1962—I would go over to the SUB and read the essay and look at the paintings and it really made a lot of sense to me. It had a large impact on my work.[47]

Jussila spoke of Robert DeWeese's teaching as something new and different, something he had never encountered in his hometown of Butte, Montana:

> [Robert DeWeese] liked the idea of the quick sketch. Bob excelled as an impeccably fine draftsman. It seems to me when I think about it, he was involved with this idea that the word *draw* means to bring forth, like drawing water from a well....His purpose was to teach people the value of spontaneity.[48]

DeWeese explained this theory in a rare essay about painting. "A teacher–student relationship in the field of painting is artificial and false. They should be considered as equal participants in the excitement of painting; the one with the greater experience which the other draws upon."[49] He continued to state that there must be a philosophy, not merely a pedagogic methodology, of painting or there is no painting:

> There must be equal earnestness and drive; there must be hard work. A teacher must stimulate by fair means or foul. But don't ask him to spoon feed or hold your hand.... the language of painting—size, shape, position, and color—is simple, but it takes many paintings to learn the language—to feel and sense it—to make it part of you. Don't be precious with your painting—you must gradually learn to see and operate in these terms.[50]

However, former students distinctly recall their teachers as being pivotal in forming the basis for not only their understanding of art but also for establishing a different way of conceiving the world of art in their own lives. As his student Jerry Rankin said of DeWeese, "His simple statements embodied huge ideas. He kept us busy with the job of seeing."[51]

Senska's student Al Tennant spoke about her ability to be tough while allowing each student complete freedom to discover their voice. "It's difficult to explain, she suggested as she talked to 'look over here' or 'think about something other than that's a piece of clay, what is it?' She'd go on for five or ten minutes. And then she would walk away. I'd sit there, kind of bewildered."[52] Tennant stated that her walking away actually enabled him to consider his work:

> But then I'd think oh, she's saying that I should explore things on my own but take these basics [with me]. If I don't my own work will be totally goofy. That's how she talked. Years later...she still had the same attitude about what I was doing, what

everybody else was doing. She'd said, "I just let everyone go."[53]

Senska grew with her students. When she first started teaching, she actually did not know much about ceramics. Only after spending a summer with Wildenhain did she begin to understand clay. As she taught, she grew as a teacher and as an artist. Tennant described her as a gregarious, kind person who talked gently about clay, romantically perhaps, but she inspired her students enough for most of them to stay with the arts for the rest of their lives. "Fifty years later, I'm still making clay because I had a teacher like Frances Senska who never discouraged me and made me kind of think about the whole process."[54] Tennant described DeWeese, Senska, and Jessie Wilber as quintessential instructors. "They did not teach you how to do something, but instead they taught you what to think about when you're doing the art." Tennant defined a good teacher as someone who could make him pay attention. "If you have the capability, and you have the imagination, you have the desire you will take this and run. If not, go drive a truck. That's kind of what they said. They were just three of the most amazing people."[55]

When asked about the most memorable aspect of Wilber's teaching practice, Tennant answered that she spoke about freedom, a very fine technique, and then she implored her students to experiment, experiment, experiment.

Tennant's memories of Robert DeWeese capture the DeWeese classroom. "He always said, Tennant if you don't understand what a line is, then you can't draw. And I thought, what the

fuck is this guy talking about. Then one day he walked by [me] and said, 'that's a line.'"[56] The story rounded out in a printmaking class. "I kept doing the same drawing and he said, 'Tennant, these are really ugly. You can't print anymore in my class until you come up with an image that has some substance about it.'" At that point Tennant thought he would never pass that class:

> I thought I was going to flunk out and everyone will be so disappointed in me. And then one day I was sitting near the college and next to me was an old Chevy pickup with an advertisement on the side that was faded. I looked over and thought, oh wow, look at this door, it has the most beautiful image.[57]

With his sketchbook tucked close by, because that was what DeWeese taught them, he drew this image. "I went back to Bob and said this is what I want to print. And he said, 'Okay, Tennant, you can print it. Those lines are important.' He was making me pay attention."[58]

DeWeese, Senska, and Wilber taught in what John Dewey called a "pragmatic environment," where reality is experienced. Every one of their students learned their art by doing the art. In nearly every case, the credo of the teacher–student relationship reflected Dewey's view of learning art experientially.[59] For example, Senska discovered her famous ceramic partridges while demonstrating how to make a bottle on the pottery wheel. When she was done, she closed the top, and in her mind, perceived the shape of the Hungarian partridge (page 60). That "learning by doing" philosophy ran deep within the entire department at the time.[60] Pete Voulkos was constantly breaking into the ceramics studio after the school closed to work on his very big pieces. When she found out, Senska gave him a key.[61]

Most students attending MSC in the 1950s experienced all three professors during their years in the art department. Together, these teachers not only introduced their students to contemporary art at the time—the Modernist movements and the avant-garde—but also enabled their students to discover what pushing the envelope of current art in their own hands meant.

FRANCES AND JESSIE: CHANGING PERCEPTIONS

Montana State College hired Jessie Wilber in 1941 as part of a very small art department. Five years later Frances Senska joined the department. Their friendship and partnership remained a steadfast aspect of the Montana art community until their deaths. They shared their work, both in teaching and in art, and they shared a home they built together, each with their own studio overlooking the Gallatin Valley. It would be hard to talk about one without the other. Wilber began her art career as a painter but became well-known for her printmaking. Senska began with ideas of becoming an industrial designer, but her ceramics grew to gain international fame. Each embodied the traits they taught their students: try something and see if it works, as Moholy-Nagy advised and, as Wilber often said, experiment, experiment, experiment.

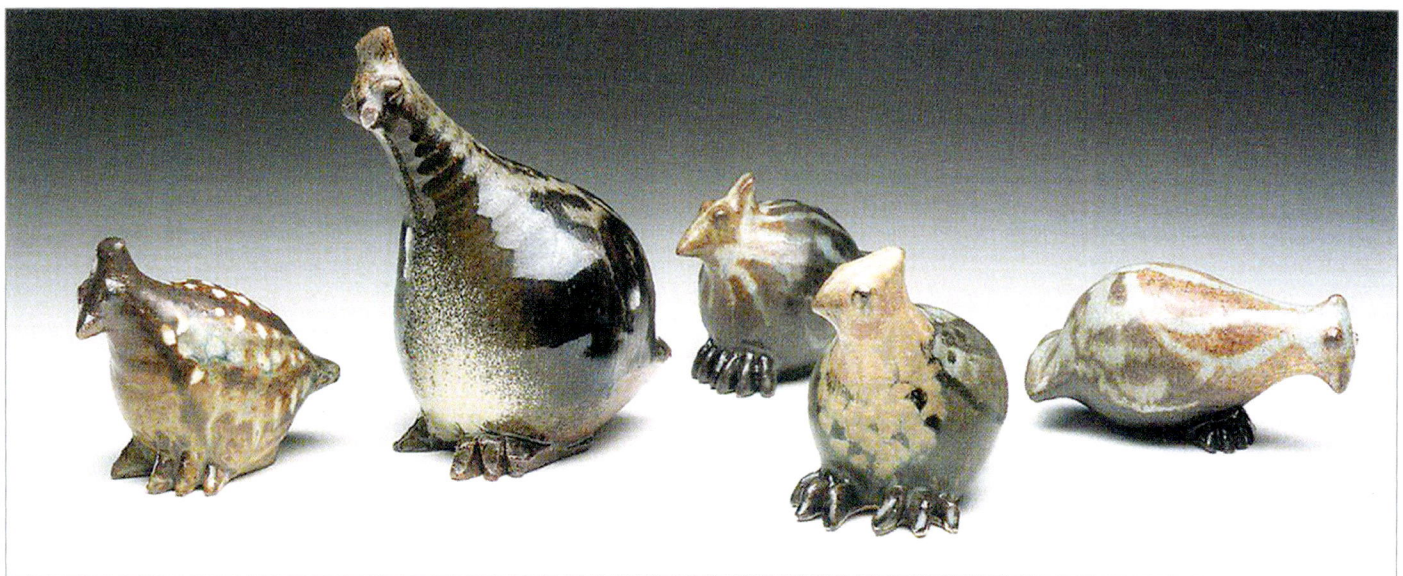

Frances Senska, *Hungarian Partridges*, n.d., stoneware, variable dimensions. Courtesy of the Holter Museum of Art.

While their work may seem vastly different at first glance, similarities emerge. Senska's partridges and the birds in Wilber's painting *Huns* (page 62), show a like-mindedness in the shape and outline of the Hungarian partridges shown in each work. It is as if the two artists, speaking the same language, created an intimate dialogue about space, nature, and Modernism. Wilber's painting portrays a two-dimensional image with the Modernist claim to a flat surface and a shunning of illusionism. Senska's partridges show the small birds in a full three-dimensional space, the glazes used as shorthand for the plumage, not as an exact replica of the huns but as way to mark them. Showing Senska's perception of a partridge without resorting to an overly realistic conveyance, she relates the birds, seen commonly from the window of her home, to one of the few pieces she made that were non-utilitarian. Since the partridges are not dated, the question of which came first, the painting or the sculpture, remains open-ended.

Jessie Wilber (1912–1989) took an art teaching position at Montana State College in 1941. That same year Wilber's PWAP (Public Works of Art Project) commission to paint a mural in the post office at Kingman, Kansas, came through. She finished the piece in 1942, after moving to Montana. The painting, *The Days of the Cattlemen's Picnic*, depicts a Western scene with fenced cattle, ranchers on horseback, and a young boy on a bicycle riding by. Slightly curved and abstracted figures perch on a jack-leg fence, watching bull riders as part of the picnic's entertainment. The colors, primarily dusty beige, burnt sienna, and green, convey a sense of late summer or early fall.[62]

Even in Wilber's early work, she picked up the mantel of Modernism by claiming a flat surface and a skewed, Cubist perspective. Each of the figures enhances their three-dimensionality.

Cubism, the style she used in her mural painting, rubbed off on Wilber when she met Estelle Stinchfield. Wilber described Stinchfield as "a fiery little Cubist whose mission in life was to bring Modern Art to Colorado in no uncertain terms."[63] At twenty-one, Wilber enrolled in Colorado State Teachers' College as a junior. While working in the art department, she took classes from Stinchfield, whose passion for Modernism slightly outweighed her "sharp tongue." Wilber adored Stinchfield because she

> deplored the reluctance and cowardice of people in the face of a new idea, she brought us the world of Paris, where she had studied for several years. She filled us with information about all the painters who were working there while she was studying—Picasso, Matisse, Modigliani, and the rest—and she made good Cubists of everyone![64]

In light of the Great Depression sweeping the nation at the time, the notion of passion and art, change and promise, elated and inspired Wilber to find meaning in her own work. "Stinchfield was not a person you could ever forget; even today, in a strange quirk of reminiscence, I smile at what she would probably say when I am working on a drawing or a print."[65] While Wilber's Cubist tendencies did not stay with her throughout her life, she carried Modernism with her when she moved to Montana.

During World War II Wilber taught geography to airmen on the campus of Montana State College,[66] but she also continued to explore her own art. While working on the Kingman mural in her painting class at MSC during her first year, Wilber noticed the students taking a "polite" interest in the work. Seeing that spark in her students spurred her to take on the project of the Rocky Mountain Spotted Fever Mural that still hangs in Lewis Hall at Montana State University, Bozeman. Wilber contacted the Rocky Mountain Fever Lab in Hamilton, Montana, and

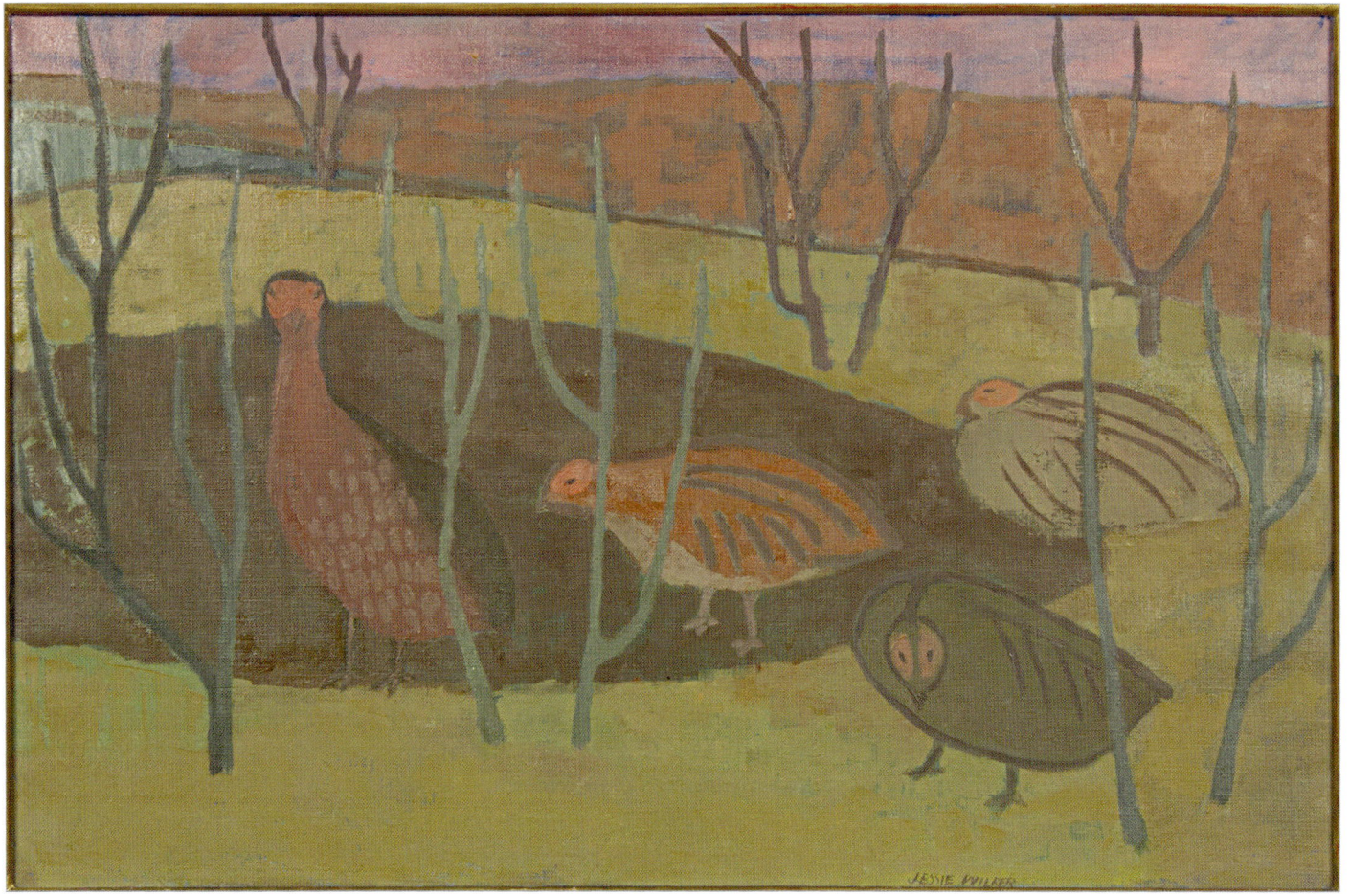

Jessie Wilber, *Huns*, 1954, 24.5 x 35 inches, oil on canvas. Courtesy of the Yellowstone Art Museum.

the scientists traveled to MSC in order to tell the students about the lab and their research on insect-borne diseases. For the mural in Lewis Hall, she used tempera directly on the wall, after preparing the area using "the traditional pre-Renaissance method" of gesso, whiting, zinc white, and water-soluble hide glue. She then asked her students to create drawings to scale, using their own ideas of composition. Each student's work was presented, and the class as a whole chose the ones "we felt were the most likely to succeed as big mural paintings."[67] This demonstrates Wilber's inclusive and democratic teaching methods, how she grasped the smallest spark of interest and turned it into a project in which all her students participated and felt ownership. This methodology, started by Wilber, spread throughout the School of Art as a community in the coming years as a few more artist/teachers and students began to take advantage of the G.I. Bill.

In 1943 Wilber accompanied watercolorist Olga Ross Hannon to the Blackfeet Reservation east of Glacier National Park to witness the Sun Dance ceremonies.[68] She and Hannon sketched and took notes. The simplified depictions of bears, beavers, snakes, buffalo, elk, deer, and mountain sheep on tipis, as well as the geometric renderings of the landscape, piqued Wilber's interest, but Hannon's interest stayed strong as she produced a number of watercolor paintings based on the tipis. Wilber did notice how the upper and lower portions of the painted lodges darkened due to outside weather and smoke from within the tipis, leaving the central area free for the painting of sacred animals particular to the tipi owner.[69]

When Hannon died in 1947, Wilber kept Hannon's tipi project alive. John C. Ewers described the project:

> [Hannon] proposed to record faithfully, in a series of silk-screened plates, the colorful murals painted on the exterior surfaces of Blackfeet Indian tipis....Another dimension was brought to the project by the research of Cecile Black Boy, a full blood Blackfeet Indian, who, during the 1940s, collected Blackfeet legends under the sponsorship of the Museum of the Plains Indian for the Montana Writers' Project of the Public Works of Art.[70]

Wilber had kept Hannon's project close to her heart and, when she retired in 1974, she decided to honor her friend and colleague by finishing the Blackfeet Tipis with a grant awarded to her by the Montana Arts Council in 1976 for a series of the silkscreened Blackfeet Indian Tipi Designs. The decision to use the medium of serigraphs to portray the tipis enabled the conveyance of the object while adhering to the images by singling out the individual differences of each person's tipi in a respectful way.[71] Wilber extracted the essence of the object while setting it up as a specimen, removing any kind of realism associated with its use. There is no sign of the smoke stains noted from her experience of seeing the tipis in person, or of the weather that should have left its mark on the fabric. Instead, her flat, clean images eschew a sense of place. Under the hand of Wilber, the forms take on a smooth, unweathered character. The prints, without a traditional pragmatist ground line, seem to float in space, caught in a web of time. Wilber's use of the silkscreen printing process elevated the bold colors, symbols, and geometric shapes used by the Blackfeet while also bringing attention to the medium.

Two of Wilber's former students, Stacy Hamm and Sage (Sigerson) Walden, graduates of the fine art program at Montana State University, helped Wilber to create the silk-screen works. Hamm and Sage established the Jessie Wilber and Frances Senska Individual Artist Award in Ceramics after Senska died in 2009. In 1973 the Montana Institute of the Arts named Wilber Artist of the Year. In 1988 she was honored with the Montana Governor's Arts Award.[72] All of these awards attest to the importance of her art around the state as well as her influence on younger artists.

THE HUMAN GAZE

In *Huns* (page 62) from 1954, Wilber's interest in painting birds comes through in her abstraction of the figural form. Her deep, saturated color announces itself before composition, line, or subject matter. A conscious use of a monochromatic theme was an aspect of Modernism, as explained in a 1943 letter to *The New York Times* written by Mark Rothko, Barnett Newman, and Adolph Gottlieb. They stated, "We favor the simple expression of the complex thought....[W]e wish to reassert the picture plane. We are for flat forms because they destroy illusion and reveal truth."[73] Within the formal aspects of Wilber's *Huns*, illusion is destroyed. There is no illusion. This is a painting. The lines are drawn, like a curtain draped across the canvas, a curtain meant to reveal, not hide, the

two-dimensionality of the painting. Wilber depicts the scene with a minimalist view of the landscape, only a single line delineating the horizon, as an oval stands in for a pond. Single brushstrokes create bare foliage. Of the four huns, two stare directly ahead, challenging the viewer's gaze. It is as if Wilber used the huns as Manet used the barmaid in *A Bar at the Folies Bergere*, creating an inverse perspective on birdwatching. Thematically, Wilber used the huns, as well as other birds commonly found in her backyard, again and again. After Matisse, the use of the window as a view from inside the studio to the outer world, or from the outer world to the subconscious world, became a well-known trope for artists. Wilber consistently explored her view from her studio, within yards of her surroundings, including her cats and her garden, in her paintings and prints.

During an examination of her works archived in the Montana State University's School of Art collection, it became clear that Wilber used whatever resources she found. Whether it was crepe paper, linoleum, or pieces of scrap wood, she created an array of prints; archival quality was not the topmost component of her process. Wilber responded to the materials on hand and, by picking up that piece of scrap wood, she thought about the wood itself, throwing out any preconception of what to do with scrap wood. Rather, she looked at the material itself, resulting in her woodblock prints.[74]

In her ca.1950 woodblock print, *Cats in a Garden* (page 66), Wilber creates a unique sense of space, the circles of cats and garden each stand their own ground. In this print she uses a monochromatic theme, so the brown of the paper—

earth and soil—become a changing background to the black ink as the viewer's eye moves from one delineated area to the next. The gouged wood creates rich texture in both the background of the cat and the leaves of the foliage. In a partial break from the circle theme, Wilber acknowledges the horizon line, but only in passing, not in an illusionistic sense. Instead, she emphasizes the flatness of the paper. Wilber also uses shallow depths to explore space and the divisions of spaces. With each circle, she draws our attention to the importance of things—this, this, this—expounding with intent each aspect of her personal world while interlacing the indoors with the outdoors, leaving only simple lines as thresholds.

This woodblock is indicative of Jessie Wilber's style. Her work isolates and at the same time unites her subjects, a personal documentation on the way she observed the world. To the viewer, it appears as one vision, yet the viewer can choose to look upon one thing at a time. Here she allows the viewer to do both, to be in the moment and to take the long view.

In 1949, after bringing Dozier in for several workshops at MSC between 1946 and 1949, she was invited to Texas to study with him and his wife, metalsmith Velma Davis, over the course of a summer. That mentorship changed her style though not her subject matter. At that time she discontinued her Cubist style and freed up her hand. No longer concerned with the idea of a three-dimensional object on a two-dimensional surface, instead she embraced the flatness of the surface. She still tended to look out her window, engaging with the birds, cats, and garden. How-ever, Wilber also brought in artworks from traveling shows, including work from Surrealist Eugene Berman, California Modernist Dan Lutz, California watercolorist Millard Sheets, and abstract painter Morris Graves, as much for her students as for herself as an artist.

All of Wilber's work modeled behavior, style, discipline, and the life of an artist. In the art department, as is true even now, professors actively encouraged students to follow their own creative paths and make art to show in the professional and academic areas of their lives. The following works by Wilber embody her studio practice, but they also stand as an example of her pedagogy. When she worked, she worked at the school with students surrounding her. After she retired, she worked at home, with students surrounding and helping her there.

Birds and Trees (n.d.; page 67), a two-color print on paper, invites the viewer to take an intimate look at how Wilber saw her world. Modernists were tasked with showing the world in a more immediate and, especially for Wilber, more personal way. She singles out the various parts of her backyard—the birds and the trees—and again allows the viewer to consider each one individually and, after that, the composition as a whole. In looking at two colors somewhat offset from each other, the eye moves around the images in a continuous narrative: a flock of birds in flight, others on the ground. While the gold-haloed trees may be bare, they tower like sturdy bystanders against the horizon.

In *Huns (on a pond)* (n.d.; page 68), Wilber used construction paper to create her print.

It must have been the right size and right tone, giving the Hungarian partridges an evening feeling. Wilber tried the same images with black and white. Hungarian partridges commonly flush in coveys and stay in Montana year-round. Wilber elegantly uses line to embrace the idea of the hun without the need to include every feather and feature. Again, her perception of a hun, not an anatomically correct bird, speaks to her shorthand descriptions of her environment. In doing this, she allows the viewer to connect with the scene in a more personal way, to fill in their own ideas of huns.

The River (Don't Dam It!) (1977; page 69), a woodblock print, incorporates the chine-collé process of using (in this case) colored paper placed directly on the black ink of the woodblock and then applying the wood blocks to the paper, creating

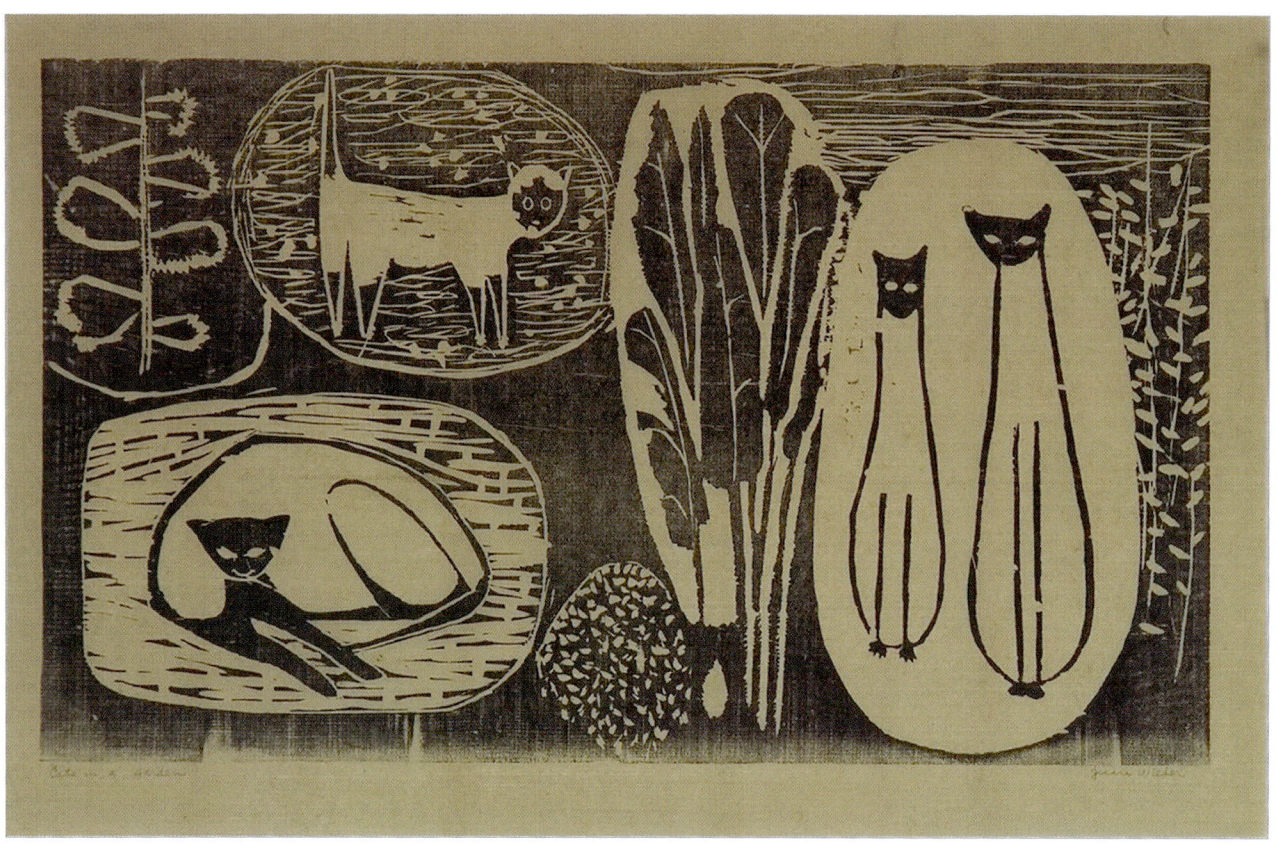

Jessie Wilber, *Cats in a Garden*, 1950, single-color woodblock print, 19 x 11 inches. Courtesy of the Montana State University School of Art.

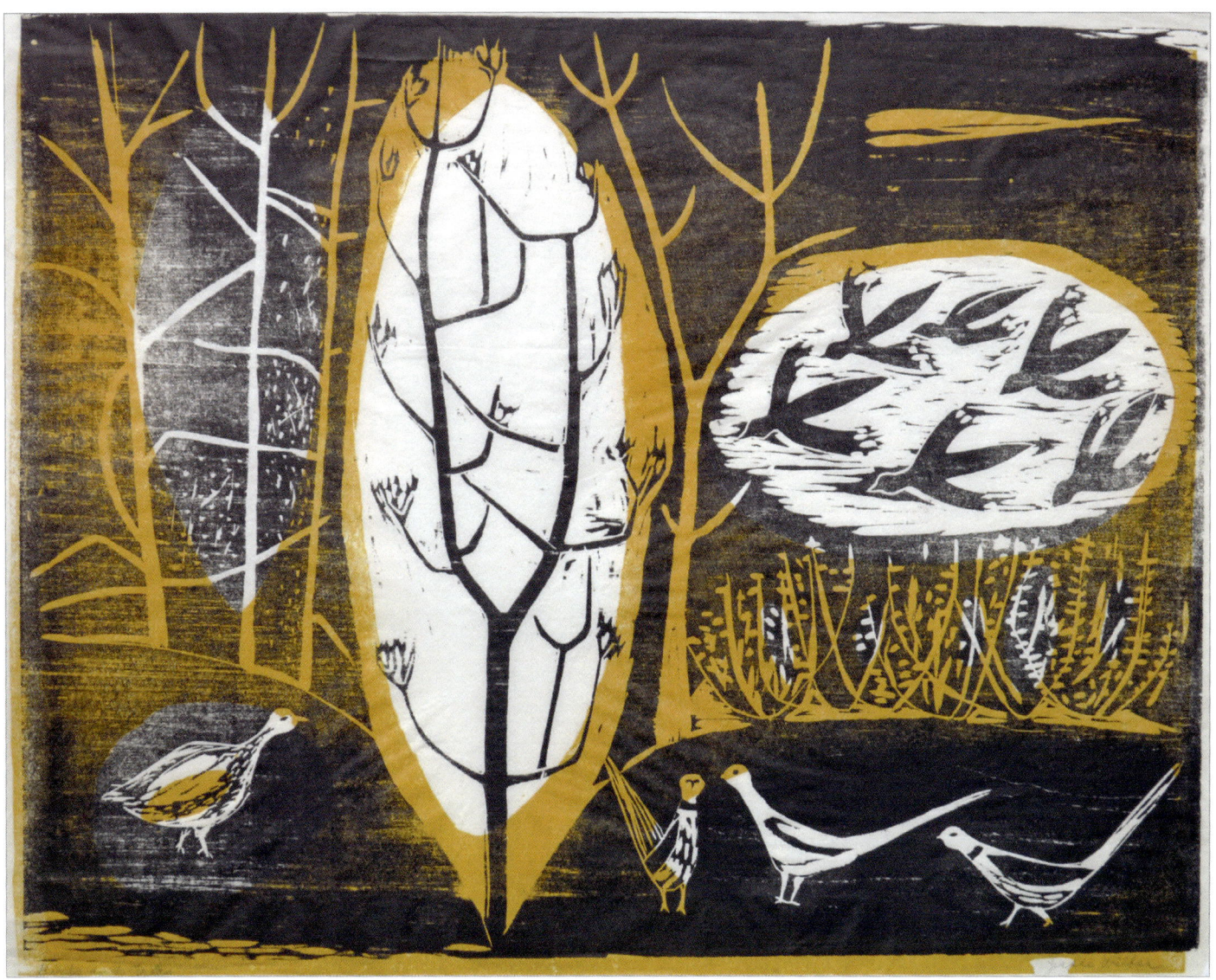

Jessie Wilber, *Birds and Trees*, n.d., two-color woodblock print, 17.25 x 22.75 inches. Courtesy of the Montana State University School of Art.

areas of color within the print. Wilber's choice of colors—orange, green, and grays—overlap to enrich the image. In the MSU art archives, the woodblock she cut and gouged for this print is available, as is a test print in only black and white, as well as the exquisite color print with the chine-collé technique. The evaluation of all three steps in the process reveals Wilber's precision as well as

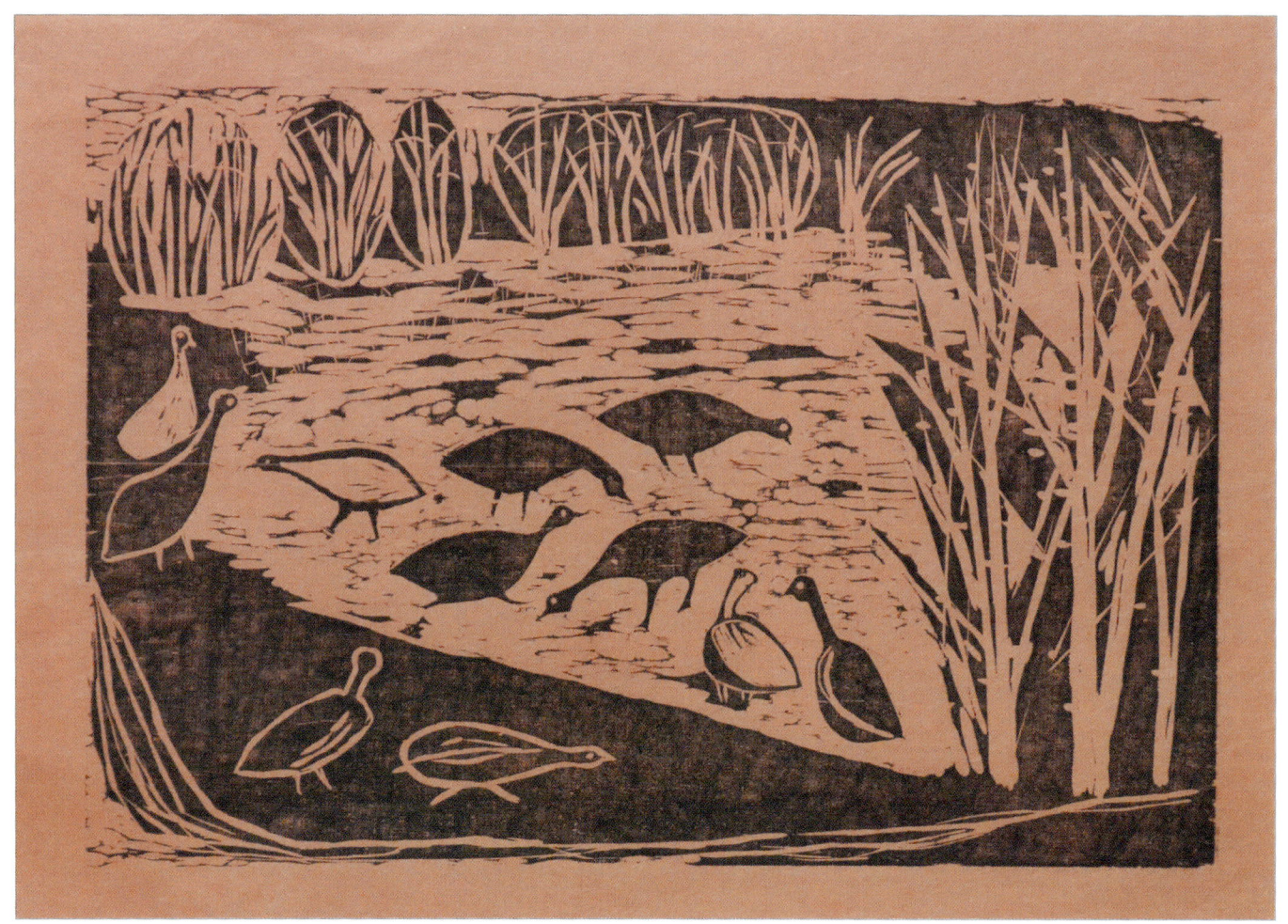

Jessie Wilber, *Huns (on a pond)*, 1956, single-color woodblock print on colored paper, 19 x 12 inches.
Courtesy of the Montana State University School of Art.

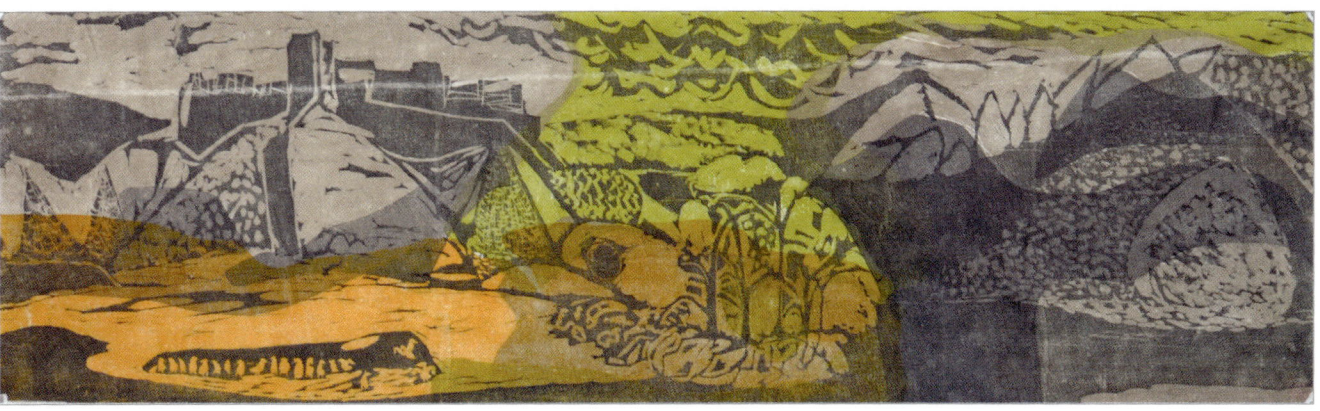

Jessie Wilber, *The River* (*Don't Dam It!*), 1977, woodblock print on paper using Chine-colle technique. 44 x 13 inches.
Courtesy of the Montana State University School of Art.

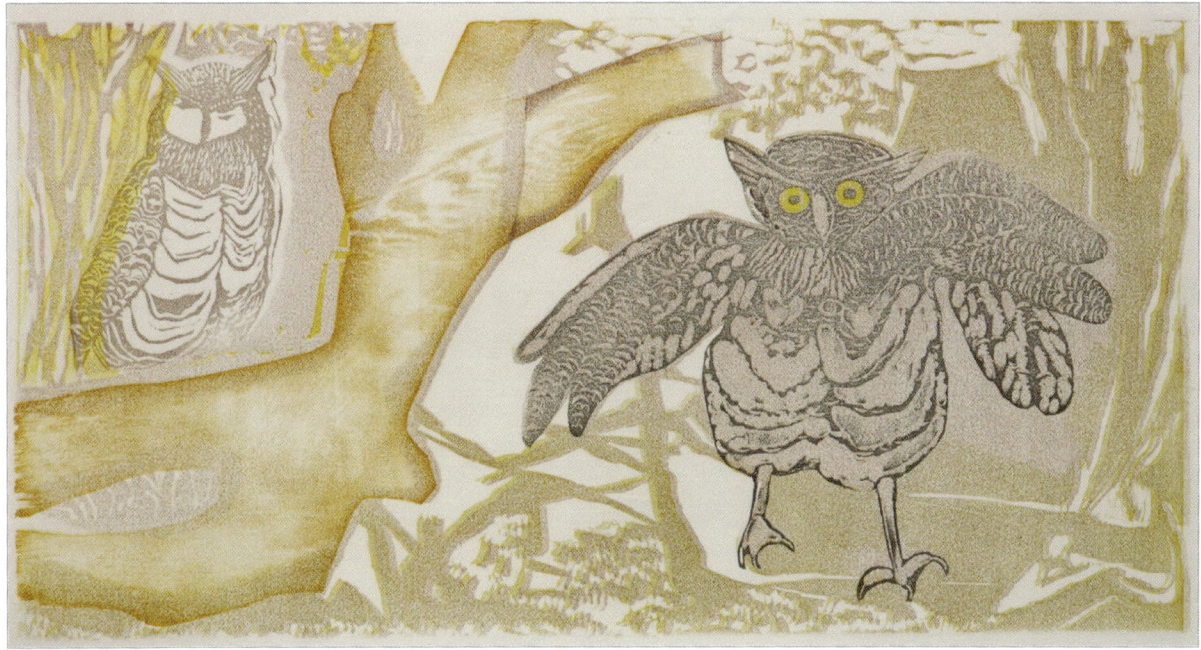

Jessie Wilber, *Owls*, n.d., five-stage woodblock print, 30 x 15 inches.
Courtesy of the Montana State University School of Art.

her experimental philosophy of trying something to see if it works. In this case the end result retains the landscape nature of the piece, but it also speaks to the continuous attention to current issues involving dams and rivers. This print commemorated a trip down the Missouri River after Wilber attended the Montana Institute of the Arts festival in Havre in 1954 and today stands as a reminder of the battles fought to preserve free-flowing rivers.[75] Between 1962 and 1963,

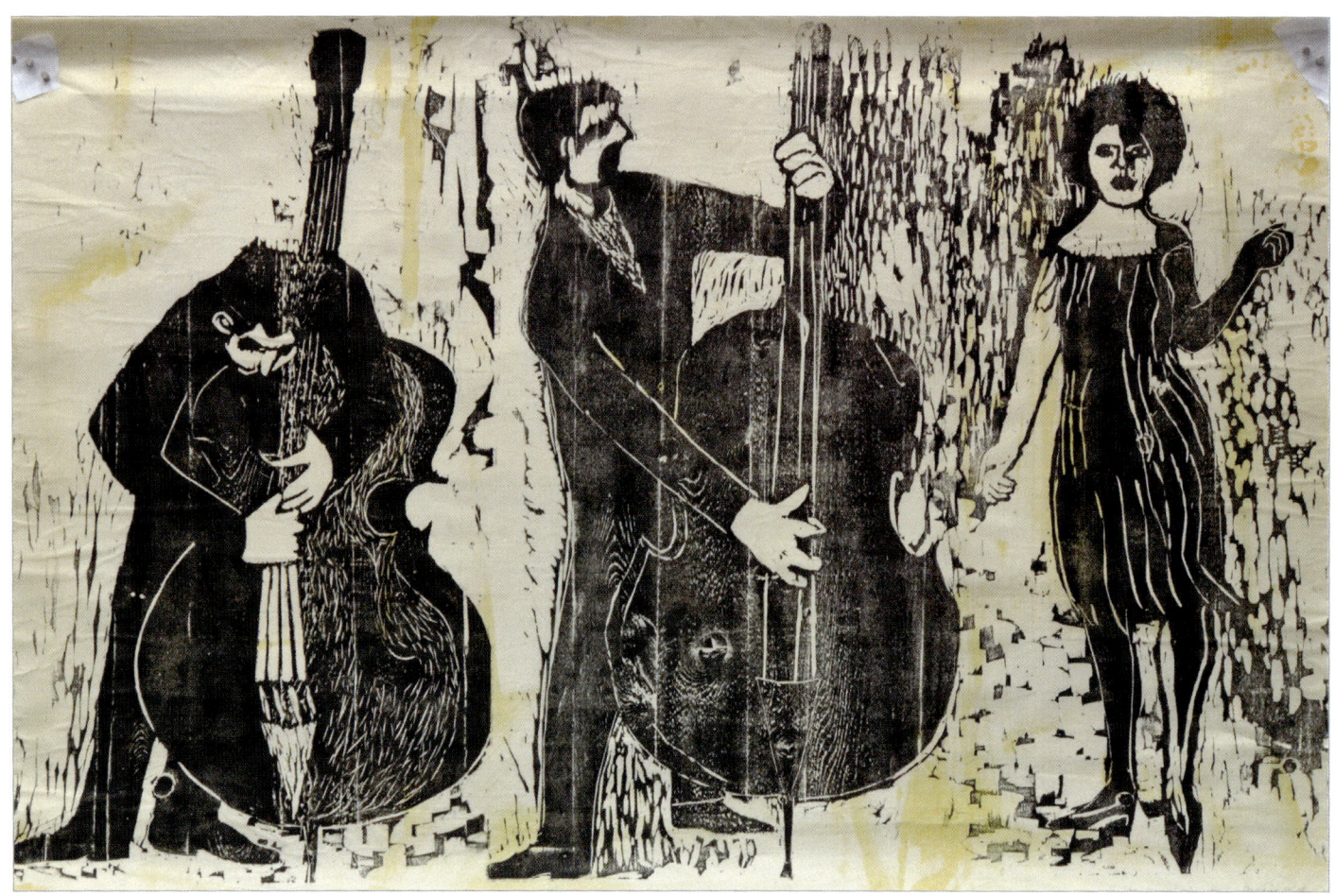

Jessie Wilber, *The Musicians*, 1965, single-color woodblock print on fabric. 46 x 30 inches. Courtesy of the Montana State University School of Art.

the Yellowstone River community made their voices heard with a huge outcry as the prospect of damming the free-flowing river got serious. There were meetings and protests, editorials, and letters to the newspapers.[76] Wilber, as well as many of her fellow artists, musicians, and writers deeply involved in politics, both local and national, used their art to contribute to the ongoing dialogue.

Owls (n.d.; page 69) consists of a five-stage woodblock print. She carved several layers of woodblocks and, using earth tones, she again played with the idea of the flat surface. Within the formal aspects of Wilber's *Owls*, she openly acknowledges the two-dimensional surface with a minimalist view of the landscape. Considering the owls themselves, of the two owls, one of them stares brazenly and directly ahead, directly at the viewer, challenging the viewer's gaze, turning the idea of birdwatching on its head, a theme she returns to time and again.

The Musicians (page 70), her 1965 single-color woodblock print on fabric, speaks to the strength of her community and the people in it. The material she utilized, a paper picnic tablecloth, was probably just the right size for her very large print. She created three separate woodblocks, one for each musician, and then printed them onto a single image. She depicted the evenings spent with other artists, dancers, writers, and, of course, musicians, as shown here. These get-togethers, one way in which the Modernists in Montana could share their work and their ideas, became instrumental in forming the kind of community that could stand up to the pushback against the Modernist aesthetic and the lack of sales.

MAKING IT PERSONAL

In Clement Greenberg's 1960 essay "Modernist Painting," he argues that "[t]he immediate aims of the Modernists were, and remain, personal before anything else, and the truth and success of their works remained personal before anything else."[77] Jessie Wilber's truth reflected Greenberg's analysis of Modernism: Birds, flowers, cats, landscapes, all represented an essential aspect of her own personal environment. Each print she made spoke to the things she loved, her own experiences, and her memories. Wilber said in a 1983 interview, "Everything revolved around what I could see out of my back window."[78] In the Bozeman home she shared with Senska, they created a garden, which they tended with care. Their personal joy derived in part from nature, from their garden, and from their work. Wilber's work evolved but never became derivative. Her experiences with the land, with the isolation of Montana, combined with the community of artists she surrounded herself with resulted in uniquely fresh and innovative Modernist concepts. By keeping to the personal, she constantly referred to her own environment. By keeping to the aesthetics of the materials at hand, she responded to that environment with immediacy. "Both Jessie and Frances were immersed in their garden," said Tina DeWeese, who knew them all her life. "Jessie and Frances always gardened and that beautifully tended space was inspiration for much of Jessie's imagery in prints and collages."[79] Senska, too, included florals and other foliage in the decorations on her pottery. The two artists' connections ran deep.

Frances Senska wrote about Wilber's 1986 *Magpies in a Snowstorm* (page 73): "The subject matter is treated with obvious affection but without sentimentality."[80] *Magpies in a Snowstorm*, one of the last prints Wilber made before her death, includes over twenty shades of white. She incorporated a technique of sketching to create a spontaneous feeling in a complicated composition. The multicolored print consists of numerous steps, each one adding to the last to complete a winter scene. A return to the olive greens of earlier prints establishes a dialogue with her past, but her lines are no longer simple. *Magpies in a Snowstorm* is a return to her silkscreen work, a tactile, unforgiving, and work-intensive method. The result is tumultuous, the magpies frantic, the snow relentless. The viewer can almost hear the cacophony of clipped calls, slightly muffled and tamped. No longer concerned with the "isms" of her youth, Wilber ended her body of work completely devoted to the process itself. Connie Lange, a printmaker who helped Wilber in her later years noted:

> She fed the magpies regularly all winter on a stump in the garden and made many, many drawings of their flight. She enjoyed the way they swooped in, courteously waited their turn, thriftily picked up pieces they dropped in the snow, and was particularly tickled by one who discovered the suet he got was a frozen chunk too big for him manage and brought it back and picked up another![81]

Wilber's unique voice comes through as recognizable as the caws of the magpies—loud, clear, and distinguishable from any other sound. Her work is as indigenous to the Montana landscape as are the birds in her yard. The strength of her work relies on her personal world, told through a lifetime of Montana Modernist aesthetics. Above all, her voice as a teacher and as a mentor echoes across time. Her students who knew her keep her in their hearts as she kept the lessons of Stinchfield and Dozier in hers. Her natural kindness and generosity, as well as her art, were handed down from student to teacher across the generations, taking the personal approach while addressing the tenets of Modernism.

FRANCES SENSKA: FROM HER ROOTS AND BACK AGAIN

Ceramic artist Frances Senska's (1914–2009) deep interest in local materials contributed to her role as a pioneering Modernist. By drawing on her early years spent in Cameroon, the daughter of missionaries, Senska learned to value place and locality, which she applied in the creation of her gouged and painted pots, as well as the figures she modeled from native Montana clay. Senska's direct connection to Bauhaus artists Marguerite Wildenhain and László Moholy-Nagy helped bring her studio practice into the Modernist realm.

Senska's father, a medical missionary station doctor, and her mother, a teacher at the mission station in the grasslands of Cameroon, contributed to her sense of community.[82] Her father, also a craftsman, earned his way through medical school as a cabinetmaker and a construction foreman. Senska learned how to use those tools standing by her father's side. Through her father's building abilities and the lifestyle of Cameroon,

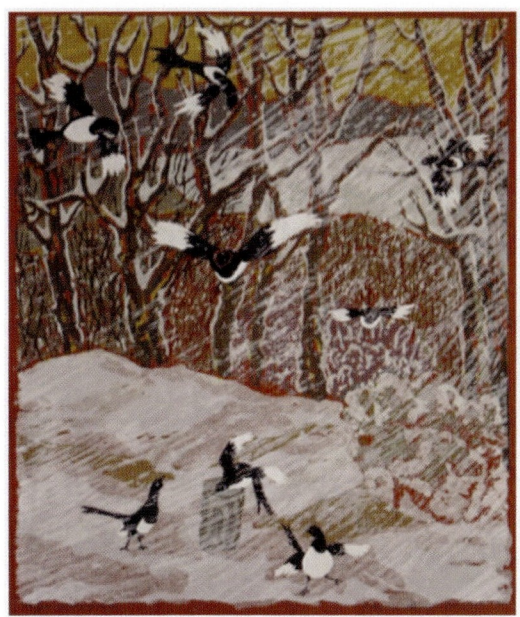

Jessie Wilber, *Magpies in a Snowstorm*, 1986, silkscreen print, 33.5 x 30 inches. Courtesy of the Yellowstone Art Museum.

Senska's aesthetic formed, specifically her lifelong dedication to functional objects:

> Everything that was used there was made by the people for the purposes they were going to use it for...you know, big vats and jugs to make the beer, and smaller pots to cook the vegetables, and smaller ones to serve the peanuts....[I]t was all clay work. And it was all for function, a use, a human use, and so that still seems important to me. I'm not the bric-a-brac type.[83]

At ten years old, Senska and her family visited Paris, France, on their way back from Africa. At the time, the *Exposition de l'Art Moderne*, con-

ceived by the French government, introduced new avant-garde styles in architecture, interior design, furniture, jewelry, and the decorative arts to the rest of the world. The experience stayed with Senska throughout her life. "I really got interested in art and design and what you might call industrial design and so forth at that exposition. So, I sort of headed in that direction when I went [to school]."[84]

She began teaching at Montana State College in 1946, where she met Jessie Wilber. Their relationship deepened as they shared a love for gardening and nature and an aesthetic derived from the Montana landscape. In a retrospective on Senska, curator Brandon Reintjes noted:

> [Senska's and Wilber's] shared subjects repeated throughout their respective careers, including a series of Siamese cats, floral décor, and garden motifs....[Wilber's] presence and proficiency with printmaking may have been the determining factor that influenced the entire suite of [Senska's] lithographs, which emerged between 1946 and 1952.[85]

The lithographs enabled Senska to explore the imagery and color that, at times, showed up on her pots. The etching in the lithographs came through in the sgraffito technique on her YaBaBo pots (n.d.; page 74), a form of decoration made by scratching through a surface to reveal a lower layer of a contrasting color, reflected both her early life in Cameroon and Wilber's exploration in printmaking. These pots developed after Senska took a trip with Wilber back to Africa as an adult in 1966. They bring to mind Cameroon water pots, not only in approximate shape, but in their use of the sgraffito technique. According to an interview conducted for her 2014 retrospective at the Holter Museum of Art, in Helena, the name of her African-influenced "good luck" pots ("YaBaBo") comes from the Cameroonian saying "it will be nine," which is a good luck chant in Basa/Bantu culture. Senska stylistically divides the space into nine segments, each depicting part of her natural environment, such as a turtle, two people in a canoe, and birds.[86] Senska's foray into printmaking became an extension of the scratch-making technique she often used in her ceramic work. The subjects of these prints and lithographs reflected her environment and embodied the African aesthetics that played a part in her own thinking about place.

Senska's use of the sgraffito technique not only connected her to Cameroonian ceramics but also grew into her existing studio practice. During a video made in her studio in 1978, Senska said, "I am a compulsive decorator. I always draw on the pots, something specific, something mine."[87] This way of seeing reflects Greenberg's assertion that Modernism stems from the personal.[88] For Senska, the personal encompassed everything she did, from collecting local clay to the designs she gouged onto the sides of her pots.

Decoration showed not only in her scored designs, as in the YaBaBo pots and on her 1966 *Ring Necked Bottle* (page 75), but in her *Chicken Wine Set* (n.d.; page 76), where she drew with glazes. In this set the pitcher took on the guise of a chicken with a beak/spout, and simple feather images drawn on the body as well as on the off-

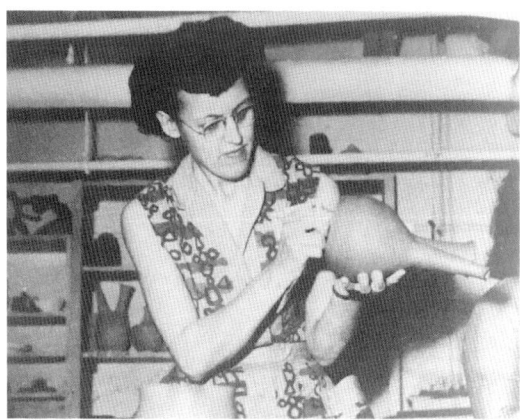

Frances Senska in her studio, circa 1950s.

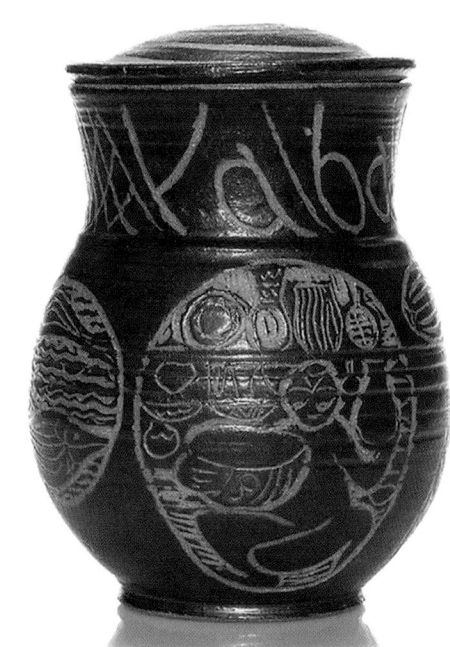

Frances Senska, *YaBaBo Pot*, n.d., stoneware, 9 x 7 inches diameter. Courtesy of the Holter Museum of Art.

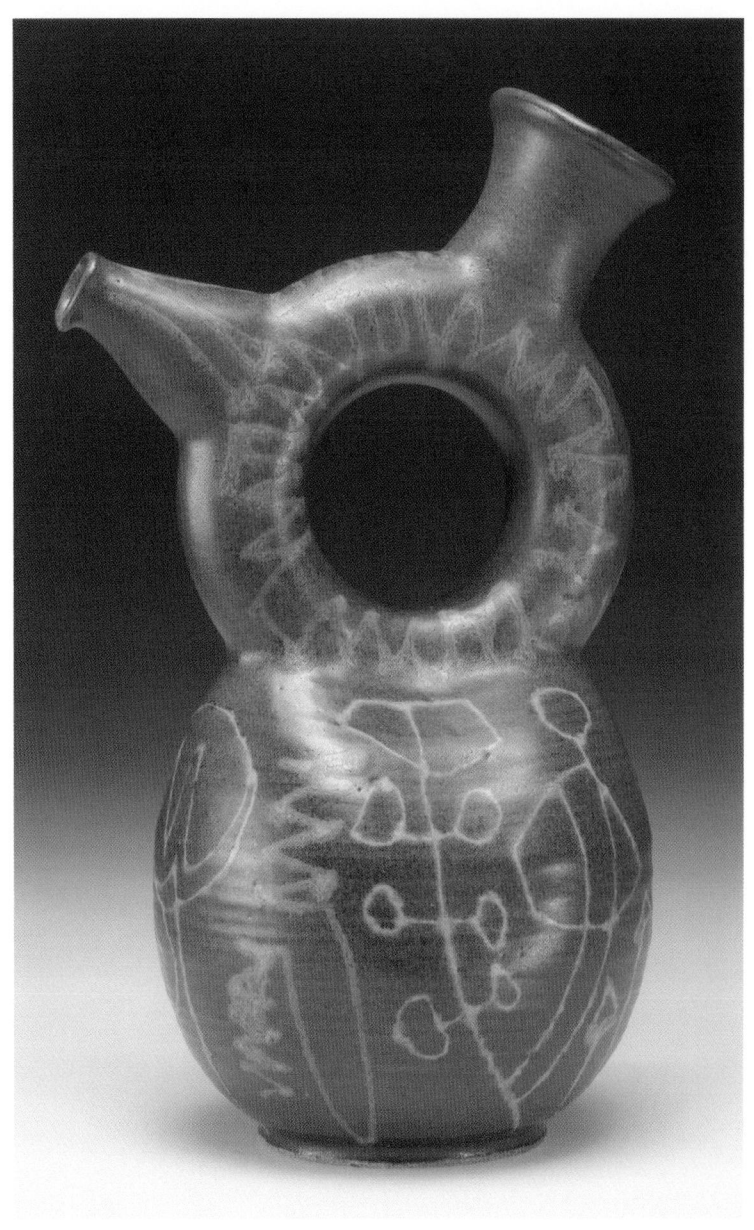

Frances Senska, Ring Necked Bottle, 1966, stoneware, 12 x 7.5 x 5.5 inches.
Courtesy of Alfred University/Alfred Ceramic Art Museum,
museum purchase, Rodger D. Corsaw Collection/#2015.16.
Photograph by Brian Oglesbee.

set mouth of the pitcher continued to portray the chicken anatomy. This way of depicting birds shows another aspect of her work: a sense of play. Her referential drawings of birds and abstract foliage recur as a motif throughout her work.

Looking at Senska's 1979 *Branch Bottle Weed Pot* (page 78), the dark outer slip allows her figures of birds and abstracted foliage to stand out through her sgraffito technique. In Cameroon pottery beer and water containers display complex decorations,

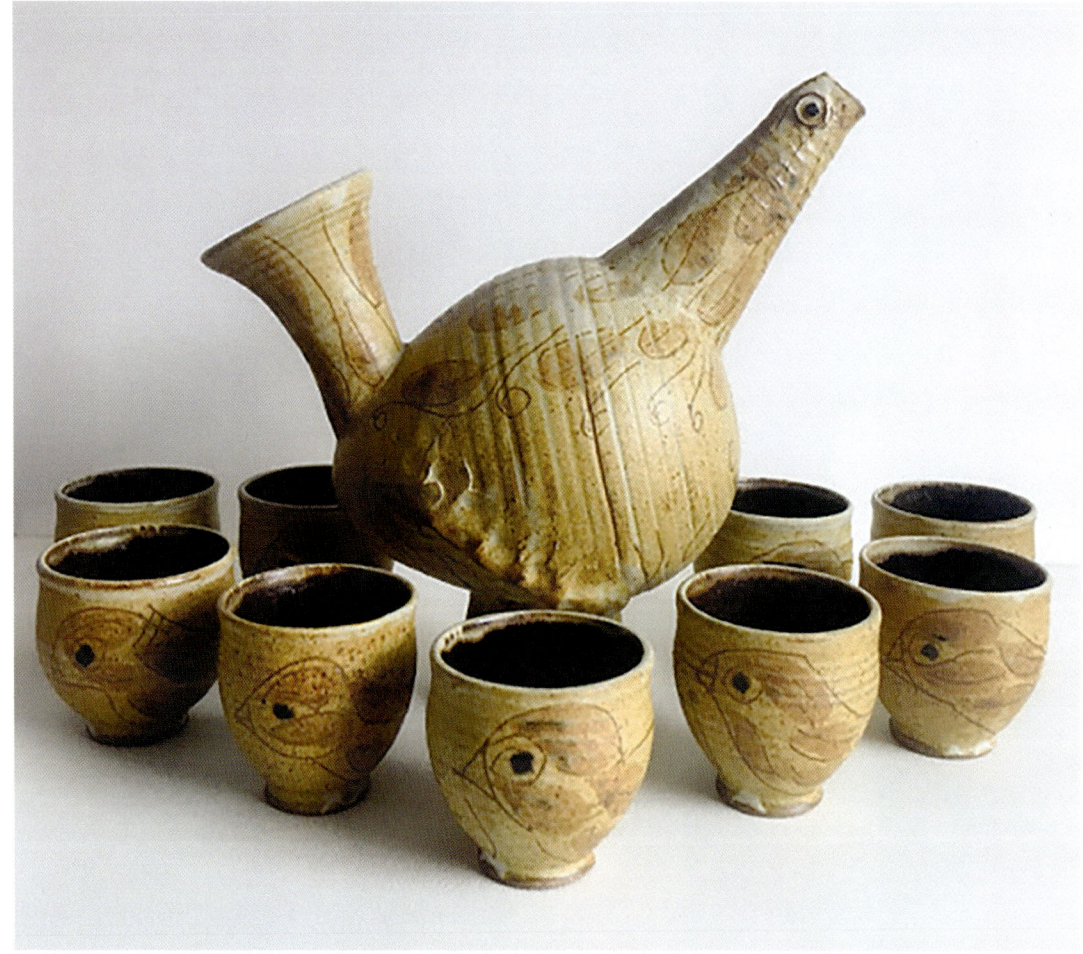

Frances Senska, Chicken Wine Set, n.d., stoneware, variable dimensions. Courtesy of Anthony Waller. Photograph by Anthony Waller.

mixing a range of ornamental techniques and images.[89] The 14-inch-tall vase with its five spouts on top speaks to a flower or "weed" vessel, animated by the birds and leaves on the body of the pot. Although utilitarian in theory, it is doubtful anyone actually put flowers in it. Senska's appreciation of shape, color, and size of an object for its own sake overrides the utilitarian uses, although those functions played a part in the overall design.

Senska preferred dark slips, which, in the case of the YaBaBo pots, gave this body of work an appearance similar to that of the clay objects of Cameroon. She likened her style of living to the dark slips she worked with by saying, "I prefer brown rice, brown sugar—all things not overly refined. I like elegance only in the sense the scientists use the term, meaning the most economically precise solution to a given problem."[90]

The communal activity surrounding pottery speaks to a more intentional connection. Its role in an exchange network in Cameroon was also important to Senska. Pottery from one area often showed up in other areas of Cameroon, playing a large role in defining regional identity. These utilitarian objects of daily life, including ritual objects, often remain prestige items in families' possessions. A pot that originated in one region of the Grasslands easily ended up in another. This exchange compares to the gifting practice of American pottery, where a wine set is given as a wedding present or, more specifically, where Senska's partridges (various dates; page 60) were often given as small presents to celebrate personal achievements. Montana State University History Professor Mary Murphy said she often gave the small ceramic birds as gifts to female colleagues who earned tenure or some other notable achievement. Exchanged or gifted pots may have been a part of Senska's early life, and it may explain her deep connection to the pottery of Cameroon as well as her preference for the dark-colored pots she lived with in her youth.

Babessi culture (of the people of the Grasslands) held potters in high esteem. Babessi pots, often described as the "wombs of women," were an important component of the community's life. The bottom of the pot, with its symmetry, balance, and regularity, relates to the center of a person and needs to be done well because it contains the potential for life.[91]

In Cameroon, clay is generally collected near the potter's home. Methods of processing the clay for modeling vary from potter to potter and remain key to the integrity of the clay itself. Senska's methods came from her own tests and trials. She demonstrated to students how to process the clay dug from raw earth, making it part of her classroom work.

These elements of clay, decoration, utility, and nature embody her African aesthetics combined with a consciousness of the Bauhaus movement. Nothing exists in isolation. Senska's work in Montana, rooted in Africa, through the schools of the Bauhaus movement, add a different aspect to the idea of what it meant to be a potter in Montana. Her combined background and education, practice and pedagogy, informed her aesthetic. As artist and Bauhaus founder Walter Gropius stated, "Every piece of work is a manifestation of our innermost selves,"[92]

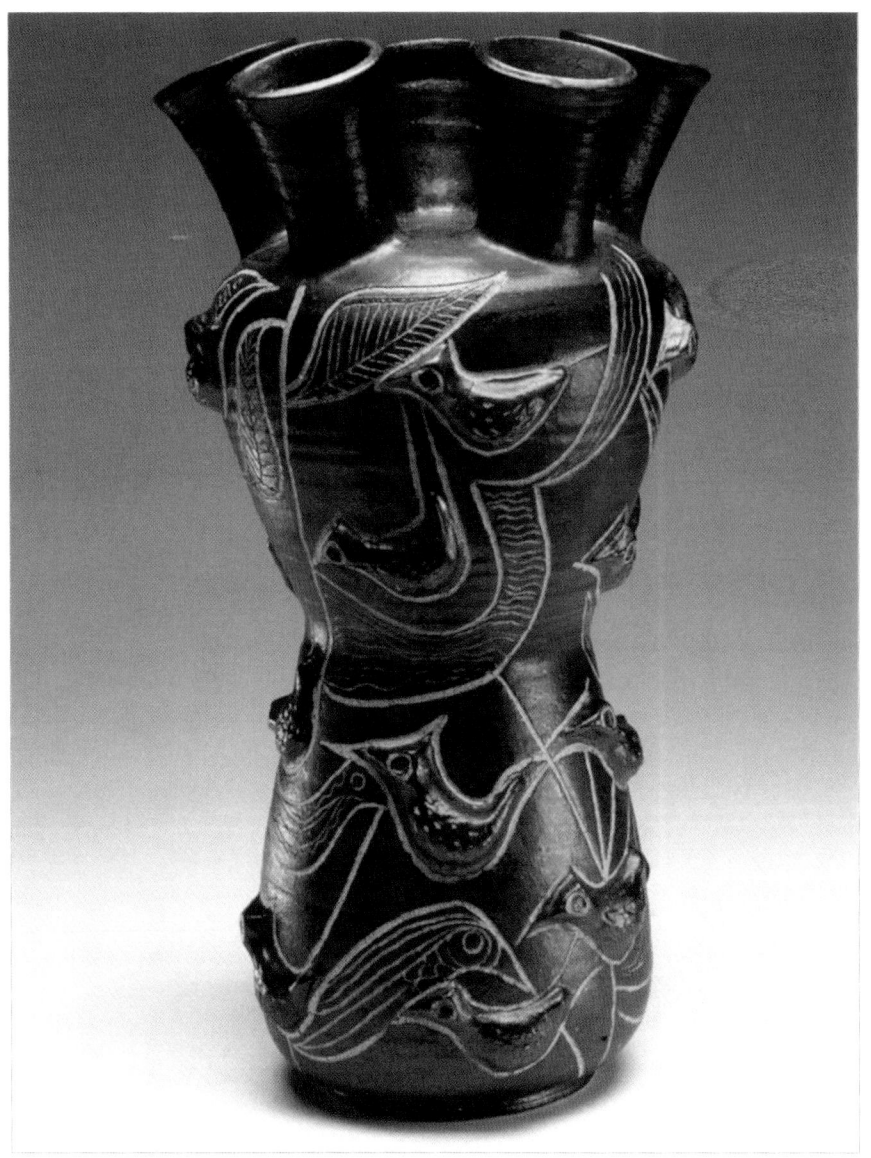

Frances Senska, *Branch Bottle Weed Pot*, 1979, stoneware, 14 x 6 inches.
Courtesy of the Senska/Wilber Collection.

clearly a reference to Sigmund Freud's psycho-analytic work as well, specifically on the Ego. As Gropius states when speaking of the analysis of the design process,

> The objective of all creative effort in the visual arts is to give form to space...but what is space, how can it be understood and given a form?...Although we may achieve an awareness of the infinite we can give form to space only with finite means. We become aware of space through our undivided Ego, through the simultaneous activity of soul, mind and body.[93]

A close look at Senska's ceramic work reveals the fundamental characteristics of her materials, the utilitarian forms (and non-utilitarian forms) as well as processes that reflect her personal perspective. Inherent in her work, as well as her teaching, is the Bauhaus theory that a basic, craft-based training was a prerequisite to being an artist. A producer of artistic work had to know everything about its production. For Senska this philosophy, reflected in her collection and processing of her own clay, became the common thread between African potters and her Bauhaus beliefs. While Senska never called herself a Bauhaus artist, the movement and her Bauhaus teachers clearly impacted her work.[94]

MAKING PRECEDES MATCHING

The culmination of Senska's work firmly positions her as an important transitional artist whose art forms a bridge between American studio ceramics of 1940–1950 and contemporary ceramic sculpture.[95]

A Modernist relationship to nature, reflective of its subject rather than naturalistic detail, characterizes Senska's work. For example, in her chicken form she referenced the natural structure of a chicken but did not describe it. Art historian Ernest Gombrich wrote about the idea of "making precedes matching." This

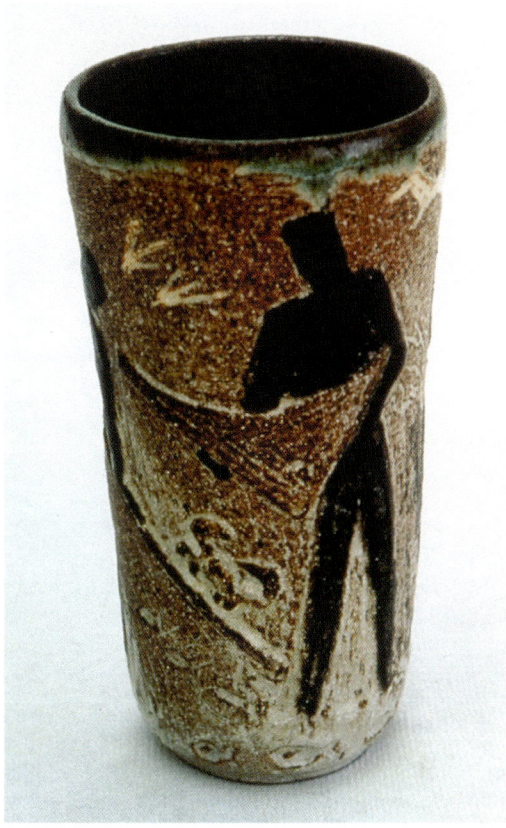

Frances Senska, *Surf Fishers* (*Pond Farm Vase*), 1950, light stoneware, 7 7/8 x 4 3/8 inches.
Courtesy of the Senska/Wilber Collection.

is shown through Senska's bird imagery, which stands as a summation of her own idea of a bird, and is not depicted by the actual bird's anatomy. Gombrich's account of the art of painting as the consideration and condition of perception reflects not only the look of things but the hidden essence of things. Senska's process, while incorporating the utilitarian side of ceramics, also feels like an intuitive process expressed through form and composition.[96]

Senska's ability to portray several strands of artistic lineage speaks to her ability to find common threads in her work and in her life. This can be traced back to the underlying principle of problem-solving. This she does by taking what she needs from each of her mentors, starting with Maholy-Nagy. Senska, quoted in *Vision in Motion*, repeats a nonsensical tongue twister in the Basa dialect of Cameroon: "*Koki umbale gogo/ tenge kule milondo/ kokroko miyombroko/ mbondo tos*."[97] The idea of her knowing this and sharing it reveals Senska's connection to both Cameroon and the teachings of Moholy-Nagy. Moholy-Nagy uses this kind of tongue twister wordplay to put a tic in the ear of the artist, to open the artist up to other kinds of inspiration and encourage a kind of sound abstraction that leads to outside-the-box creativity. Senska said she often listened to African music in her studio while she worked, Moholy-Nagy's "tic in the ear" influencing her practice.[98] Senska's collage work, published in *Vision in Motion*, depicts a visual demonstration of art in a solution-based form:[99]

Somewhere along the way I took a course in design taught by László Maholy-Nagy and that was a lot of fun, and I got a lot of ideas about how to teach from him, because he was one of these people who—he gave us all the material to work with and tools to learn.... You know somebody would say, "Well, I'd like to do thus and so," and he'd say, "Well, try it and see whether it works. See what you get." He'd never say, "Well, you can't do that." He'd say, "Well, try it." And so I thought that's the way to go, so that's the technique I used on my students, too.[100]

Senska said her early instructors stayed with her, especially in her approach to clay. "It was important then to learn to use the technology and the materials which were available to solve the problem—and that seems even more valid today."[101] Moholy-Nagy brought the ideas of function and form, as well as creative ways to solve problems through intuition instead of planning. In Moholy-Nagy's own words, "The problem of our generation is to bring the intellectual and emotional, the social, and technological components into balanced play; to learn to see and feel them in handling human affairs, a rigidly stifling biological and social impulse; a memorized, not a lived life."[102] However, another teacher was instrumental in introducing Senska to the life of a potter.

Marguerite Wildenhain believed that the best teacher was nature itself, but a ceramic artist needed a strong foundation in technique. Looking at Senska's 1950 *Surf Fishers* (page 79) and Wildenhain's *Tall Footed Vase* (n.d.; page 81), the impact of Wildenhain's work becomes clear.

Wildenhain, the Bauhaus-trained potter who taught at Pond Farm, promoted a community-based potter's school in Gurneyville, California, where, in 1950, Senska spent a summer under her tutelage.[103] Wildenhain said in the book *The Invisible Core*, "Pond Farm is not a 'school' it is actually a way of life."[104] This kind of atmosphere, as well as the back-to-the-land philosophies of Pond Farm, contributed to Senska's overall teaching and lifestyle. According to Senska, Wildenhain's lessons stayed with her throughout her teaching career. "Marguerite wasn't into high-tech at all, it was just sort of a shed with some wheels and there was clay, and we mixed our clay, and made our things and fired them. It was the way she'd been taught."[105]

Senska recalled how different Wildenhain was from Grotell:

> [Grotell's] students were just as devoted to her, or more so, than [Wildenhain]'s students, but it was a completely different thing, because she wasn't there. [Wildenhain] was there all the time and she was giving you instruction and she was telling you stories about this, that, and the other thing, if it would help you out and you know, she was just a teacher from the word go.[106]

Comparing Wildenhain's *Three Necked Vase* to Senska's *Branch Bottle Weedpot*, the resemblance comes through in design and coloration. According to ceramic artist and Professor at Montana State University Josh DeWeese, who knew Senska, Wildenhain remained an important figure to Senska throughout her life.

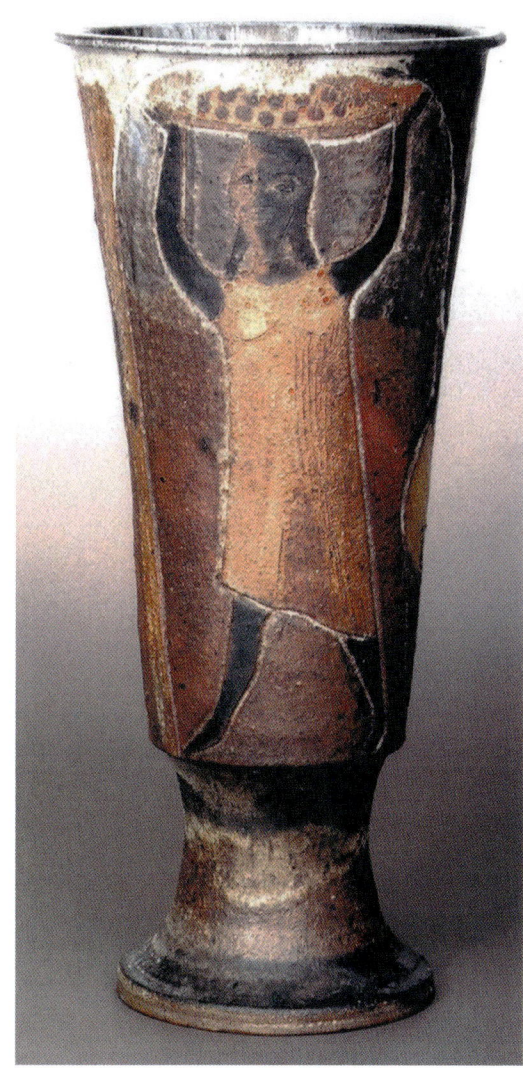

Marguerite Wildenhain, *Tall Footed Vase*, n.d., 13 1/4 x 6 3/8 inches. Courtesy of the Luther College Fine Arts Collection.

Once at Montana State College, Senska fully appreciated the land and the environment where she lived and worked. The art department, called the "Department of Applied Art," was part of the Home Economics curriculum and did not split off to form its own department until years later. At the time, Senska said, "I started teaching ceramics with the merest little scrap of knowledge. I had had just two quarters of ceramics when I started teaching. I just learned it right along with the class."[107] Senska cleaned out an old storage room in the basement of Herrick Hall where she and her students built a ceramics studio, which included several small electric kilns, and a few kick wheels she bought with a grant of $300 from the department. "I managed to change the curriculum," Senska said. "They hadn't tumbled to the fact that ceramics was going to be a big deal."[108]

Due to the purpose-built spaces, the culture of ceramic studio art (as well as printmaking) is more communal than a painting studio.[109] Because of the cost of building such spaces, sharing it becomes a necessity. In additional to the convivial atmosphere of working together, Senska added field trips with her students to collect clay and process it.

The clay, dug from a railroad line cut near Lewistown where an outcropping of the Kootenai formation lies exposed to the elements, offered up some of the best stoneware available in the state, according to Josh DeWeese, who, in later years, once accompanied Senska on the trip. She also found, along with Voulkos, a closer source in Bear Canyon, where she took students. One of Senska's favorite stories about Voulkos is how he stood guard beside a filthy, mud-covered, pickup truck parked on Bozeman's Main Street until the owner returned. "'Where did you get stuck?' he demanded, intrigued by the clots of good red clay clinging to the vehicle. And so Peter discovered Bear Canyon clay."[110]

For Senska there was no question of ordering clay; even one of her glazes, her Trail Creek Glaze, came from a nearby drainage, while others came from all over the state. Her deep connection to the land grew to become as important as the forms she used to create the vessels and objects. For Senska digging the clay and processing it for use in the studio embodied the experience of being a potter. It contributed to developing an awareness of surface and materials. It also helped to create a tighter-knit ceramic community, as she invited her students to experiment alongside her in the studio.

Senska's life as a potter and her life as a teacher often intertwined. In a video of her taken in her studio she said, "You have to be patient when you're dealing with some inanimate objects. You can't hurry a pot….[Y]ou have to coax it and assist it and direct it where you want it to go…and if you make a sudden move, the pot just goes."[111] She likened pots to people and by extension revealed her attitude toward her students. "What you're doing is passing on what you have gotten to someone else so that they can use it. Sometimes they use it in very original ways, not ways you had anticipated—but which appeal to you."[112]

A 1978 video of Senska shows her at the potter's wheel, disk spinning as she sits with her elbows tight to her sides. Her hands cradle a solid block of clay as she presses down on it. "I'm a maker. I make things with my hands," she says, her voice light and smooth.[113] "Pottery is something you can do yourself, from collecting the clay to forming it, to [choosing] the glazes and firing it…the whole works." She impels the clay downward as her fingers apply pressure coaxing a shape upward, pulling gently. "There's a sympathy, an empathy for the natural. What [the clay] wants to do and it does what you want it to do." One hand reaches deep inside the nascent vessel while the other matches it on the outside, pinching, shaping, almost without effort, as a spout forms. She lays her vessels and sculptures— bowls, pitchers, small partridges—into the kiln, like a mother putting a near-sleeping child to bed and closes the lid on the electric oven. "Glazing is your last choice, and you have to make that decision, and that's hard. I'm a compulsive decorator—that may be part of the African influence. In Cameroon I don't think I ever saw an undecorated pot. I always draw on the pots…make it something special, something mine."[114] Upon opening the kiln, a larger one, she turns to her notebooks to make a notation of the glaze finishes, the firing temperatures, and times. "[Pottery] shows an actual living person…[Y]ou can reach out and shake hands with it and know there was someone else who had their hands on it, too."[115]

Senska's work embodies the Montana Modernist aesthetic, from its reflection of the land in the clay and glazes she made to her playful partridges and wine sets. Her ability to place making before matching incorporates Gombrich's notion of what makes Modernism more than a mimetic practice of recreating the world. Instead, her work showed students how to express themselves in ways that did not imitate the landscape but instead revealed it in a more personal way.

Senska's work and life crossed the frontiers of ceramics. She learned from those who taught her how to live the life of an artist and how to become a teacher. Senska passed both of those qualities down through the generations of ceramic artists that followed her. The life she instilled into her ceramics speaks to the culture of Cameroonian exchange traditions as well as the Modernist attention to materials. A potter's life may seem simple, but the strands that create an artist are not. Each piece Senska made holds tight to the experiences of her life: her childhood in Africa, the teachings of the Bauhaus's form and function, Wildenhain's demands to master the technique, and her own years of generosity through teaching. For Senska, even if she never made a dime from her art, her happiness derived from a life with her hands in clay.

FROM BRICKS TO CERAMIC ARTS: ARCHIE BRAY AND OTHER CHARACTERS

Although the Archie Bray Foundation did not begin as a school, it served as another sort of learning institution stemming from the work done at MSC. An extension of both the power of community and the strengths of the teachers connected to the foundation, the Archie Bray Foundation's origin story contains both legend and truth. Archie Bray, Branson Stevenson, Henry and Pete Meloy, Sister Mary Trinitas Morin, Frances Senska, and Jessie Wilber all had a hand in turning the dying brick manufacturing business into a world-renowned incubator for ceramic artists. The Archie Bray Foundation became a significant part of Montana's artistic legacy, bringing in ceramic artists from the world over, helping to change the paradigm for ceramics.

The Archie Bray Foundation had its beginnings in the time following the Great Depression and Helena's three earthquakes in 1935, the largest of which registered a 6.3 magnitude, contributing to the shrinking brick business in Helena.[116] After World War II, with the advent of new technologies for building structures, brick manufacturing fell on even harder times. During this period, the upward surge in American-made ceramics, helped by the scarcity of pottery and porcelain from China, Korea, and Japan due to the devastation of the war in those countries, created a viable ceramic market. For Bray, this became an opportunity to use the brick yard and to encourage art in Helena.

According to Senska, happenstance also played a large role in the creation of the Archie Bray Foundation:

> Pete Meloy and Branson [Stevenson] and Archie were all good friends because Archie ran the Community Concert and local theater...they were all interested in the same thing. Then came along Hank [Meloy] who would come down and visit [Montana State College], and sort of got acquainted with Pete [Voulkos] and Rudy [Autio], and the other students, and we had a nephew and niece of Pete Meloy's here...[T]he way it all got pulled together and started was the summer between Pete and Rudy's two

years in graduate school, they came out here [to Helena] looking for a place to have a studio."[117]

The short stride from brickyard to ceramic artist incubator happened when Voulkos and Autio teamed up to work at the Bray and create art there, when not working on the brick business. Author Janet Koplos states:

> Rudy Autio and Peter Voulkos were brothers in spirit in the early days of the Bray, although their careers diverged strikingly. They were both Montana boys, both sons of immigrants, both attended Montana State College (now University), both were in the art department, where they discovered clay with Frances Senska, and together they became the first artists in residence at the Bray."[118]

During that summer of 1951, Senska and Wilber brought Voulkos and Autio to Helena to meet Archie Bray. Once Senska's group arrived in Helena, Pete Meloy took Voulkos and Autio out to the brickyard. As long as they "nipped brick" to help with the brick business, Autio and Voulkos could use the studio at the brickyard as needed:

> They had all night to work in the drying shed where there was a lot of room, and they had all the clay they wanted....[T]hen they went back to their graduate schools and finished up their degrees and came back out to a job at the Bray and you know, sort of became the first directors there."[119]

Voulkos recalled the first summer of the Archie Bray. "Rudy [Autio] came out and we set up a temporary pottery and a workspace in that old tile shed. We had a couple of wheels and they started getting material to stock the pottery building they were going to build that summer." Both he and Autio ended up working during the day on the bricks, and at night they would work on their own art.[120]

That summer Senska and Wilber made several trips to Helena to help lay brick for the pottery. She also noted that "so many amateurs laid brick for those walls, it's a wonder they remain standing."[121] The idea was to sell the pottery made at the brickyard to help fund the artistic endeavor, but the artists disagreed with the factory mentality of stamping everything with the Archie Bray Foundation mark "ABF" and wanted their own work to have their own marks. Regardless of these differences, the Archie Bray Foundation opened its doors on October 13, 1951. Viola Lindley, a Helena resident, wrote in 1951:

> The Foundation is the answer to the lifelong dream of Bray, who as a boy tried to construct a potter's wheel—although he had never seen one—a dream that persisted even after he worked his way through Ohio State College to receive a degree as a graduate ceramicist and after he had traveled in the Midwest and had seen the small man-made wheels driven by waterfalls.[122]

However, the Bray Foundation also answered Branson Stevenson's dreams. Bray and Stevenson both envisioned the pottery, beginning in 1947, as a place for people to "leave the cares of the day outside the pottery while they examined the potter's work or watched the throwing of pots," as Stevenson once said.[123] Bray strove to create a place of art for everyone. Also in 1947 Stevenson took a ceramics class from Sister Mary Trinitas Marin from the College of Great Falls. Sister Trinitas was the art department head. She and Stevenson bonded over the importance of art in people's lives. For Trinitas, as for Stevenson, experimentation played a big role in their work. Stevenson tried using native Montana minerals for his glazes and created new ways to decorate his pots. He worked for the Socony Vacuum Oil Company alongside his brothers, but, in his heart, he lived for art. While maintaining his full-time job as district manager for the oil company, he served as Vice Chairman for the American Artist Professional League.[124] Former Yellowstone Art Museum director Terry Melton remembered Stevenson as "suave and elegantly complimentary" when he was a visiting artist at the College of Great Falls:

> He wowed the nuns, of course, with his *savoir-faire* he slid his way into the librarian's best graces and convinced her that the unprinted fly leaves in these very old books would be wonderful to print on. Elegant papers they were. So, the nuns with razor blades extracted certain front and back leaves, and they would present them to Branson.[125]

Melton noted that many of the papers bore watermarks. "It's always delighted me to think of archivists and historians in years to come, examining a contemporary print of Branson's on a paper with a watermark of the eighteenth or nineteenth century."[126]

In 1952 Branson Stevenson convinced world-famous potters Bernard Leach, Shoji Hamada, and Soetsu Yanagi to come to Montana. He asked *Time* magazine to put him in touch with Leach after reading an article in 1950. Stevenson had invented a new kind of emulsion wax that "can be readily and easily brushed on the cold pot without hardening immediately." [127] That wax resist method caught on and changed the way potters around the world applied their glazes. When he first met with Leach in St. Paul, Minnesota, in 1950, to convince him to visit the Bray Foundation, Stevenson introduced Leach to his wax resist:

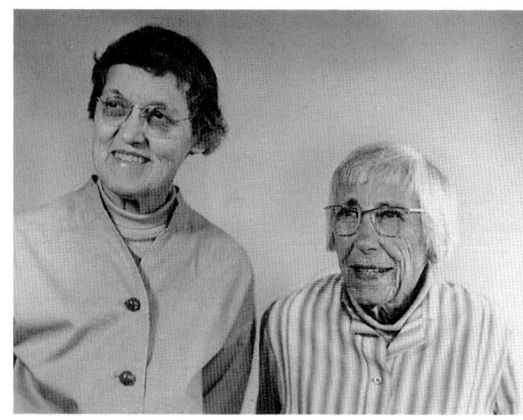

Frances Senska (left) and Jessie Wilber in the mid-1980s.

> Leach was delighted with its use in place of the cumbersome and fire-hazardous melted wax method and, of course, found it ideally suited to brush decoration because it applied fluidly without congealing, just like painting with oil or water color, unlike the melted wax, which congealed the moment the hot fluid contacted the cold pot. [128]

Impressed by Stevenson's wax resist method, the famous potters were convinced to make a two-week stop in Montana. After visiting the Bray, Leach, Hamada, and Yanagi took Stevenson's wax resist and introduced it in Japan. [129]

The workshops the three famous potters conducted put the Archie Bray Foundation on the world map.

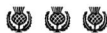

By following the various strands of Modernism and by taking a look at the combination of aesthetics that form the Montana Modernists, reaching back to Cezanne himself, we see how the lineage of these artists aligns with their pedagogy. From the egalitarian nature of their teaching style and the atmosphere of learning in the classroom, they modeled a behavior conducive to forming bonds with their students, yet they also took on the mantle of creating an avenue for Montanans to see themselves in their work. Through Wilber's prints and paintings and Senska's playful pottery inspired by her African roots, they invited people to see themselves as gardeners, as women, and as thinkers. As art professors and women, they also modeled a professional behavior not prevalent in the 1940s. Women in Montana may have been tough, but few taught art at the college level. This became another way for women to see themselves, not only in art but in the lives of these artists.

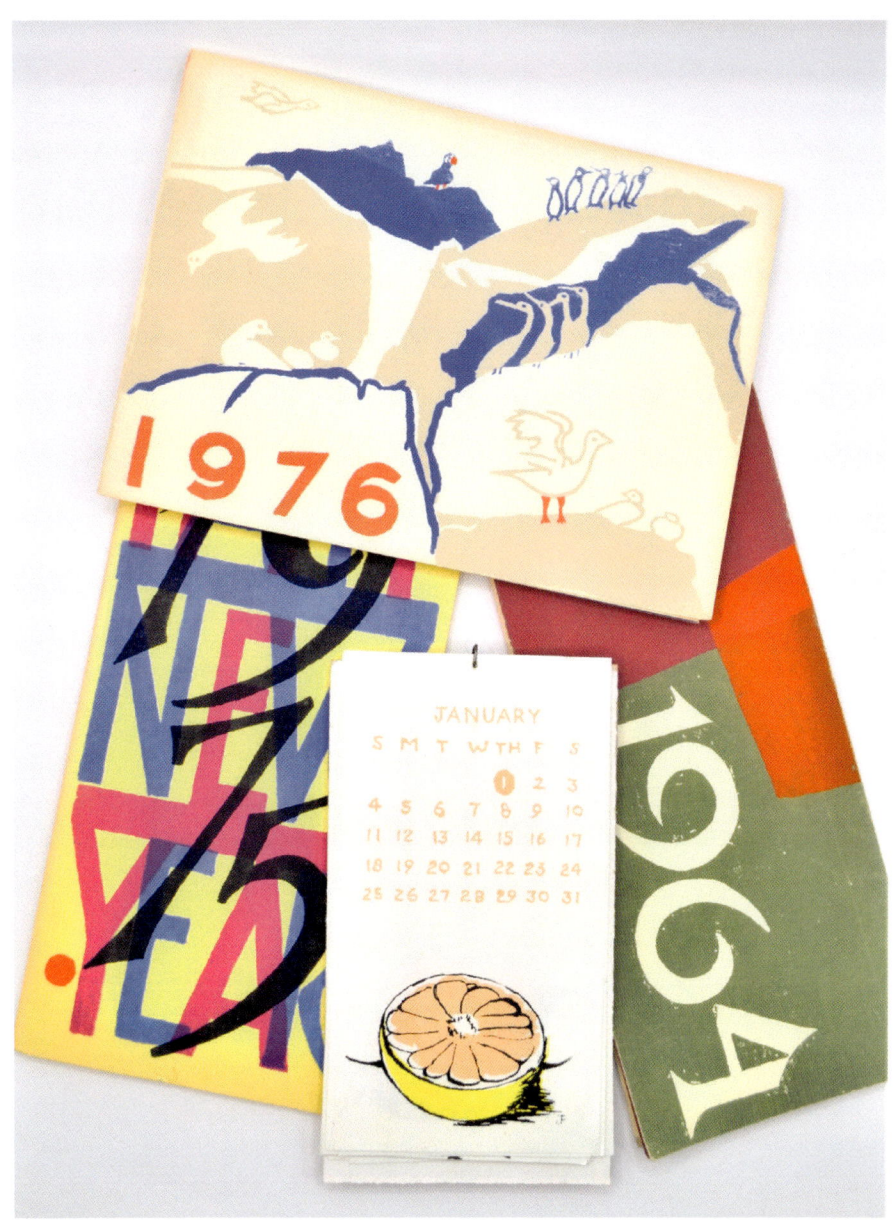

Samples of the handmade calendars Frances and
Jessie created each year and sent to friends.
Courtesy of Kenda Minter.

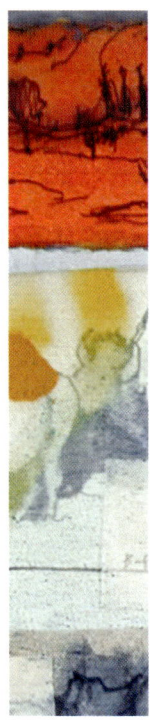
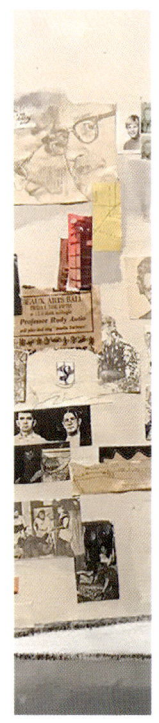
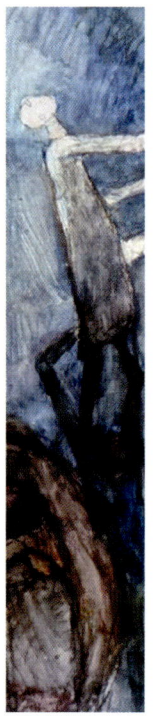
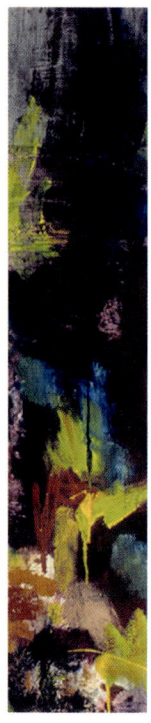
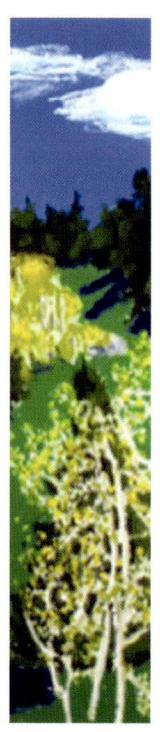
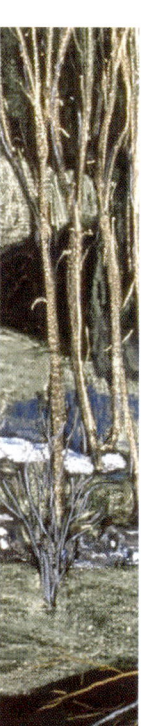

SECTION THREE: COMMUNITY

Reading culture as text is, in many very ordinary respects, what each of us does every day in order to live in the world.[1]

—Anne Norton

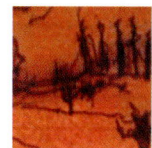

PATRONAGE, ART MOVEMENTS, AND THE G.I. BILL

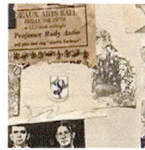

Since the Renaissance, patronage has played a large role in the survival and recognition of artists. Historically, patronage opened possibilities for artists to explore their own voices and media without worrying about survival as long as the work did not stray too far from the patron's taste and requests. Patronage in the sense of financial stability offers a metaphor for the financial security delivered by colleges after World War II. The G.I. Bill sent a flood of students to college, including art students. Colleges needed teachers to work in America's expanding academia. This new influx provided financial security for artist-teachers, if not directly for their art, then by giving them a paycheck, allowing them the freedom to create art without worrying about a steady income.

Even before the G.I. Bill, at the peak of the Great Depression, President Franklin D. Roosevelt enacted the Federal Art Project (FAP) as part of a national work relief program. In 1935 the FAP, under the authority of the Works Progress Administration, instituted the idea that artists produced work, like the bricklayer or the shoe-

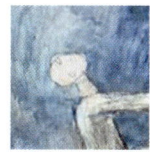

maker. By putting artists to work, the program redefined the role of the artist in American society. It also offered artists a way to gain the financial stability offered by a patron. The government paid the artists, and the artists produced work for cities or towns. After the war the G.I. Bill impacted the Modernist art movement in a similar way with a similar effect, without the direct payment to artists for their art. Instead, the G.I. Bill, by offering government-paid tuition, encouraged a burgeoning veteran population to enroll in colleges. In turn this produced the need for more college teachers, especially in areas where there were few before the war. Through the hiring of artists with Master of Fine Arts diplomas (the terminal degree for art), they found steady work, which enabled artists to continue their exploration of Modernism. While they taught they also made work, explored genres, and learned by visiting other artists. In an extended way, the college took on the role of patron.[2]

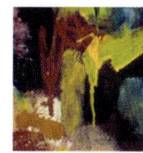

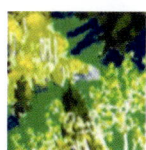

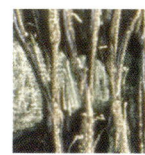

THE DEMOCRATIZATION OF ART

Support for art in America prior to 1930 fell under the purview of the social elite.[3] The FAP shuffled the position of artists and art by making it more accessible to the population as a whole. Through the employment of artists tasked with creating art for public buildings, including post offices where all classes could be exposed to art on a regular basis, viewing art became an egalitarian experience, not confined to private residences or museums. The US Treasury's Section of Fine Arts hired or commissioned artists to paint murals for Post Offices across the country. In Montana it took until 1937 for murals to be funded. The state's sole congressman, Jerry O'Connell, felt Montana had been neglected in the process and so went about procuring funding for public art in the state. The Montana jury, including Montana State College art department chair Olga Ross Hannon, met in Dillon where they decided upon the artists. In the end six post offices were awarded their own murals: Billings, Deer Lodge, Dillon, Glasgow, Hamilton, and Sidney. Most of the art not only depicted a historical perspective but also tied the mural to the places in which they were displayed.[4] While the murals may not have furthered the idea of Modernism—it was too early for that—they did expose people to public art, adding to the art on display in churches and courthouses.

In New York the FAP set up an "art caravan" that carried a complete art exhibit, touring communities around the state. In New York City, exhibits spontaneously popped up in alleys and grew the public's interest in art. Artists around the country visited schools and guided the creation of student art projects. "By recognizing the American artist as a legitimate worker, Federal Art Project programs challenged the idea of art as a sacred object and the notion of the artist as a social outsider," art historian Joan Saab states.[5] The FAP operated from August 1935 until June 1943, costing $35 million and employing over five thousand artists. According to art historian Irving Sandler, the FAP played a vital role in the development of a purely American art, in part because it was paying artists to work, not only on public art but on their individual art. As part of the FAP, in communities where many artists were employed, artists met once a week to organize the work for the upcoming period. In New York City this enabled the New York School artists to collaborate. Many met after work to discuss their direction, visiting the Museum of Modern Art and critiquing each other's work in relation to the work shown at the museum. As Sandler said:

> A by-product of the Project experience, and that which proved its most lasting legacy, was the art community it gave rise to, particularly in New York. Unlike earlier American artists, who tended to be loners, the WPA employees were thrown together of necessity. Daily meetings on the job encouraged contacts that cut across aesthetic positions and produced a constant exchange of ideas, generating a sense of community similar to that in the Paris cafes.[6]

Just as the WPA/FAP contributed to the formation of art communities in New York City, for example that of the Abstract Expressionists in the

1930s and 1940s, the G.I. Bill's combined effects on student enrollment paved the way for the formation of Montana Modernists in the postwar years. After World War II the G.I. Bill enabled veterans to get an education. The bill paid veterans' tuition and living expenses while they went to college, high school, or a vocational school. In the years following the end of the war, land-grant universities across the country saw a significant increase in enrollment due to the attendance of veterans. While the G.I. Bill did not provide money for art projects per se, it did enable soldiers to enter colleges in order to obtain art degrees, which required artists to teach them.

Art education historian Frederick M. Logan found that, in the aftermath of World War II, veterans returned to college in droves. "Art departments and art education areas expanded overnite (*sic*) and never did settle back down to the enrollments of 1945."[7] He observes that colleges where only two or three people had taught a few art classes suddenly began to offer art degrees, including the new expanded Masters of Fine Art (MFA) and Masters of Art degrees. He linked the benefits of the G.I. Bill to the growth in the number of associations for art teachers, including those at high schools, and the creation of the National Art Education Association in 1950.

For artists an MFA opened up the teaching job market, which guaranteed artists a salary, and often came with a studio on the college campus. In Montana the consequences of the G.I. Bill included attracting young artists to teach art. These artists came not only from Montana, but from other areas where modern art and avant-garde thought influenced their work as well as their teaching style. In 1946, the year the G.I. Bill went into effect, Montana State College found itself bursting at the seams. It also saw an increase in enrollment in the art school, as did many other land-grant universities around the country. Eastern Montana College, Billings, began its Fine Arts Department in 1950 and, in 1967–68, the Department of Fine Arts moved to the Division of Humanities where a student could major in art.[8] The New Mexico College of Agriculture and Mechanical Arts established its art department during the 1949–50 academic year.[9] Colorado State University's art department developed fully in 1950.[10] Montana State College's art department originally fell under the Division of Household and Industrial Arts with courses available to graduate students beginning in 1939, but those courses were suspended due to the war and did not reopen until 1946.[11]

Not every college became the seed for a new art movement. The chemistry between the incoming professors needed to be one of camaraderie, inclusivity, and sharing in order to create an atmosphere where students and teachers felt a kinship through their self-expression and were confident enough to expose themselves to new ideas and experiments in style. It also helped when the Bauhaus philosophy of combined disciplines enabled artists to work together, thus encouraging the growth of new ideas.

Montana State College expanded its roster of art teachers, hiring Frances Senska and Robert "Bob" DeWeese. Robert DeWeese came to MSC accompanied by his wife Gennie DeWeese, who also taught as an adjunct as needed. Isabelle Johnson began teaching at Eastern Montana College in 1949. Jessie Wilber came to Montana in 1941 and became instrumental in the expansion of the art program at MSC. This atmosphere of new voices and new ideas became fertile ground for the development of Modernism in Montana.[12] The New Deal legislated programs that put artists to work; this allowed them to continue working on their own artwork and led to the Abstract Expressionist movement, or the New York School. In a like manner, the G.I. Bill expanded art education. Both federal initiatives helped create the foundation for a new art movement in rural areas of the country, like Billings and Bozeman.

COMMUNITY: STRENGTH IN NUMBERS

Up until the 1940s, the remoteness of Montana contributed to the abutment placed before Modernism, keeping the status quo of illustrative nostalgic Western imagery in art. After 1949, however, artists' awareness of their isolation from the art world became a factor in creating art communities. Their small numbers did not deter the artists from seeking each other out but had the opposite effect: It united them. Due to their separation from the art world, they intentionally sought out other like-minded artists, no matter how far flung.

The Modernists in postwar Montana fought against the illustrative and romanticized Western paintings typical in the Rocky Mountain region. Keeping to the tenets of Wilber's "experiment, experiment, experiment" philosophy meant rejecting the dominant cultural stereotypes, as well as much-hoped-for commercial success. Just

as teaching offered these artists the monetary security of a steady art patron, the "art colony" climate offered by a community of artists, dancers, musicians, and dramatists drew on the members' commitment to push back against the prevailing conservative meta-narrative of the West.

The community, especially at Montana State College, played the role of an art colony in that artists, musicians, dancers, and writers could interact, supporting each other's forays to the edges of modern art. No local art market existed at that time.[13] In solidarity and support of each other's work, trade between artists became the norm. The act of bartering for art served an important purpose: it validated their continued work and helped to create a bond between the artists. These factors allowed Modernism a foothold in the state.

Teachers such as Wilber, Senska, DeWeese, and Johnson added another dimension to the aspect of community. Each one encouraged their students to create expressive art and supported their art by inviting them to show their work to the public and to each other. Moreover, they worked together to form a fertile artistic environment unique to that place and time. Together, they created a paradigm in which an art movement could thrive, even though there was no patronage or market for their work.

Eventually, this community encompassed both students and other artists cropping up around Montana. Ray Campeau—artist, teacher, and student of Senska, DeWeese, and Wilber—noted that "Those were the people that were the glue that kept the arts alive in the state. There became a beauty [to it]—everybody in the arts was one big family."[14] Due to the scarcity of art galleries in Montana, the only venues where Modernist art showed were directly connected to the Montana Institute of the Arts or on the MSC campus.[15] "The leaders were the teachers, the people in higher education, and they would exhibit too, not just the students...[Everyone] became part of it. They'd give lectures, give demonstrations, share their beauty."[16] Campeau, who was closest to Senska and Wilber, spoke of them as tough and loving. He also described the kind of nurturing community created by all of them, which allowed their students to feel safe enough to explore new ways of expressing themselves.

Campeau described the time he bought his first painting, while still a student: Jessie Wilber's portrait of the DeWeese family. "[My wife] Kay and I had an agreement that anything we made in art we'd spend in art. During the first student show at Herrick Hall somebody bought a few of my lithographs."[17] He continued, "Jessie painted a painting of the DeWeese kids and Kay and I fell in love with it, but we couldn't afford it. We saw it in a couple of shows, one of the MIA shows, and we wished we could have had it." Campeau and his wife left their kids in Bozeman one year and hitchhiked to see the World's Fair in Seattle. "And there was Jessie's painting again, in the Northwest Pavilion, and we thought, oh god we really want that painting. Everywhere we went that painting would appear." He remembered the day he came running home and told his wife he had sold a couple of those prints. "Then I had to find the phone to call Jessie and tell her I could make a down payment on that painting." When Wilber answered

the phone, she told Campeau she had just sold the painting...to his wife! "We both made the same decision only she got to it before I did. That's the way we felt about both Jessie and Frances. I would have run through a wall if they told me I could run through a wall."[18]

The idea that Campeau, still a student without much money, spent his savings on a painting whose subject is Robert and Gennie DeWeese's two children speaks to the power of the painting as well as the strength of community. To hang a painting of someone else's children in their home reflects the closeness of the artists. Campeau recalled the time in his life when he and his wife struggled to make ends meet. "We had this association with teachers that a lot of people don't have anymore. They helped us. Not just with our art, but with our lives."[19] Senska and Wilber actually lent the Campeaus the down payment on their Bozeman home. "Frances and Jessie knew we were going to get [the house] before we did. I was going crazy working on my masters. I bought that place for $9,000 but I didn't have $9,000. I asked them if I could get a loan and they said, 'certainly.'"[20] Campeau paid them back almost immediately, but the situation had needed instant action, and, without that loan, the Campeaus would have lost the house:

> Frances and Jessie were the catalyst for so many things happening. It's like the Archie Bray Foundation, Frances was one of the founding members there. They had this connection all through the state with people; they were an inspiration, not just teachers, and they did their own work.[21]

Senska, Wilber, and the DeWeeses all understood their role in creating a strong art community. "They said 'I'm a teacher, an instructor at the university and I instruct art and I make art,' but they knew how to work with people. There are a lot of people doing art out there because of them."[22]

When Robert DeWeese applied for the position of art professor at Montana State College, he corresponded first with Cyril Conrad, head of the Department of Applied Art, and later with Jessie Wilber. Over the course of three months, as DeWeese considered the position, he inquired about the housing situation, the weather conditions in Montana, and his expected teaching load. The letters, beginning June 4, 1949, started with DeWeese's qualifications and ended August 19, 1949, with his resignation at the Texas Technological College, Lubbock. They reveal an open back and forth between DeWeese and Wilber. DeWeese worried about an array of logistics, from moving his family from Texas to Montana in an old car to the precarious nature of owning a gas stove and bringing it with them if gas hookups were available. Wilber warned DeWeese about living on the main floor of the student housing units (very cold in winter), the high cost of good tires in Bozeman, and the "strip-house" apartments in the Veteran's Village. "There might possibly be some other apartment or house in town… my students are all trying to keep their ears to the ground too."[23]

In July 1949 a Western Union telegram from DeWeese to Montana State College stated, "Happy to accept offer of position," followed by a telegram from Wilber acknowledging his accep-tance. Wilber then sent him a "hurrah" letter, wherein she stated that she and "Miss Senska had difficulty wording the telegram to you this morning because what we really wanted to say was 'Three Cheers!' I am so glad you decided to come to Bozeman, and I hope that it will turn out to be a fortunate decision for you."[24]

In subsequent letters Wilber reported that she had called a car dealership, gotten a quote on good tires, and included a newspaper article warning them about ticks and Rocky Mountain Fever. She then told DeWeese, "You won't have to go over many mountains getting here—in fact I believe the only really high grade is the last 25 miles, and if necessary you can call us up from Livingston and we will come over and pull you over the hill."[25] Preparing themselves for the worst, the DeWeeses inquired about the availability of antifreeze, surplus furniture, and warm coats. Again, Wilber offered her services in getting the DeWeeses settled and answered any questions large and small. The correspondence reveals the gentle beginnings of what would become a lifelong friendship, but, more than that, they offer insight into Wilber's generosity of spirit and the DeWeeses' acceptance of an unknown future.

Once ensconced at MSC (subsequently MSU), the DeWeeses quickly found themselves with likeminded artists and creatives. They soon became central figures in the circle of artist gatherings. Every artist in the state would show up at the DeWeeses', especially at the Fourth of July parties at their Cottonwood Canyon home. Joel Jahnke, hired by MSU in 1976, recalled, "I remember pockets of artists talking about what they were doing, sharing, not their art so much, but their love of each other. I don't think there was a standard artist in the group, they were all of the avant-garde."[26] Jahnke, who taught theater design and later spent thirty-six years as artistic director for Montana Shakespeare in the Parks, came to the group before he realized what he was getting into. Ben Tone, Charlie Payne, the DeWeeses, Jessie Wilber, Frances Senska, and Ken and Mary (Tata) Bryson got together weekly:

> They were always doing some wacky bohemian thing: they would read a play together, discuss some philosopher, some artist. And it became a drunken brawl, but it always started with a theme. I think really, in those moments, they were globally shaping art in this valley and then that ultimately spread throughout Montana and became huge.[27]

Added to that group were a few students, but mostly people from the university. "But then Bill Stockton would show up, and all these people—whoever was in Montana around the Fourth would show up. It was so much fun to be a part of that wackiness."[28] Tone, a good friend of the DeWeeses, who ran the theater department at the same time as Jahnke, brought him into the group. "Ben was always lighting off fireworks with the children. He would create toys. He was a woodworker, and he'd created a cannon with a cork in the end. You'd put a firecracker in one end, and it shoot the cork out and then spend most of the day trying to find the cork."[29] Jahnke immediately felt a part of their community. "It was beyond belief." He recalled one Fourth of July party when

the actor Bill Pullman attended. "All the kids had decided to do a little play and a parade to commemorate the holiday. They made their own costumes. Frances and Jessie were there. Pullman loved them." Pullman spent two years on the faculty and three years in Montana's Shakespeare in the Parks. "We just all became part of this group of people who shared each other's work. There was always a party going on at the DeWeeses. It was a grassroots movement."[30] Jahnke did not remember any one particular person taking the lead. "They were all just doing their work, talking, and sharing, and all was well. There was equality between students, teachers, and artists in the community no one was above anyone else."[31]

Jahnke recalled everyone talking about their production of the *Three Penny Opera*, although it had taken place in the early 1960s, before Jahnke came to Bozeman. "Bob had a studio at the end of Main Street, and I know they did it there at his studio."[32] Bob's studio was located in the old Moose Lodge above the VFW. "Gennie played the lead, Ben played the lead, Ken was in the play, [Charlie Payne played the piano, Bob did the set design and he was the Street Singer in the play]. They talked about it from the time I met them to the time they took their last breath."[33] Theater became a collaborative effort, where they could all contribute to the piece. "I was never part of those bohemian parties, but they talked about it a lot, about how it made them all broader thinkers in their field. Jessie and Frances were a part of it. They ended up being the greatest audience for that bunch of yahoos."[34]

Upstairs in the storage loft of Gennie DeWeese's old studio in Cottonwood Canyon, a cardboard box packed with postcards and invitations to art openings around the state, covering decades, evidenced the strength of the community the DeWeeses and others created in Montana. All the artists in the state attended each other's openings even when the weather seemed prohibitive.[35] The DeWeeses, Senska, Wilber, and others created an environment of artists supporting artists, a comradery, a profound indication of their dedication to the careers of their friends, colleagues, and students.

Another string pulling the pockets of artists together was Branson Stevenson, who traveled all around the state for the Saxony Oil Company. As he traveled from town to town, he brought new artwork with him, his own ceramic art, and pieces he would borrow from people like Senska and Wilber, presenting them to the far-flung Montana art community during a lecture or slide show. Aside from spreading art news, in his role as vice chairman of the American Artists' Professional League, he invited artists to Montana to speak and give demonstrations, such as in 1952, when internationally renowned potters Bernard Leach and Hamada Yanagi conducted workshops at the newly minted Archie Bray Foundation. As Senska said years later in a 1998 interview, "That was a good boost and we've been reaping publicity from it ever since."[36]

Word of art doings from around the world also came to Montana through people like groundbreaking ceramic artist Pete Voulkos, who spent time teaching at Black Mountain College,

occasionally returning to Montana after interactions with artist Robert Rauschenberg, musician John Cage, choreographer Merce Cunningham, and poet Charles Olson. Artist Henry Meloy, an art professor at Columbia University in New York City, originally from Townsend, Montana, visited with the DeWeeses, Senska, and Wilber as well as other Montana artists on his trips west. This was evidenced in the booklets (*Figures, Notes,* and *Portraits*) by Meloy that the DeWeeses kept. When Meloy came back to Montana in the summers, conversations among all of these artists often spurred all-nighters. Sculptor Paul Harris, another artist who visited during summer breaks, brought news from the West Coast and from his experiences teaching at the Berkeley School of Art and the School of Arts and Craft, in Oakland. Ideas of Modernism from coast to coast as well as politics stirred the pot.[37]

POLITICS AND THE POLITICS OF ART

Much of the literature, films, and television shows surfacing during the postwar years sought out the white hat/black hat scenarios reflected in classic westerns and comic books. The need for creating heroes, whether they wore cowboy hats or capes, signaled a search for an American identity where the rules were easy to follow. It took until the 1970s when the environmental movement took hold in Montana to break out of that genre, as stated by historian Michael Malone. "The simple frontier nostalgia of previous generations has given way to a subtle reflection on the land and its people and their doubtful future in a society dominated by consumer individualism."[38]

In Montana artists were very aware of the status quo and did not rely on selling art, Modernist or otherwise, to make ends meet. In 1953 Robert McCraig explained the Montana Institute of the Arts' goal of not bucking the status quo but conceded artists needed to make art for art's sake, since commercial success was unlikely. He said:

> It would be smug and ridiculous to assume that from our efforts will come any great and world-striking results. Few of our writers will ever find a place in the world's libraries, few of our painters will receive recognition by famous museums; but we can give to many people the chance to round out their lives to a greater fullness by providing them with the opportunity to create something themselves, perhaps unique, perhaps beautiful, but in any case, no matter how crude or amateurish the product, something that is their very own, with the resultant satisfying uplift to soul and ego. [39]

He noted that life is often a compromise, but the role of the organization did not depend on the commercial success of its members. "If we in the MIA can approach or even make a start toward any of our high objectives, we will have done something in which we can feel satisfaction."[40]

The underlying tone of McCraig's essay implies a kind of pessimism about the arts in Montana. He states the low odds of anyone making it beyond Montana's borders, or even within its borders. His voice permeates with undertones of nihilism. The same year McCraig wrote this piece, the C. M. Russell Museum opened its doors, celebrating the romantic, illustrative art usually associated with Montana and the Old West. While raising money for the C. M. Russell Museum, organizations asked for money from donors "who have enough interest in our state" to contribute a thousand dollars. The plea included a lightly veiled threat that, if the museum did not succeed, Charlie Russell paintings would begin to leave the state. The plea insinuated that the way Montanans looked at themselves, through the lens of Western paintings, would be lost as well.[41]

In 1951 James Dew, a founding member of the MIA and art professor at the University of Montana, Missoula, felt it necessary to write an essay explaining modern art to the people of Montana. As the membership of the MIA consisted of artists, writers, and musicians, it is even more important to note that Dew felt the need to explain Modern art to the readers of their own quarterly magazine—in other words, to the artists themselves. He stated:

> It is common knowledge that the majority of people will react favorably to factual paintings, paintings which are close copies of nature. However, if we begin with the idea that art is a copy of nature and is created with the single purpose of decorating a living room, we are using a false premise. Pictures should be observed as entities, things in themselves.[42]

Almost a decade later, art critic Clement Greenberg said, "Modernism used art to call attention to art."[43] Dew and Greenberg voiced the philosophical difference between Modernism and Naturalism or Realism. Modern art, particularly Abstract Expressionism, asks the viewer to consider the painting as an object, not as a picture of an object. For people in Montana at the time, a population drawn to the paintings of C. M. Russell and Edgar S. Paxson, this required explanation. Dew went on to say, "Without an open-minded attitude or an honest desire to enjoy modern paintings, this source of enrichment of life will never be ours. The process takes time."[44]

Up until 1959, print media and newspaper content came from the Anaconda Company headquartered in Butte, Montana. The company controlled nearly all the newspapers in the state. Starting in the 1920s, the Anaconda Company bought up newspapers, including *The Anaconda Standard*, *The Butte Daily Post*, *The Montana Standard*, *The Billings Gazette*, *The Missoulian*, *The Missoula Sentinel*, *The Helena Independent Record*, and the *Livingston Enterprise*. Through this heavy-handed method of controlling the political dialogue, objectivity took a backseat, especially in politics.[45] In addition to conservative power brokers, the state also boasted a considerable population of laborers and union members, from workers in the mining and timber industries to railroad and farm workers. Montana teetered between conservative and liberal perspectives.[46] In presidential elections, Montana voted Democrat from 1940–1948, Republican from 1952–1960, Democrat in 1964, and Republican from 1968–1988.[47] The conservative trend began in the 1950s with the "Eisenhower Equilibrium," a balance between war hawks and peace doves, a philosophy that brought a balance to politics. Montana voted for a Republican Governor, J. Hugo Aronson, and Democratic Senator, Mike Mansfield. In 1941 the Malmstrom Military Base served as the first B-17 bomber base and continued to so serve throughout the Cold War. The flood of military personnel created a steady flow of conservative ideology in Great Falls.

During the 1960s Gennie DeWeese attended political rallies, holding signs and protesting the use of nuclear weapons. According to her daughter, Tina DeWeese, "Gennie was a feminist before the word was really used. She was not going to go quietly into the role of a hushed faculty wife."[48] Tina also said that not many people in Montana spoke the language of art in the way that her parents understood Modernism. "They always recognized they were outside the mainstream, but they didn't care. That's why those connections with other artists were so powerful."[49]

Bill Stockton, with a permanent attitude of anti-government interference, often groused about the number and placement of missile silos situated near Grass Range. Jessie Wilber was concerned with conservation and the misuse of natural resources, as evidenced by her print, *The River (Don't Dam It!)* (page 69).

Politics often undergirds art. In Montana the Modernists understood that their politics were not always popular, but that made the community they created even more important. The gatherings became a safe place to express opinions, popular or not, and be guaranteed a robust exchange of ideas.

BOB AND GENNIE

When Bob met Gennie, the relationship began as two artists fascinated with the creative process, struggling to find their individual voices. The notion of anything more than a friendship, albeit a deep-connecting friendship, did not occur to either of them until, separated by World War II, their correspondence built up over time and revealed something that might be long-lasting. First and foremost Bob and Gennie were artists, and that seminal position became the basis for the rest of their lives.

Robert "Bob" DeWeese (1920–1990) and Gennie Adams (1921–2007) met at Ohio State University, where both earned art degrees. Bob, president of the Art Club and Gennie, president of Art Honorary, both graduated in 1942. Both Bob and Gennie took classes from Hoyt Sherman and experienced his unique classroom, the Flash Lab. Bob's exchanges with Sherman's theory of "perceptual unity" would later enable him to further explore his own philosophy that "responsibility equals the ability to respond." Gennie's

experiences with the Flash Lab took the path of experimentation with depth and perception in her non-objective paintings.

Hoyt Sherman's Flash Lab[50] at Ohio State University, conceived as a way to mediate the "schism" between thought and feeling and between science and art, asked his students to draw what they saw.[51] The Flash Lab implemented his theory of perceptual unity, a way to interpret how the mind sees images through the human eye, in an effort to help students see the whole field of vision simultaneously in relation to a single focal point.[52] It was not only the flash art but the notion of introducing exciting new ideas in a classroom environment that both Bob and Gennie carried over into their own work. Sherman also influenced Bob as an art teacher, and once at MSC Bob adopted some of Sherman's techniques in his practice and in his classes.

After college Bob enlisted in the United State Army Air Force, where he held a position of flutist in the Air Force Band, stationed in Hawaii. He kept up his art practice, completing a large mural in a church in Hawaii as well as several paintings. Gennie went on to receive her teaching certificate from the University of Michigan in Detroit. She moved to Wilmington, Delaware, to help her sister when her brother-in-law joined the navy. There, she worked as a junior high school/high school teacher, but this took much of the time and energy she would have preferred to spend on art. She briefly moved to New York City. With few prospects at that time, she decided to enroll in an occupational training course offered to artists by the army, working with head and

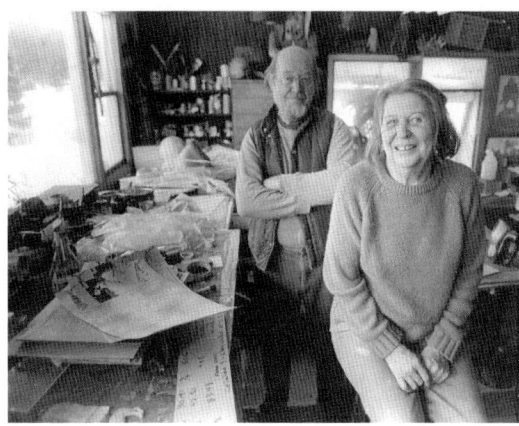

Bob and Gennie DeWeese in the 1980s.

nerve trauma patients at the army hospital in Battle Creek, Michigan. When the war ended, she moved to Detroit so she could substitute-teach three days a week, which enabled her to paint the other four days. Throughout the war Bob and Gennie, though not yet romantically involved, corresponded regularly.[53] They shared a need to take what they learned in school and apply it to life, or, as Gennie would often write in those letters, "LIFE!"

In one of Gennie's letters to Bob, she wrote about art and its ability to reflect on the times: "No wonder they speak of chaos, nearly every generalized subject which comes to my mind—I can think of 10,000 variations pertaining to it—all in conflict with each other—so it all becomes jumbled—no wonder so many have turned to symbols."[54] As an artist trying to be true to herself and yet also record a response to her surroundings, she said:

> When something tries to center itself in the form of an honest reaction to a given thing it's lost in a maze. Sometimes I think trying to somehow record that confusion would be the most honest. It seems that this present is more marred by hatred and indifference than love of any kind.[55]

In another letter her struggle to tap into her own creative process clearly comes across: "The amount of time I have to spend *seeing* to make the entire thing, is a farce." She then references Hoyt Sherman's lessons on seeing: "The realization that it is defeated by time makes the task seem too gigantic to undertake in spare moments."[56] She expresses concerns for friends and family, but more than that, a desperation about her own place in the art world:

> You can't do 10 things and worry about 10,000 and get results. I defeat myself at every turn—unfortunately I can't get it all in—actually it's such an infinitesimal part of the original conception I feel contempt for it—and myself—physically—and emotionally. I'm not up to it.[57]

Her voice cries with frustration about making art while at the same time surviving during the war without any financial support from her family.

Over the course of three years and more than fifty letters, their platonic relationship deepened and, although hard to pinpoint, something more happened. His voice comes across as a mentor, friend, and, later, a hint of something deeper. The tone of their letters seems confessional, not love notes so much as expressions of artistic tendencies, frustrations, and experiments. In the beginning Bob played the part of mentor assigning books and movies for Gennie to read or watch, as he too struggled with his creative direction. Once, clearly missing the camaraderie of his fellow art students, he wrote:

> Tonight, I met an infantryman outside the big post's library who had been looking through the art books also...[O]utside we got into a discussion that lasted about two hours. It was strange for both of us at first to be talking art, and at first my usual guard was up but eventually we had a very good time...[N]othing destroys my confidence so much as talking (usually unsuccessfully) about art to only mildly

interested (or politely interested) persons of another field.[58]

Although seemingly well-situated in the visual arts, Bob often considered a future in writing, not to mention his professional position as a flautist in the Air Force band. DeWeese discussed his attempt to write stories and in one letter even stated, "I am a writer."[59] In another letter he wrote about the success of his watercolor paintings, trying different instruments aside from the flute (the oboe, for example), and the feeling that his future, though somewhat unclear, brimmed with possibilities. However, in another letter, he cried with desperation:

> I got your letter today and again it mirrors what has been going on with me. I think it quite [unsatisfying] that thinking is a damnable part of us. Now and then it might come out in imagination, and then it is good; but all too often it is that damnable eliminative destructive analysis that one by one picks off the hopes, talents, and gives way to despair.[60]

The end of the war on September 2, 1945, brought about a change in the tone of the letters. Whereas, in earlier letters, Bob seemed the more pragmatic and stable of the two, later letters show Gennie taking the reins. She advised Bob to take advantage of the G.I. Bill and to apply for unemployment the minute his discharge came through. His letters betray a bit of nervousness about coming home as her letters take on the tone of planning for the future. "I'm keyed up enough to do something—complacency is out the window," she wrote.[61]

They married in 1946, the same year Bob returned home from the war. Bob joined Gennie in her apartment across the street from the Detroit Institute of the Arts until he attended the University of Iowa, Iowa City, on the G.I. Bill, earning his Masters of Fine Arts degree.[62] Through the births and upbringing of their five children, both Bob and Gennie pursued their own artistic processes with equal perseverance: Bob taking the position of art professor at Montana State College and Gennie eventually taking on the role of advocate for the Montana Modernist movement.

ROBERT DEWEESE: RESPONSIBILITY IS THE ABILITY TO RESPOND

Making art is problem-solving. The entire process involves taking an idea and making it concrete. Problems of the flat surface in two-dimensional art concern the materials, the space, and the formal aspects of creating art, such as line, form, and composition. Art historian Michael Baxandall addresses the painter's goals and situational conditions beyond the initial creation of art in his 1985 book, *Patterns of Intention*. Baxandall describes the expectations from the artist, what the artist wants from the work, markets, the artist's relationship to other painters, and how to make use of the contemporary philosophical and/or scientific ideas of the era—in other words, the problems artists are trying to solve. Moholy-Nagy's Bauhaus philosophy also addressed art as a set of self-generated problems the artist must solve, and was utilized by Robert DeWeese as well. DeWeese's investigations into the honesty of a line and how a painting can resolve the artist's

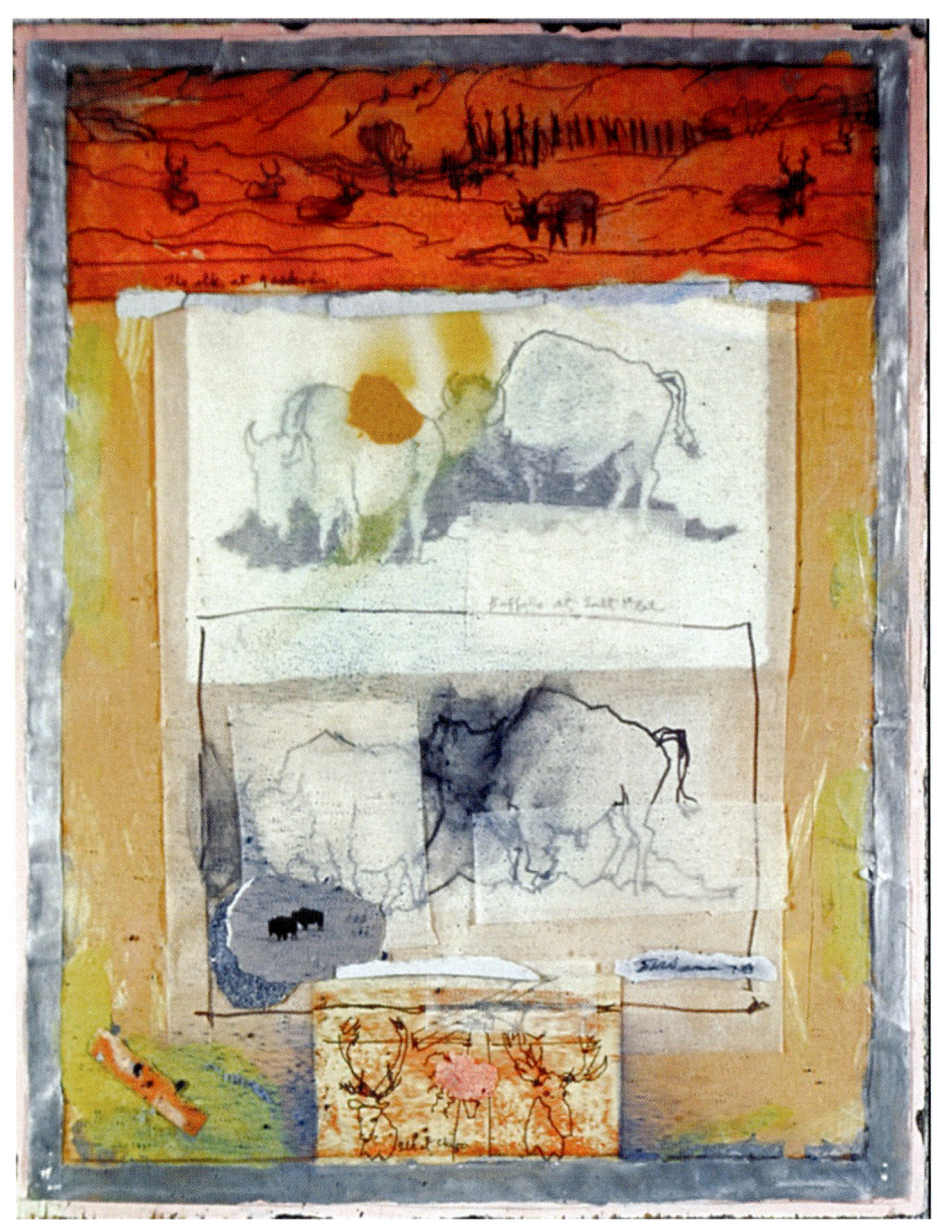

Robert DeWeese, *Western Painting*, 1976,
collage and mixed media, 15.5 x 12.25 inches.
Courtesy of the DeWeese Family.

responsibility to respond to his surroundings, with an emphasis on cultural and societal barriers, was his "problem," and that comes across in many of his works. In DeWeese's 1976 *Western Painting* (page 102), he included a series of sketches and drawings of buffalo, moose, and elk with the barest outlines of a natural environment. As discussed earlier the art market during this period in Montana consisted mostly of traditional Western paintings, replications of wildlife in paint, as well as bronzes, depictions of romanticized Native Americans, stereotyped cowboys on horseback, and historical portraits carried forward from the late nineteenth century. *Western Painting* feels like a comment on the art market at the time. Rarely did DeWeese sell a painting to anyone outside his circle of friends and peers. DeWeese did not expect his work to sell. However, he did expect it to be seen, and, as a statement, a political and even a cultural statement, his use of the present moment enveloped much of his work. Here, especially with this piece, he exposed a new way that Montanans could identify themselves. By using images of buffalo in an ironic context, he freed Montanans from the image that seemed to hang like an albatross around the necks of artists.

Most Montana artists taught for a living, and, for them as for DeWeese, teaching and making art became one and the same. "My paintings and teaching were inseparable, and like the growth of everything in those years, kept a focus. Excitement piled up in the corners, and Gen and I ran out of space three times before anyone bought a painting."[63] *Western Painting* comments on the culture at the time, the mythology of living in the

West, and how art needed to heed the status quo in order to be accepted by art buyers. The non-archival materials DeWeese used in this painting and in many of his works barely stood up against the elements of his home/studio. Fragile crepe paper, markers, sketches with frayed edges, and peeling paint reflect a tendency to use whatever he happened upon at that moment. These actions indicate an immediate response to the artist's responsibility as he saw it and a purely instinctual action.[64] He simply grabbed whatever materials were at hand and sketched, painted, or collaged his responses.

A look at his drawings shows an intentional language of line and gestural responses to his environment, including his family and colleagues, road trips and, underlying much of his work, the Montana landscape where he lived. Through these sketches DeWeese translated the world. Through these drawings he drew in a close circle of friends, colleagues, students, and fellow artists. The underpinning of DeWeese's "Responsibility to Respond" philosophy can be seen in his sketches, and reflects his training in Sherman's Flash Lab.

For example, DeWeese's series of sketches from the 1960s showing his daughter moving about the room may be related to a specific class exercise executed by Sherman (page 104). As Elizabeth Clymer Okerbloom wrote in her essay on Sherman, "The end of the course includes drawing a dancer flashed in action."[65]

By the time DeWeese created this series, his sketches continuously portrayed the instantaneous imprints of reactions that inferred a rapid

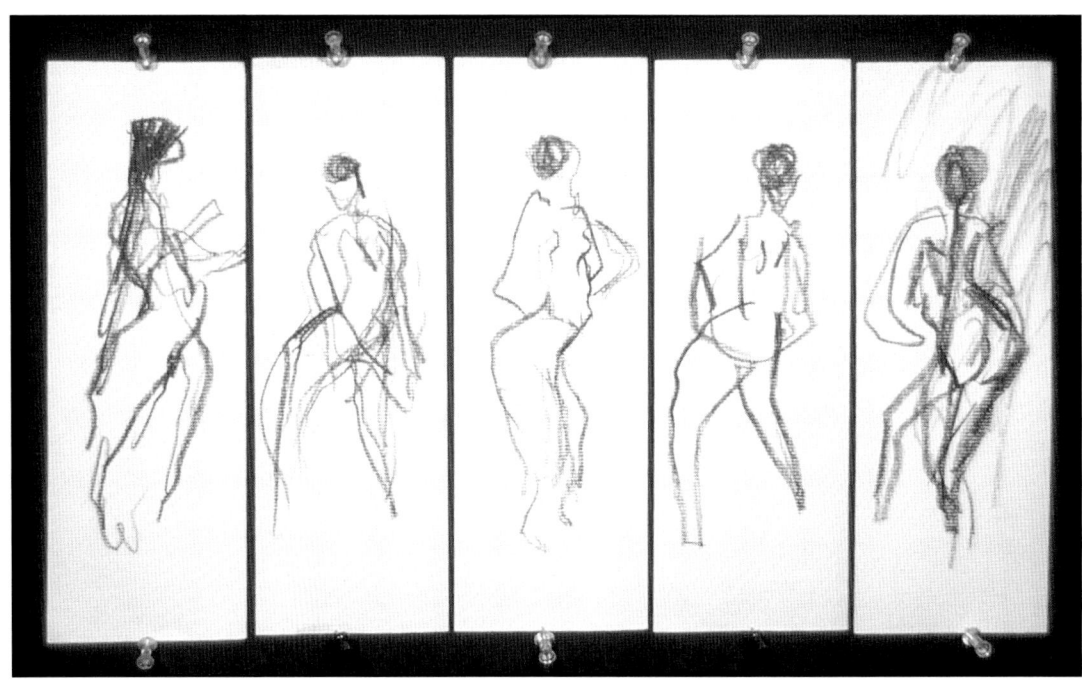

Robert DeWeese, *Figure Dancing*, n.d., drawings on paper. Courtesy of the Holter Museum of Art.

execution of a drawing to convey the moment, an idea, or object.[66] Even in social situations, he responded by sketching. In every situation, he drew. His sketchbook is a window to his world. His sketching, like that of Wilber's prints, reflects an interpretation of the things and the people he saw every day. Moving the trope of a window into the metaphor of his life, he leaves out only the frame of the glass. *Portland* (page 105), *Between Three Forks and Toston* (page 106), and *Bill's Lil' Trees* from the 1980s are examples of his immediate responses to his environment.

Artist and curator Terry Karson wrote in a 1991 exhibition catalog, "[DeWeese] was always drawing: in a car flying down the highway; at a family gathering; on a subway in Paris; at the dinner table." He notes that his peers envied his devotion to drawing as well as his devotion to being a teacher. "[He] inspired his students to higher levels than they had ever reached." Karson called attention to DeWeese as a prolific artist, "producing over 500 known paintings and constructions, some 1600 formal drawings and many hundreds of impressions from many dozens of printing plates." After DeWeese's death Karson

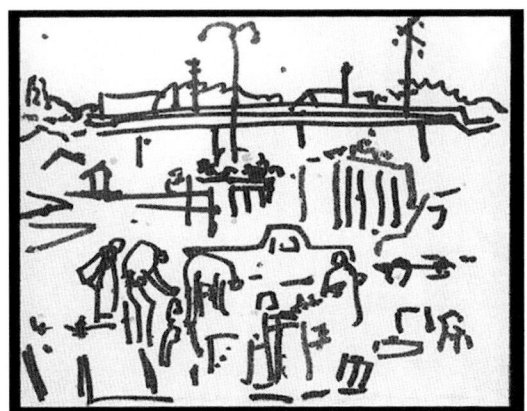

Robert DeWeese, *Portland*, 1980s, felt marker on paper, 12 x 17 inches. Courtesy of the Holter Museum of Art.

went through his entire body of work and came away inspired. "He was always exploring, always pushing his own personal boundaries, always renewing himself."[67]

Autio said the DeWeeses played a big part in the lives of the artists and students in Montana, especially Bob, "I always admired Bob DeWeese a lot. The guy was always drawing. He was like a kid. You know, he was so joyful about everything around him all the time, he'd draw like crazy. In a space of time, he'd be sitting there, he'd probably have us all drawn in this unique situation… [H]e was like a kid in a toy shop. All the time. You couldn't miss his exuberance. It affected me, I think it affected Pete [Voulkos], it affected a lot of people over the years."[68]

For DeWeese every day brought new opportunities to record his children, his wife, music, trees, and the road. Sketch after sketch shows a development of a language without words, his quick marks

of impressions. DeWeese's drawings depict honest portrayals, connecting the artist to the world, connecting being in time with being in place. For DeWeese Montana's landscapes became another avenue for him to talk about his responses to the land and his range of perceptual engagement.

Artist and former gallery manager at Montana State University Dennis O'Leary wrote, "Bob's art over these thirty years is about his life. Portraits of family, friends and localities describe his surroundings. With these, in combination with his non-representational works, we clearly see his conceptual attitudes."[69] O'Leary saw DeWeese's work through the lens of an artist's quest for fulfillment. "For Bob, [these responsibilities for spiritual fulfillment] are within himself, his family, friends and environment. For Bob DeWeese, art and life are most certainly one and the same experience."[70] Some of his sketches, simple and clear, later became paintings. Other artists influenced his work as much as his work may have influenced them, as evidenced by the painting *About Wiley* (1972; mixed media on Masonite), included in the catalogue *Robert DeWeese: Work since 1949*. DeWeese pasted the typed words of visiting artist Bill Wiley on the cover, as one of his many homages to other artists. It stated, "What we will attempt to learn though we may not know it is to learn that we are who we are and that it is all right to be who and what we are."[71]

Robert DeWeese not only created art; the openness of his studio helped to create an art community. Just as Senska's ceramics practice embraced a natural, communal environment with the group collection and production of clay and

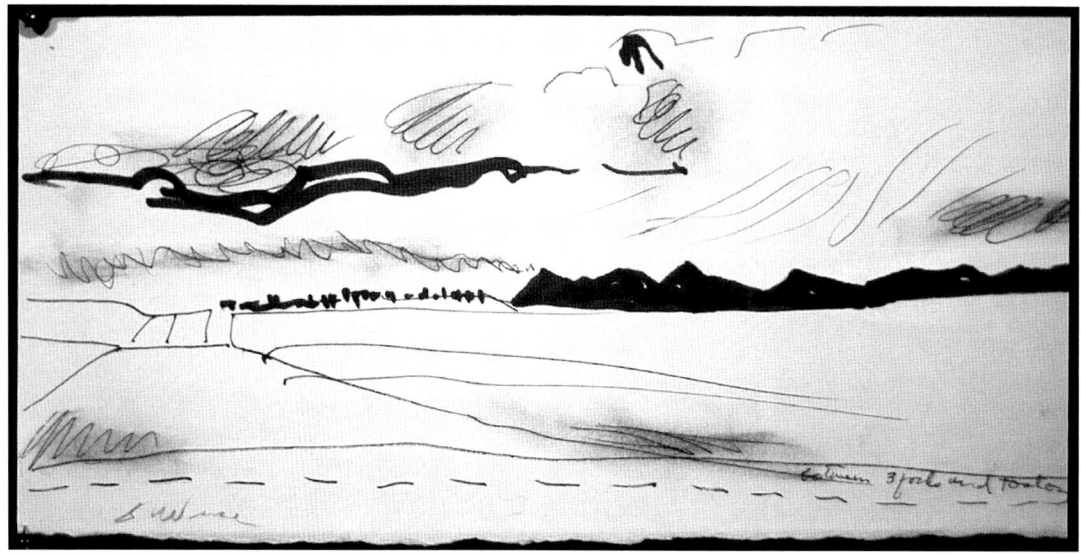

Robert DeWeese, *Between Three Forks and Toston*, 1980s, felt marker on paper. Courtesy of the Holter Museum of Art.

nights spent over a kiln, DeWeese brought artists, friends, colleagues, and family into a fold he called "art" through his constant sketching. According to the curator statement by Terry Karson for *DeWeese's Legacy*, a 2006 catalog comprising his students' work and their students' work,

> DeWeese was more than a teacher he was also a progressive thinker, a beguiling provocateur, and a seminal figure in the spread of modern art and philosophy in Montana. It was a new day for art, and a new teacher/student relationship was dawning with it. The master/pupil approach was being abandoned for a more egalitarian style.[72]

He noted that, in 1949, DeWeese brought with him a stream of steady, new, and exciting ideas as well as an exuberance about teaching. "As fate and fortune would have it, here would thrive fertile, eager minds responsive to his teachings, hungry for new ways of thinking and seeing."[73]

It is clear from DeWeese's work that his connection to art history, past artists, and art movements influenced his work. In his paintings, which are a step away from the immediacy of his sketches, he takes the time not only to explore more deeply the issues of line, color, and composition but also to nod to the classics and leap forward with current commentary.

Thematic work, or series, seems to be part of DeWeese's art exploration. Whether it was men's ties, the Rapture, homages, or Wolny's Hill, his ability to grab onto an object and dig deep and nose around until he was satisfied became another reason to paint. "Any incentive to paint is as good as any other," DeWeese once said. The tendency of art critics is to try to understand these forays in terms of their symbolic nature, which may also be there, but DeWeese's intention was purely in terms of line, composition, color, and form. That said, it is nearly impossible to study his work without a bit of interpretation.

DeWeese's fascination with art history can be seen in his complex 1988 painting, *Flight (Red Boy)* (page 108), where the figures rise in joy, sail across the sky, and fall from grace. In the center stands "red boy," represented as a placid faceless embodiment made of lines. Here DeWeese points to the classics, referencing Atlas, using a female figure holding up her "world" (a child on her shoulders) as a Greek chorus huddles in the background. His use of muddled colors activates the images. Within the painting DeWeese recalls Titian's *The Rape of Europa* with his contemporary use of mythological images to modernize the legend.[74] In the foreground all the figures remain nudes, another nod to classical painting, while all the figures in the background appear blanketed in clothes. This delineation causes a separation between them, again similar to actors in a play and the off-stage chorus. The figure flying overhead like a zephyr adds to the overall feeling of a mythological allegory. In this way DeWeese takes the ever-timeless nature of Greek/Roman mythology and translates it into a modern-day interpretation. At the same time, it was one of a series of paintings exploring the idea of The Rapture, another subject that held DeWeese's interest over the course of time.

As some of his work is more abstract, *Flight* offers a deeper reading of representational images. The brushstrokes, clear and active, support the multiple narratives going on in the piece. The eye moves from the "red boy" to the other figures and back around again, constantly supporting the motion of the work. In some of his works, DeWeese underlines the contemporary philosophical ideas of the era. *Flight (Red Boy)* was painted in 1988, when George H. W. Bush won the presidential election after eight years of Ronald Reagan, a time of the Iran-Contra investigations and televised hearings, and DeWeese's politics come into play in the piece. Politically, it was a dark time for liberal-minded artists. DeWeese died in 1990, and this painting feels autobiographical. The Red Boy may be a version of DeWeese himself. DeWeese loved the theater, and this painting reflects on his life as a Greek play.

Other pieces employ the collage technique made relevant by the Dadaists, such as Hannah Hoch and Max Ernst, whose work spoke to the changed relationship between objects and humans.[75] These issues still held relevance to the Modernists in Montana. Dadaists focused on creating artwork that questioned societal roles, the role of the artist, and the purpose of art. DeWeese also questioned the role of the artist in relation to current events and the politics of the day. By the time of DeWeese's *VFW Studio Wall* (page 109) in 1973, mass media were running rampant. The large, mixed media on canvas work included advertisements, newspaper headlines, Matisse-like cut-outs, school photographs of his children, and pages seemingly torn from notebooks. The piece, localized with Bozeman-based headlines

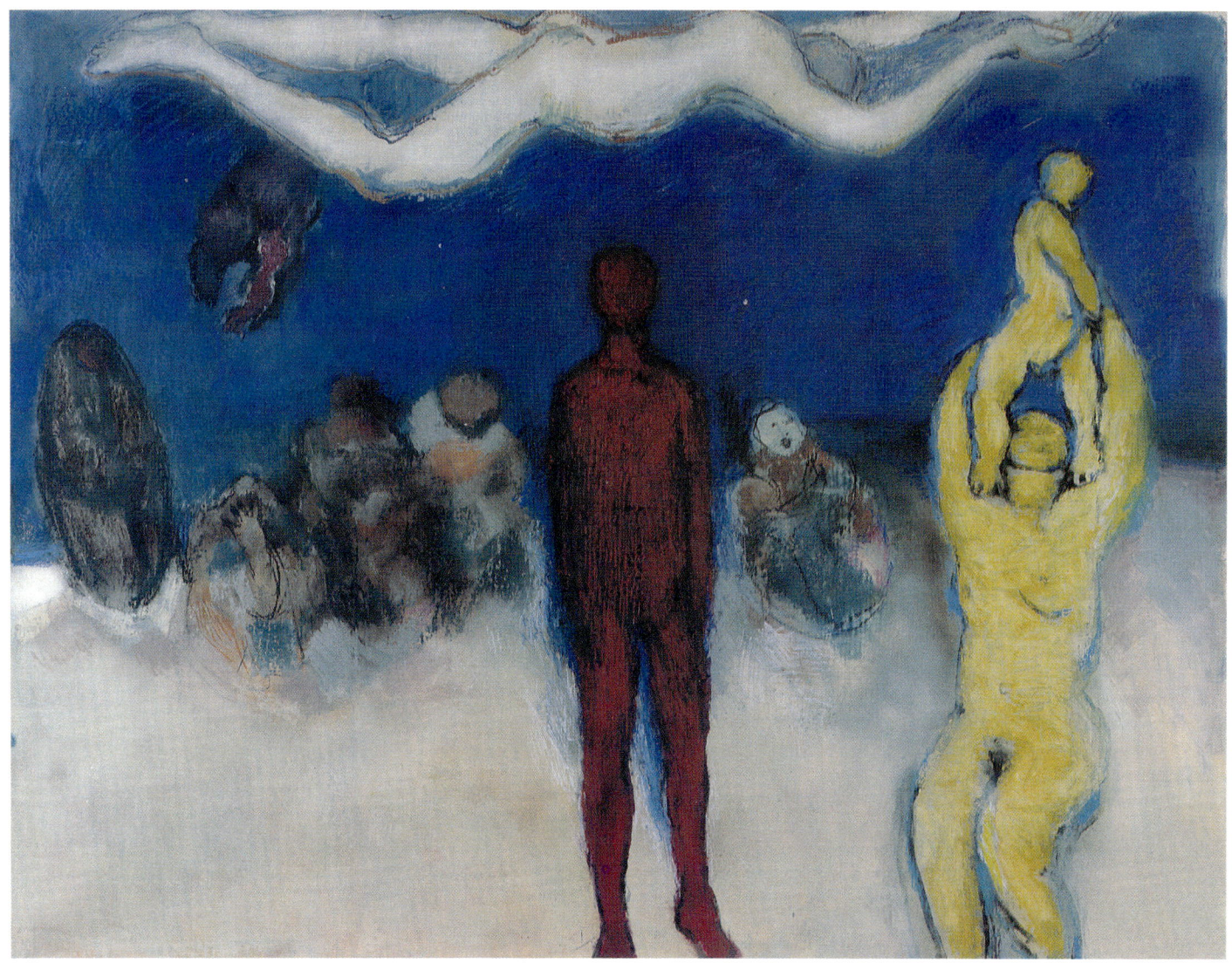

Robert DeWeese, *Flight* (*Red Boy*), 1988, mixed media on paper, 62.5 x 80.5 inches. Courtesy of the Yellowstone Art Museum.

and nationalized with images of well-known figures, includes colors and lines for the sake of composition. It stands as a portrait of his studio and as an artist's statement for his work. The openness of the piece conveys the presence of painted walls, suggesting limits to the openness. With greys and offset lines, he creates a sense of place, a place where anything goes.

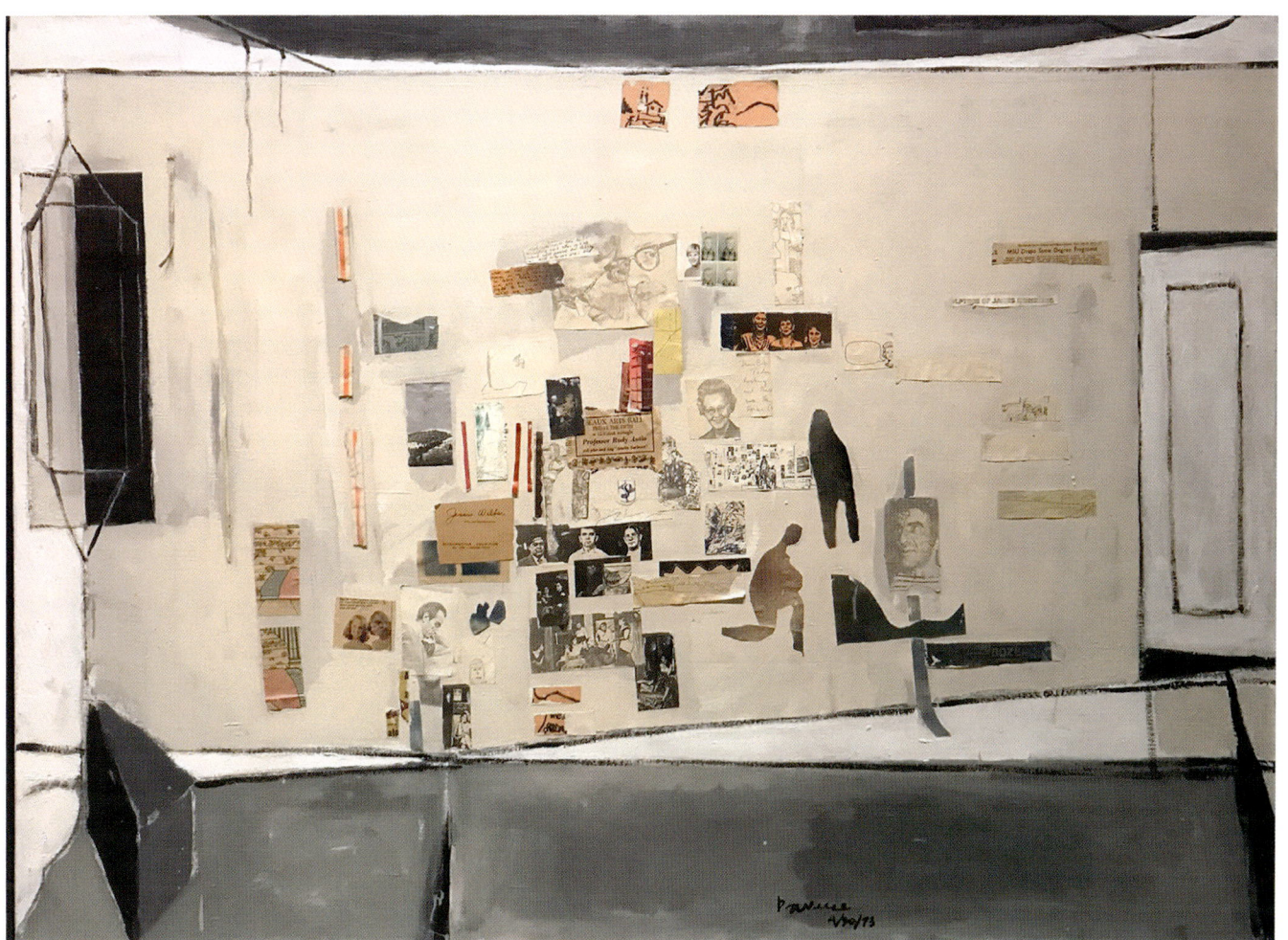

Robert DeWeese, *VFW Studio Wall*, 1973, mixed media, 49.5x69 inches. Courtesy of the Yellowstone Art Museum.

Former student and artist James Reineking explained what it was like to be in Bob's Bozeman studio:

> Bob shows me his studio above the VFW. There's a huge wooden chair with red velour covering that looks like a throne. (Is Bob the king of painting?) The studio is full of art—floor, table, walls, everywhere. It's wonderful. At some point there's a production of The Three Penny Opera. So much enthusiasm, so many people, the sets, the music.[76]

In the early 1960s, DeWeese experimented with spontaneous brushwork and collaged paper in a seven-piece series (page 113). The thick dun-colored paper absorbs ink while the oil sticks stab and drawl across the surface haphazardly delineating abstract boundaries. White paint jumps to attention while scraps of odd-shaped construction paper, intentional symbols, feel like weights placed to balance the chaos. These pieces do not represent a departure from his more figurative work but instead add a layer of intensity and perhaps a hint at what may have been going on behind the curtain.

Another theme of DeWeese's collage work appears in the series of paintings he devoted to men's ties. He said, "The last few years I have been doing that old unoriginal icon of uniformity, the necktie. Why? Well, I felt some kind of need for such an outrageously simple form no matter if it becomes an interpreter's delight."[77] The visual fact of the tie and its symbolic meaning became an object (not a subject) for DeWeese to draw upon. As DeWeese stated:

> It is something to count on, something to play upon, something really there. But then there are things that seem not to be there (in the visible world) at all—dream, fantasy, myth, allegory, symbol...Idea...Made Visible. The thereness and the not thereness all part of the same thing, eh?[78]

Curator Elizabeth Guheen noted of his tie series:

> DeWeese was not looking to surprise his audience, but to surprise himself. For him art was an adventure, from beginning to end, and the journey was one and the same with his family and friends and students— who were also his friends, because that was unavoidable—the travels, crisscrossing the state to attend every art opening, the teaching, sharing meals, talking over coffee—[he'd said], "Actually it is all the same thing."[79]

In *Nine Ties, Seven Chains* (1988; page 111) and *Circus Ties* (1986; page 112), DeWeese uses this everyday symbol of what it means to be a man, the man made visible, for a series he cannot break away from. It occurs in dozens of pieces, some of which contain actual ties and some use tie chains; in others, as in *Circus Ties*, the objects appear within the painting bigger than life. Here, he mixes his figural abstraction with a symbol of a tie as a tree that humans enslaved by society must climb. DeWeese often used satire in his work. In this instance the ties stand in for the flags of a circus, but they bring to mind crucifixes, hung with sides outstretched like Christ on the cross. In putting the ties so high that the figures need to use ladders to adhere the ties to their stands,

DeWeese replaces the Romans with the Ringmaster. The connection to art historical references and the Passion of the Christ jumps out. How many men in suits and ties have been sacrificed to the god of status quo or felt like they worked in a three-ring circus?

DeWeese says the following in his University of Iowa graduate school notebook from 1946: "Anyway of seeing is abstraction—to make any sense we select—thus abstract…keep clear Naturalism is abstraction. Modern art paints things we know about, [whether we] do or do not see."[80] These notes provide some insight into his later

works. The naturalism he refers to shows up again and again in his sketches as well as his paintings. *Flight (Red Boy)* gives a nod to Renaissance naturalism, but it is also combined with the Abstract Expressionist style of a distressed figure, especially those of Willem de Kooning, Matisse, and Picasso. "Modernism is philosophy," DeWeese wrote in his notebooks, and the word "eloquence" appears again and again. It seemed that, in order to understand his place as a modern artist and as a graduate student, he looked to the differences between Impressionism, Realism, and Surrealism. Later, he would also look at the New York School

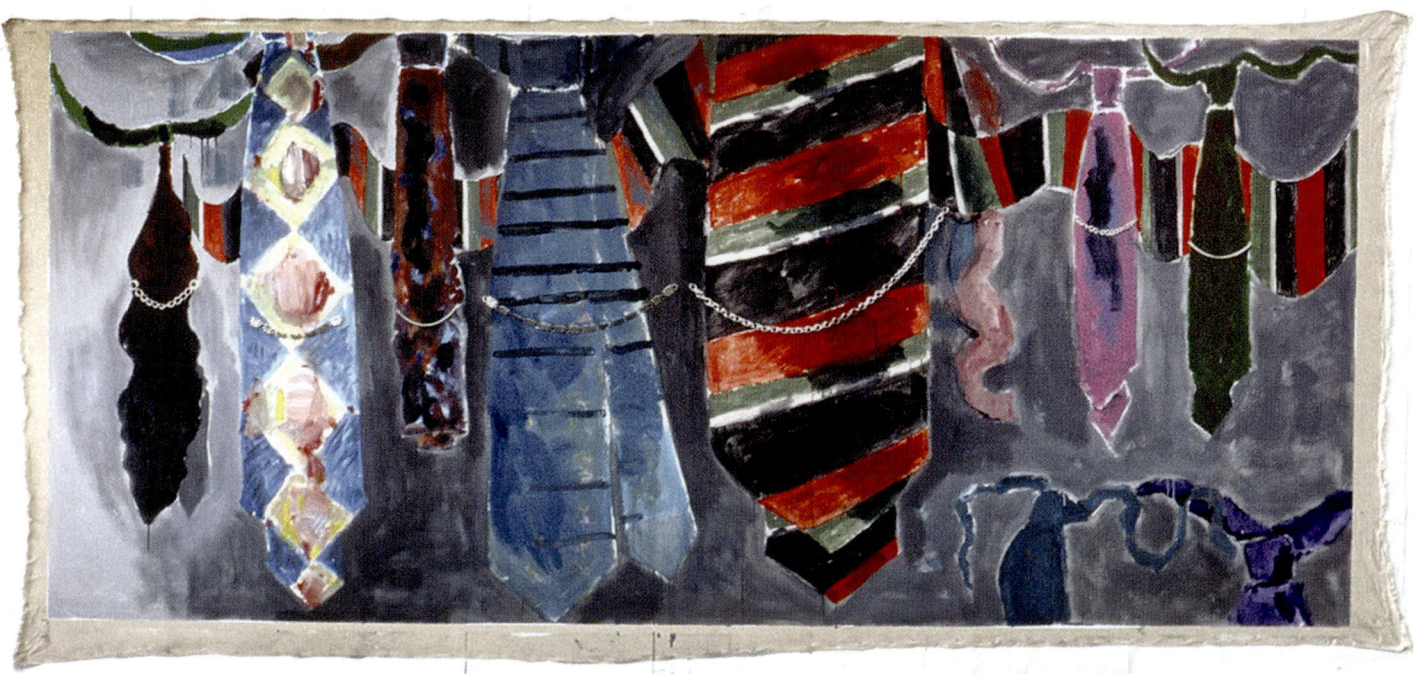

Robert DeWeese, *Nine Ties, Seven Chains*, 1988, mixed media on canvas, 5 x 11 feet. Courtesy of the DeWeese Family.

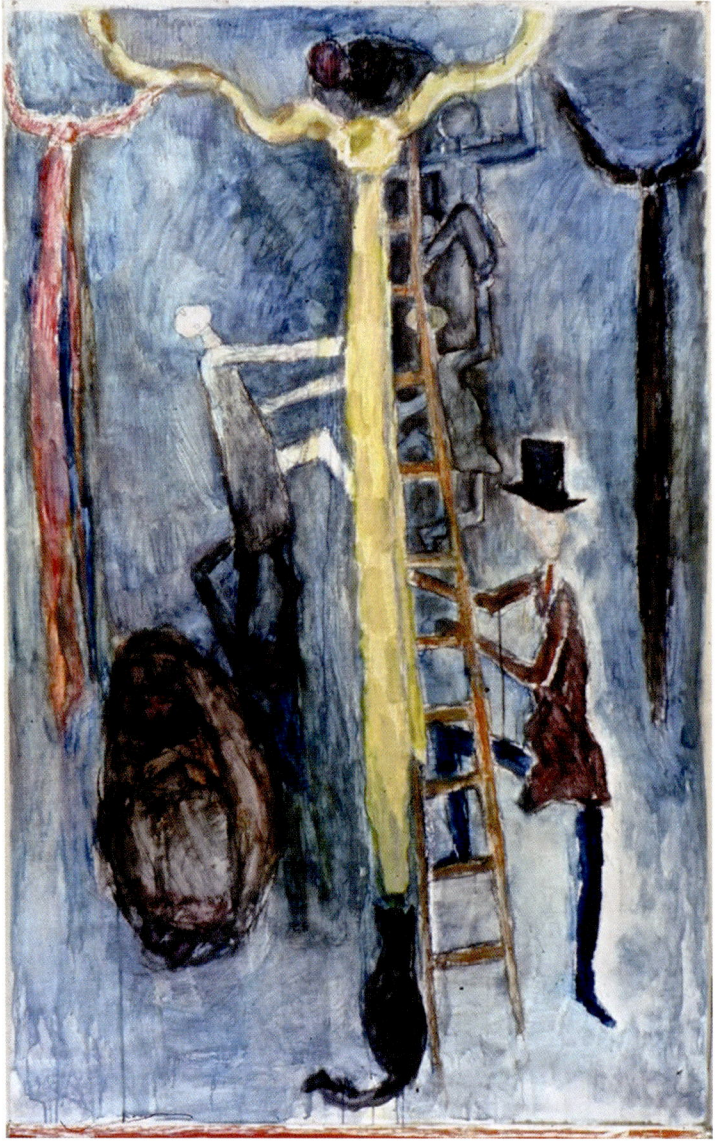

Robert DeWeese, *Circus Ties*, 1986, Caron D'Arch crayons on gessoed window shade, 73 x 47 inches. Courtesy of the DeWeese Family.

for ways to express contemporary issues within the context of painting.

As in many of DeWeese's paintings, he shows he is a painter and a teacher. His paintings tell the story of the past as they point to the future. By bringing other art references into his work, he engaged a Modernism that presented a two-fold purpose: to create art *and* to teach. In the 1970 essay "On Painting," he stated the importance for art students of knowing and understanding the masters of the past because "they are your teachers and mine, too." He spoke further about non-objective paintings and how they use the qualities of nature, but the source is "within the artist or in the painting-action itself…[I]t is pure painting—and in this sense the most realistic painting. It makes concrete such ambiguous, non-objective terms as delicate, heavy, slow, fast, hot, cool."[81] He reminds the reader that "A painting is a visual statement—no more—no less. Like a verbal statement, it can be clear, concise, and to the point; or it can be muddled, befuddled, wandering, weak, and beside the point." He notes the university did not hire a Charlie Russell painter:

> This is because the State of Montana saw fit to hire teachers from all over the country and from many different schools and universities and traditions. Charlie Russell was a good story teller and in his younger days, a pretty fair painter. He was authentic, but he's dead and his era is over.[82]

He added that there is no such thing as a realistic painting, quoting a friend who said, "The only way to get a realistic painting is to hang an empty frame on a wall." DeWeese continued to note that even a photograph is not realistic but only a mechanical way of recording the infinite value range in nature. "All painting is abstract or non-objective…[N]on-objective painting uses the qualities of nature—space, color, movement, and space relationships."[83]

In his painting *Plains Sunset* (1963; page 114), one of his earlier and more abstract pieces, he taught even as he created. His thick brushstrokes evoke the horizon, although the dark blues, gray, black, and bit of blood red negate the typical "inspiring" vista that would come to mind in a painting of a sunset. Instead, it is heavy

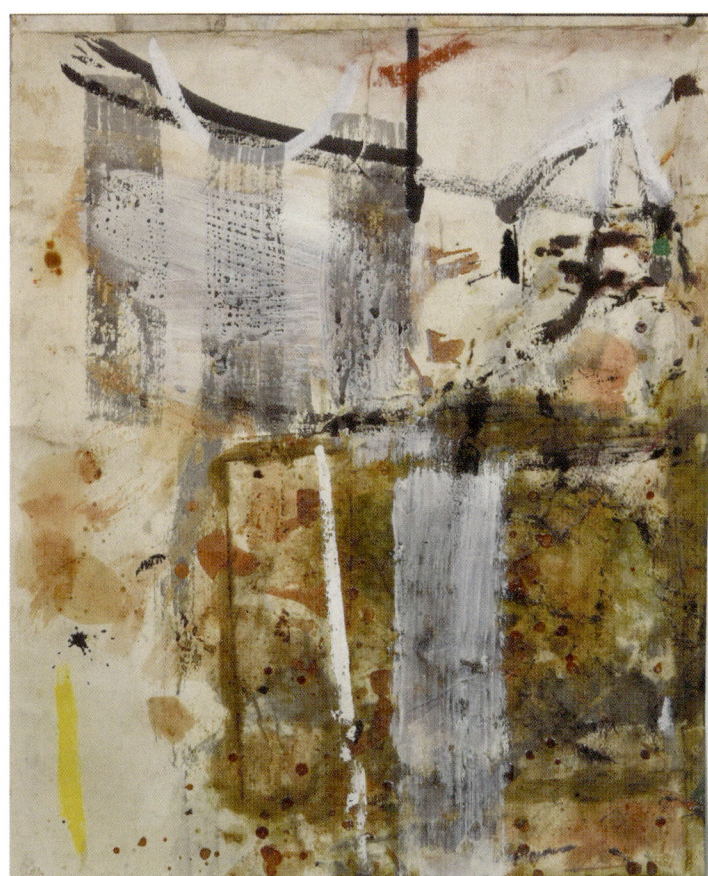 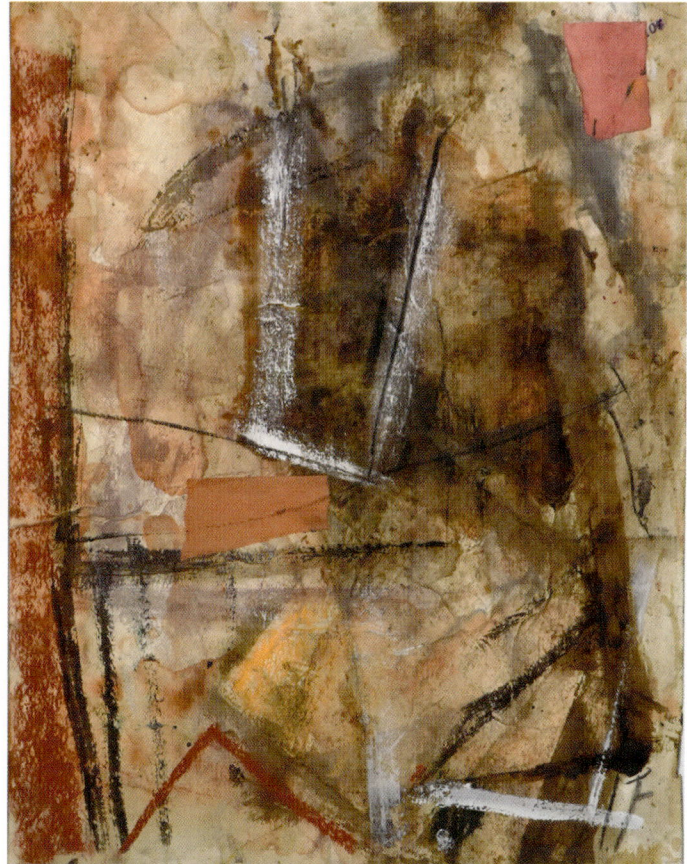

Robert DeWeese, Collages, ca 1960s, mixed media on paper, 23.75 x 19 inches. Courtesy of the DeWeese Family.

with dripping paint; the viewer's eye, while being pulled across the plane, drops into pockets of timelessness, areas of gray, and, like a game of Chutes and Ladders, zips the viewer up again. The piece is more of a journey than an observation, more of a dialogue than a meditation.

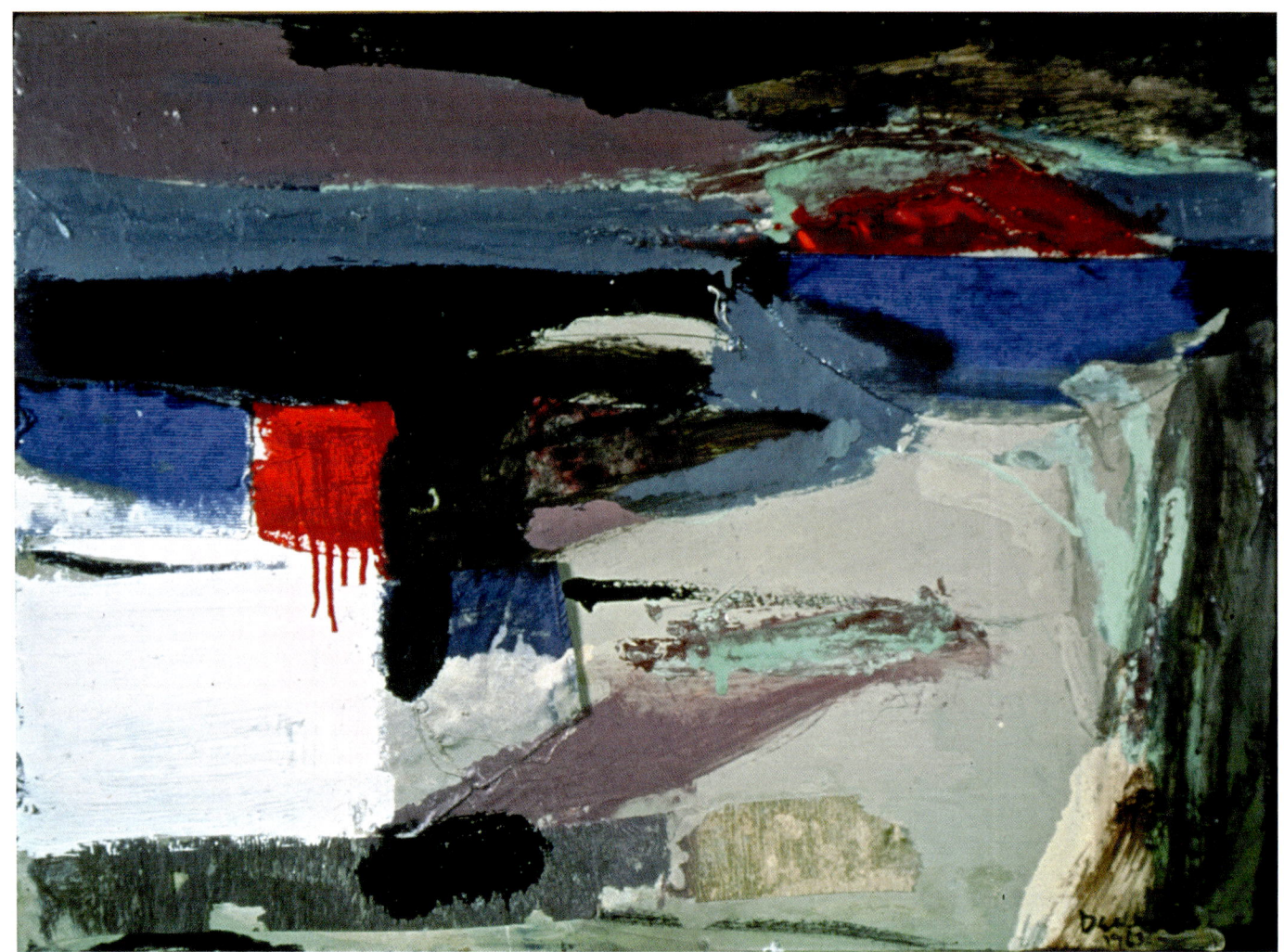

Robert DeWeese, *Plains Sunset*, 1963, oil on Masonite, 19 x 26.5 inches. Courtesy of Zak Zakovi.

DeWeese taught his students to see. "Seeing" included the landscape.

In a 1983 essay he wrote about his introduction to landscape painting, "It took a long, long time for the Montana landscape to imprint on me enough for me to be hooked on one shot. But in the last year or so it seemed to happen with Wolny's Hill, at the entrance to South Cottonwood Canyon where we live."[84] He goes on to say that he sat in the back of his pickup truck painting while the postman and the neighbors drove by bemused. "Well, what I'm doing is trying to turn de Kooning's famous 'glimpse' into a 'stare'. Not in an exact way, but in a way that will show my gratitude for the hill being there and allowing me to 'take off' from it so many times."[85] Illustrative of this stare, the painting *Wolny's Hill (One Cloud)* (below) takes the notion of de Kooning's "content is a glimpse" and moves it forward. DeWeese's content contains a series of place-markings, quick lines of indication, short strokes making an acronym of hillside, rock, and pasture, to be decoded at leisure in the future. The one cloud hovering above the horizon is barely there; the thin, white brushwork is not white enough to cover the blue behind it. This painting reminds the viewer that a scene observed every day can be new each time.

Circled twice in one of his notebooks is a quotation from Kenneth Burke: "We cannot call a man illogical for acting on the basis of what he

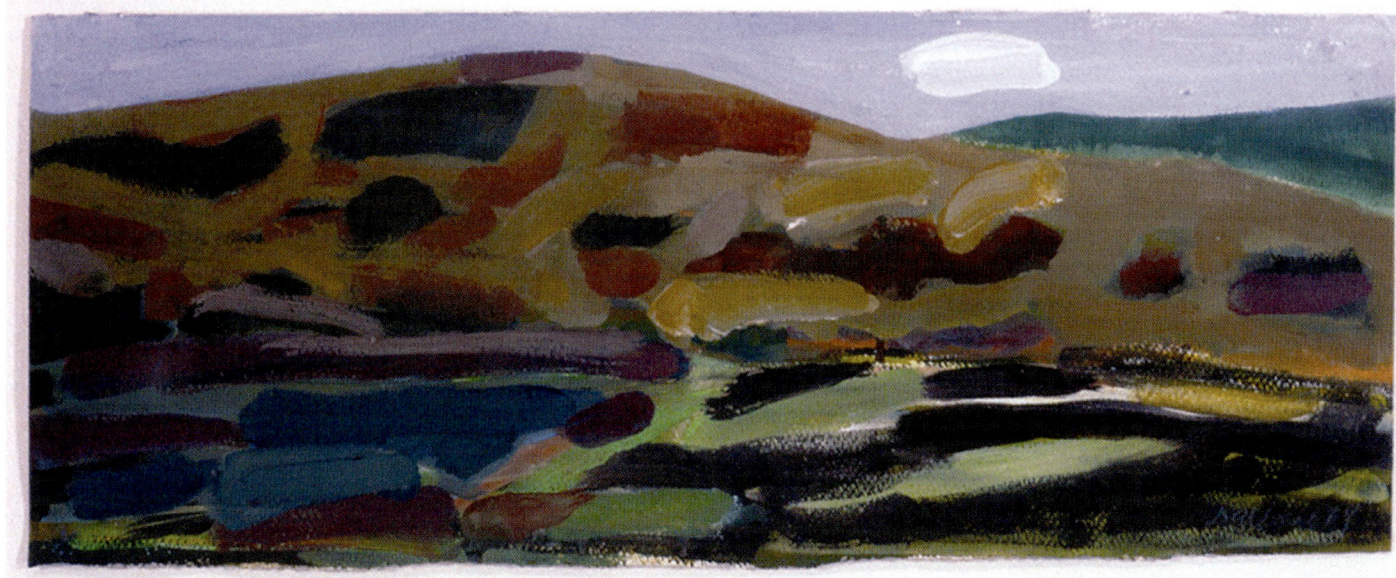

Robert DeWeese, *Wolny's Hill (One Cloud)*, 1984, gouache and enamel on paper, 9 x 23.25 inches. Courtesy of the Yellowstone Art Museum.

feels to be true."[86] Burke was a literary theorist, and, from his notebooks, it appears DeWeese regarded art as a kind of language to be understood through the literary theorists of the time. DeWeese added in his own words underneath the passage from Burke, "Both poet's metaphors and the scientist's abstractions discuss something in terms of something else—and the course of analogical extension is determined by the particular kind of interest uppermost at the time."[87]

His reference to art (and science) is a kind of metaphor and hence an arm of language that allows a direct line into Ludwig Wittgenstein's discussion of "family" relationships.[88] As DeWeese's artwork glides from sketching to painting and assemblages, underlying all of them rests the unique hand of a Modernist artist. Wittgenstein looks at the definition of games to show that not all things can be strictly defined. In his 1953 book, Wittgenstein suggests games are a kind of unspoken language with unwritten rules, yet the logic persists beneath the seemingly randomness of playground antics. The rules of art in modernity as practiced by DeWeese may seem to some to be without logic on the surface; in looking deeper into his work, however, it becomes clearer where the lines of reason are laid down.

DeWeese's work falls into the open concept of Modernism in a variety of ways and forms. Above all, there is always an acknowledgement of the surface, the character of the paint, the impact of mixed media, and his political comments on society.

As a teacher, especially a teacher in Montana, dealing with students who had little contact with or knowledge of anything other than the art

that portrayed the West romantically, DeWeese brought in notes from other Modernist painters to inform his work and to show his students the extent of Arthur Danto's "artworld," which referred to the ongoing conversation of past artists with present artists, but he did so with a consciousness of geographical context and an understanding of his students. Without prior knowledge of theory and practice, it is nearly impossible to go forward in dialogue with art. In another notebook, DeWeese wrote, "There isn't any one right way to paint—if so, it could be standardized…Must be true to yourself—learn through study of similar."[89]

Former student and internationally renowned ceramic artist Rudy Autio summed up DeWeese in a 1991 retrospective catalog. "He was an artist's artist. He was past the need for fame or fortune. Each day was a new event for him. A day for painting, worrying about things, great or small, but which fit into his heart and imagination."[90] He went on to note the thousands of drawings DeWeese left behind. "People will pass on. But Bob will fill our hearts with warmth whenever we think of him."[91]

DeWeese's paintings, sketches, homages, collages, and assemblages, like the overlapping of many fibers twisted together, strengthen his body of work and combine to create the tapestry of life and art. In 1983 *Newsweek* published an article called "Art Under the Big Sky," naming Rudy Autio, Robert DeWeese, and Gennie DeWeese as older artists "who never succumbed to the clichés of Western art or the allure of the city."[92] DeWeese, when asked about the usual fare of Western art depicting cowboys said, "It isn't like that out here." This remark, above all else, denotes DeWeese as a Modernist whose concerns of his current everyday make up the spine of his work.

After DeWeese retired from teaching, he and Gennie opened GB DeWeese Gallery in their Cottonwood Canyon home. For two years they showed the works of nearly every artist they knew and some they got to know through their work. Gallery openings pulled in over 200 people, crowding the space with intense conversation and avidly contemporary artists. Gennie explained why they opened the gallery: "We decided we wanted to show artists who were good, who lived in Gallatin County, and who didn't teach at the University, so couldn't exhibit there. We sat down and made a list, and in no time, we thought of several dozen artists we felt should be seen."[93]

In 1995, after Robert DeWeese's death in 1990, both Robert and Gennie DeWeese won the Governor's Award for the Arts. That same year Gennie DeWeese was awarded an honorary PhD in Fine Art from Montana State University.

GENNIE DEWEESE: I PAINT WHAT I SEE

Gennie Adams DeWeese (1921–2007) grew up when jazz, unfettered freedom in literature, and a number of "isms" in art influenced the culture in both America and Europe. It was a time when art and philosophy, politics, and the power of primitive expression filled the heads of artists. Although the Great Depression still pressed on everyone, starting art school in 1938 meant opportunity, a wide-open "anything goes" kind of opportunity. "Hoyt Sherman kept us coming back, we couldn't wait to get to the next class," Gennie DeWeese

said in a 2001 interview. "He was a Cezanne guy. Everything went back to Cezanne. He was an influential teacher."[94]

As Gennie wrote in a letter to Bob during the war, things were chaotic. War, Gennie began to see, might best be expressed through abstraction and non-objective art. Non-objective art is a type of abstract art that is usually, but not always, geometric and aims to convey a sense of simplicity and purity. It was initially inspired by Plato, who believed that geometry was the highest form of beauty, yet Gennie struggled to make art that felt right to her. She fought with herself over the work she created and strived to find time between teaching and living to paint. As she came into her own, after moving to Bozeman and having a family, she recognized the importance of continuing along her artistic path. Raising five children on Bob's professor's salary at MSC, Gennie DeWeese persevered to carve out time in her studio and follow her innate need to make art. As her daughter Tina DeWeese said, "Despite being a mother of five and keeper of the domestic front while Dad was slaying dragons in the halls of MSU, *Equal Studio Time* was the dictum by which our home established peace and equilibrium. And she did it!"[95]

In 1949, when she first arrived in Montana, she brought with her the spontaneous yet complicated ideas of the Abstract Expressionists—Jackson Pollock, Willem de Kooning, and Franz Kline—but she also carried the lessons of Post-Impressionist Cezanne, Fauvist Henri Matisse, and even the Impressionists like Claude Monet and Pierre-Auguste Renoir. Included in the mix were the influences of Abstract Expressionist Hans Hoffman and Nicholas de Stael, known for his thick impasto landscapes, and the teachings of Hoyt Sherman, who introduced the idea of using the flat surface to convey dimensionality without resorting to shadows, lighting, or traditional perspective. "It was fresh and new and it was all right to look at things in a different way," she said in a 1996 interview.[96] Once she settled in Montana, her impetus to reach beyond the traditional lines and composition of landscape came from other artists in her circle:

> Being out here in Montana, we were so isolated from what was going on we didn't feel the impact [of the art world] as much as those people [in larger cities] did. I don't know. There were so few of us in the state that were working in a contemporary vein. That's where our excitement came from— being in contact with those people, rather than keeping up with what was going on in New York or the coast.[97]

Her non-objective paintings, a consistent part of her body of work, were sparked by her reading of the abstract artist Wassily Kandinsky's *Concerning the Spiritual in Art* (1913), which explained his series of paintings based on musical compositions. "I liked what [Kandinsky] said, the idea of it being like music. That [a painting] didn't have to be about something. It could just be a response of some kind."[98]

In her undated, untitled, non-objective painting (page 51), DeWeese speaks to both Kandinsky's philosophy and Hofmann's ideas on color by incorporating geometric forms and floral-like biomorphic shapes. Delicate lines stand out from the squared-up reds and oranges. While the yellow pushes the image to the forefront, the darker reds recede. Inspired by Carl Orff's 1936 epic choral composition *Carmina Burana*, the painting is part of a series. The spectacular opus by Orff becomes the perfect vehicle for DeWeese's interpretation of Kandinsky's theory of visual music. The brushstrokes, as well as the colors, create movement. The black underpainting pulls the eye around the canvas. DeWeese reveals the character of the paint with a sweeping irregularity that enables the spaces to move back and forth, in and out. This painting also conveys a sense of intimacy, like the whispering of a growing chorus. A hint of chaos depicts a dialog between lusting angels and spiritual demons, thus creating a kind of transcendent tension.

She experimented with media, using cattle markers, oil sticks, oil paint, and, in this case, a series she worked on in the 1960s using aniline dye for brush drawings (page 128). Aniline dye, originally used on fabrics at the turn of the twentieth century, offered a vibrant set of colors, and DeWeese used them almost as a nod to Japanese Sumi-e ink drawings. Her gestures, spontaneous and measured, balance the white space. The water-infused mauve-pink feathered edges bring the piece into the Abstract Expressionist world, echoing the works of Helen Frankenthaler with her lyrical washes. Bright areas of red ground the drawing, seeming to anchor it with the weight of saturated marks.

Tina DeWeese sees her mother's non-objective work as marks from a direct impulse and passion to express a response:

> These gestural forms developed and delineated into often voluptuous, organic, and distinctly feminine almost figurative forms, derivative of the natural world around her. Although she was deeply influenced by the works of the modernists who came before, I would suggest that she was inspired by those rhythms of nature that once compelled her, in her younger days to yearn to live closer to nature...[S]he found her way to the heart of the natural world, not as a rancher, but as a woman immersed in the flow and gesture of the aesthetics surrounding her, through the eternal round and shift of the seasons, reflective of her internal emotional, physical cycles, and impulses.[99]

Bare Trees (1954; page 120) continues the geometric aesthetic bridging DeWeese's non-objective work and that of her physical surroundings. In this painting DeWeese integrates Hoyt Sherman's idea of Perceptual Unity. In *Bare Trees* DeWeese put herself back in Sherman's Flash Lab. The broad patterns play the lead in this piece. Fundamentally, the elements of line span across the canvas. Again, in her use of Hofmann's push-pull in regard to color, her palette reveals a space between the lines of the trees, while the steady tones of the foreground become foundational. The linen blue and violet of sky fit like puzzle pieces across the top of the painting. However, as DeWeese noted of her landscapes, you could turn it upside down

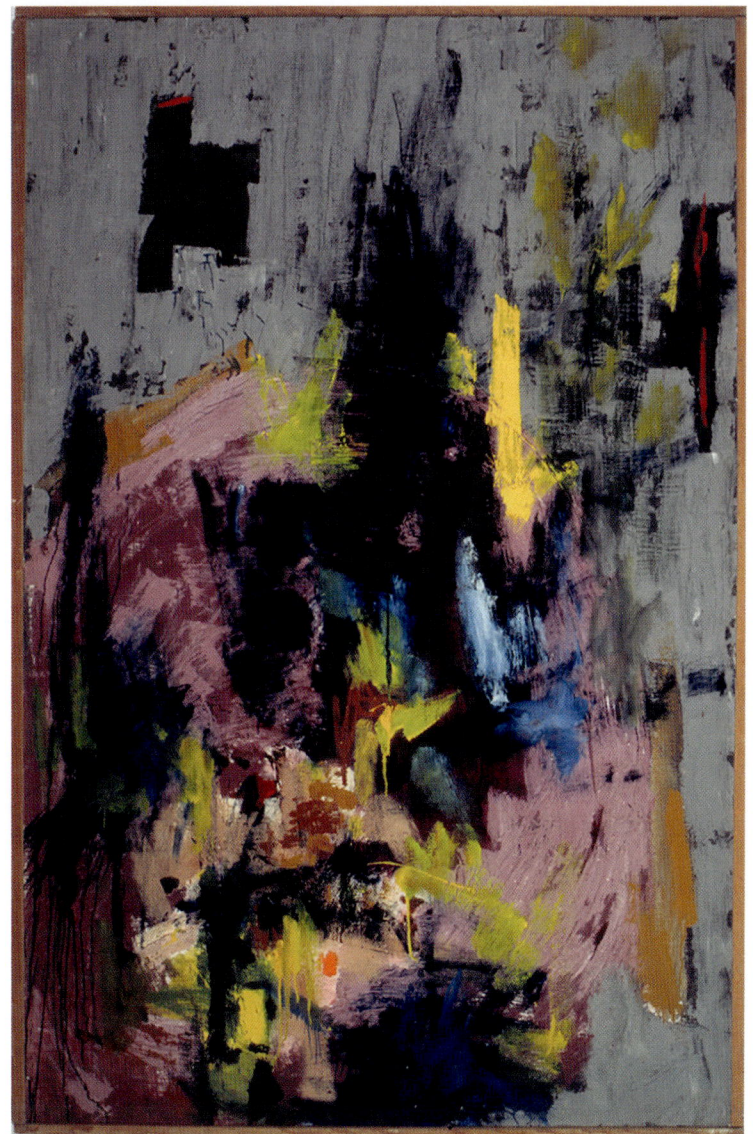

Gennie DeWeese, *Non-Objective Painting* (*Choral Composition*), 1950s, oil on canvas. Courtesy of the DeWeese Family.

and it would be a non-objective painting. She said in a 1998 interview, "To me there is only one line of requirement for the visual arts…[A]ll the parts are related…that's it, period. Subject matter is personal. If you care about it the parts will fall into place."[100] Ten years of painting only non-objective pieces enabled her to see the world through shape, line, and composition, no matter the subject. "I'm convinced they opened up avenues of visual awareness in the landscapes I returned to when I moved to the mountains and was daily confronted with visual feasts. What became important was to try to transmit that impact."[101]

In a 2000 documentary, DeWeese said, "I think the non-objective painting was a very, very strong influence on me. So that when I work now, I'm almost as close to that as I am to painting what I see out there, but I still paint what I see."[102] When she said she paints what she sees, she did not paint plein air, trying to capture the light of

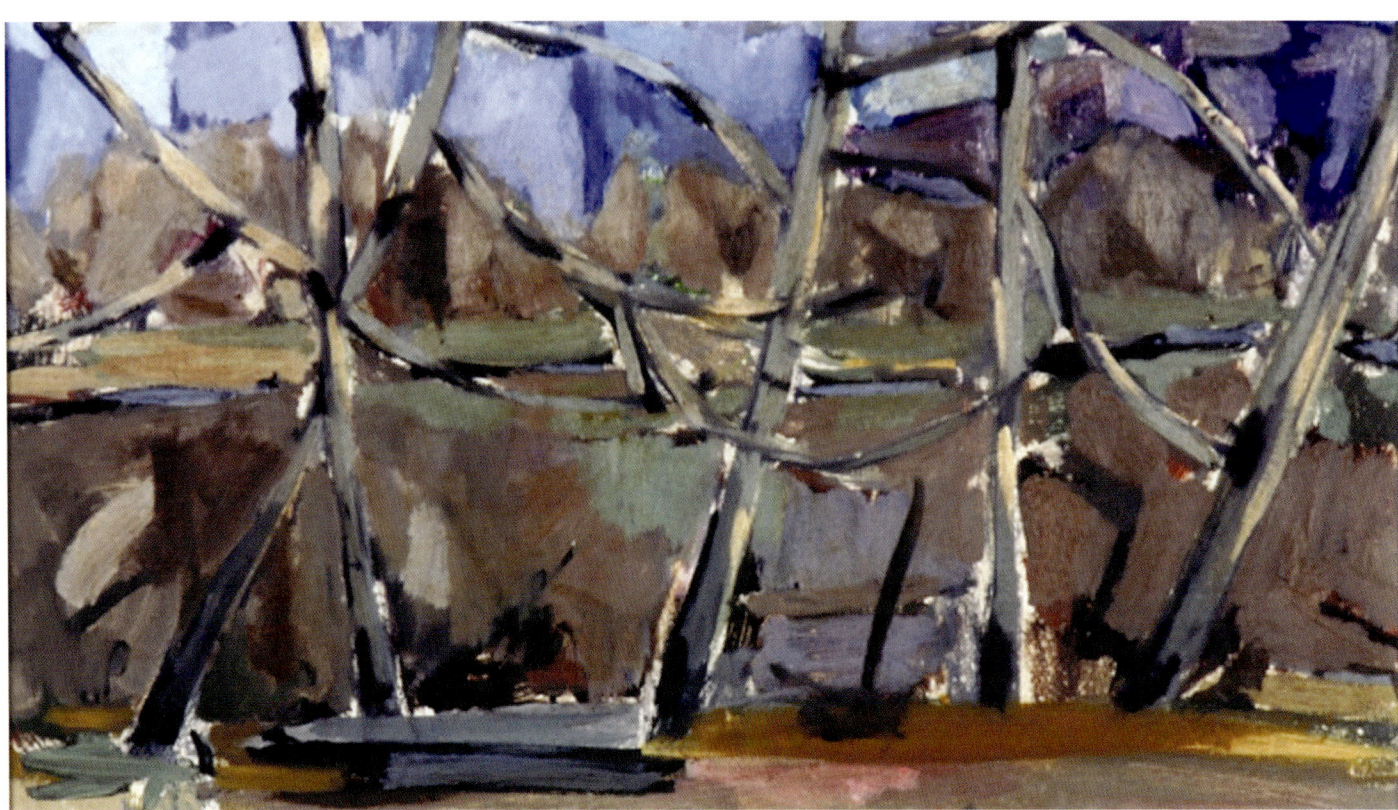

Gennie DeWeese, *Bare Trees*, 1954, oil on Masonite. Courtesy of the DeWeese Family.

the moment or the shadows as they lingered in the late summer afternoon. First, she sketched, and then she sketched some more. After each drawing, she remembered what she called the "essentials," the parts she believed to be important for what she wanted to say. It is this idea of getting to the bare essentials that speaks to her painting philosophy. When she painted objects, they were the essential parts of the objects, what she needed: the line, the form, the color, the texture. Details faded and the final painting resonated with her voice. Painting non-objectively, she said she got to a place that expressed her idea that "what was going on inside was more important than what was going on outside."[103]

In *Winter Willow Grove* (1971; see below) the all-over pattern, like a maze, carries the viewer from edge to edge. The influence of her non-objective work clearly comes through. The abstracted forms coalesce to bring the viewer

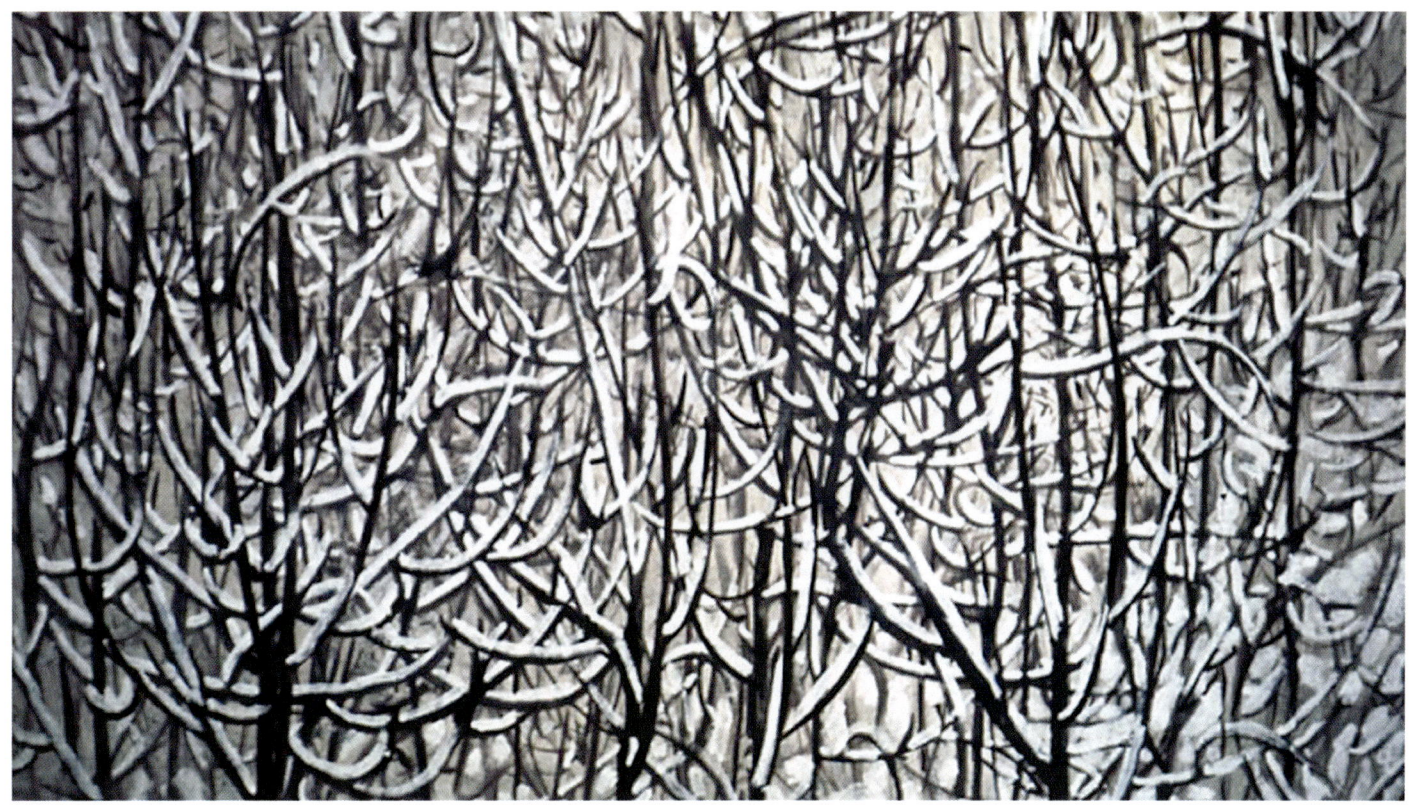

Gennie DeWeese, *Winter Willow Grove*, 1971, oil on Masonite, 3 x 4 feet. Courtesy of Mary Langan and Wally Hansen.

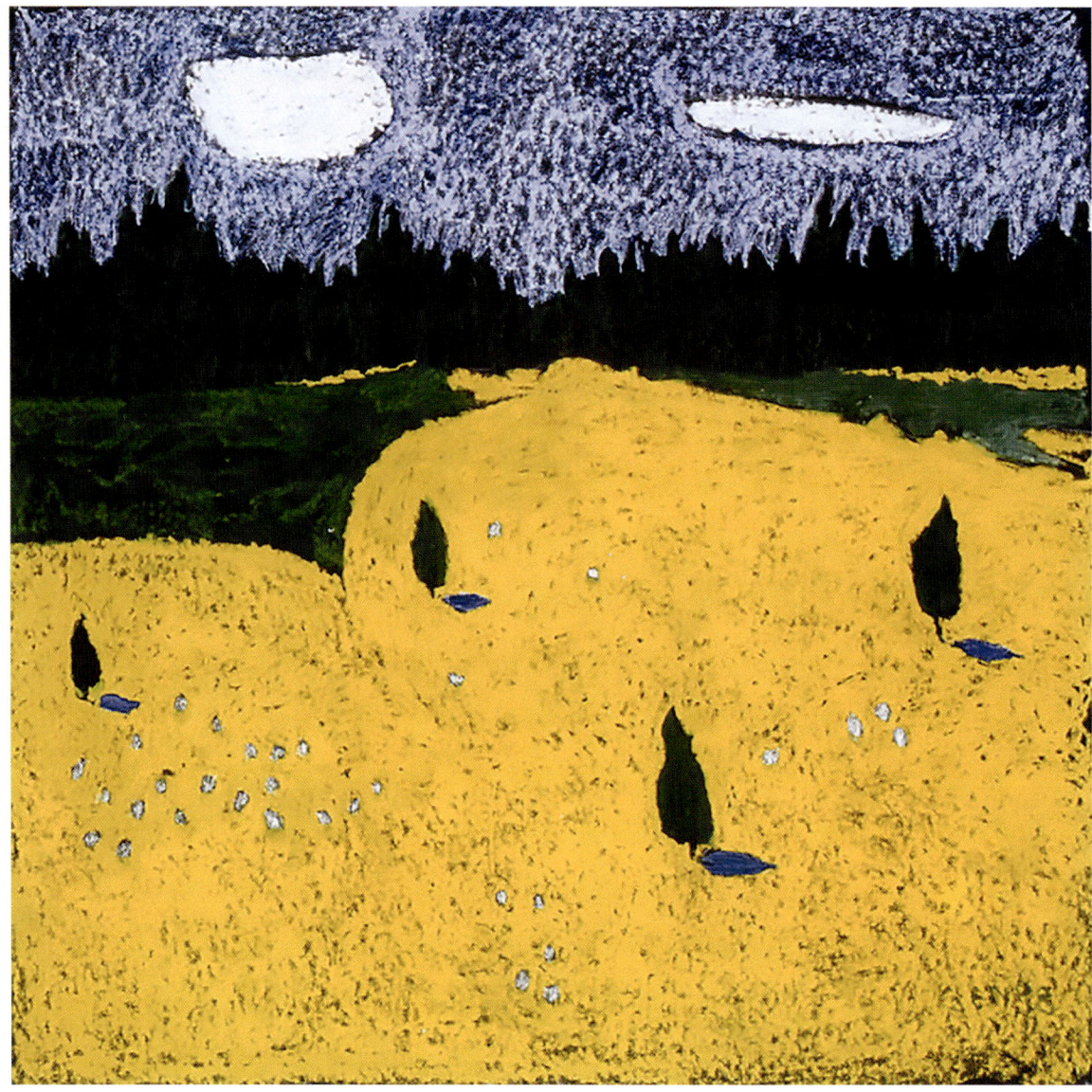

Gennie DeWeese, *Clover Year*, 1998, scroll, oil bar on canvas, 70 x 70 inches.
Courtesy of Eric Overlie.

into a conversation about place, about time, and about confluence. Her graceful lines intersect, snaking branches mingle. Like a spell-bound garden, the entangled limbs entwine seemingly in real time. The present dances with the past, and winter's weight accumulates. In this piece, a cross between landscape and non-objective painting, she examines a flattened perspective, as the viewer travels through the trees, between the branches, and maps the unseen undergrowth. This image speaks to a continual sense of place, one considered and explored yet forbidding and infinite. It is a wandering piece, a painting that speaks to time *as* place.

Beginning in the 1970s, DeWeese's work contemplating the Montana landscape deepened. Later, when she began to paint on extremely large-scrolled canvases, incorporating lush, sensuous colors, she fully embraced the genre. In one of her large scrolled paintings, *June Patterns* (1994; page 129), DeWeese combines those non-objective forms, seeing patterns in the landscape, and conveying those patterns into a composition. With the snow on the mountains implied by jagged white marks against the darker shapes, she has no need to depict details; this piece is all about gesture and color. June in Montana brings the lushness that later browns, but, for now, in this moment, DeWeese surprises us with more than alfalfa fields, with offerings of robin blue and fireweed red in the borders between dairy cows and the beyond. Again, the non-objective way of seeing plays a large role in allowing the eye to

grasp intention and feel joy in the vastness of an approaching (short) summer.

In *Clover Year* (1998; page 122), she portrays a bit of playfulness with each lone leaf-like pine tree amid a flood of yellow clover. The three trees bring to mind children in a field, each casting a shadow uniquely their own. The clouds overhead keep watch as a mustache of forestry lines the horizon. This level of interior space extends beyond the threshold of the home and into the wild, open outdoors. It speaks of freedom and responsibility, of nurture and nature, of play and of work, combined strikingly in a single scene.

Like all Modernists DeWeese did not try to create the illusion of perspective. Instead, through the use of sumptuous color and texture, and, especially with her scrolls, the mere size of them, she unearths the truth of the work by opening up space through her attention to line, shape, and composition, which in turn convey distance, scale, and structure. DeWeese said of her transition to scrolls:

> Because I tend to work on as large a scale as my space allows, I became intrigued with the idea of doing scrolls rather than framed paintings both from the practical standpoint of ease of storage but more importantly to introduce the Japanese tradition of changing displays according to seasons, moods, or whims. It allows more personal contact and decisions from the observer.[104]

In *Springtime in the Rockies* (2005; page 125), the sky envelops the viewer and somehow evokes both sunshine and evening. In the same way the promise of spring pulls at that loose string of hope, DeWeese pulls the viewer into a sense of calm, a feeling of assurance. DeWeese's colors repeatedly range from the natural to the exceptional. *Spring-time in the Rockies* presents the view from her studio in Cottonwood Canyon, showing evidence of the verdant undergrowth saturated in deep blue shadows, the stretch of willows and aspen reaching for spring. The experience, the location, and her personal dialogue delineate her work. Terry Karson noted:

> Her paintings are not tentative, cool observations of a detached person looking at the landscape from a distance, nor are they renderings of personal sentiment. These are paintings of a person knee-deep in mud, thorns and thicket. These are paintings of a person who loves the land, who perceives a oneness with it and expresses her sense of place with lusty grit.[105]

In *Winter Morning* (1984; page 130) DeWeese uses cattle markers on milk carton paper; the oiliness of the markers glides easily onto the waxy canvas. She used cattle markers to express the Montana nature of her work, while the combination of milk carton paper and cattle markers speaks to dark brutal winter mornings. In this painting the perspective drops the viewer directly into the image, which conveys a sense of immediacy. The markers seem to slide like mud across the surface in a frigid atmosphere lacking sunlight. Both Bob and Gennie used milk carton paper, as it was cheap and came in large rolls they were able to get from a nearby source. The non-archival nature of the paper did not concern them. The driving force behind all their work was to just make art, no matter what happened to the pieces

after the art was made. They often piled their art into a horse trailer that stood outside their home in the elements, covered with snow, drenched with rain, or dried in the August heat.

DeWeese's *Spring by Karl's Bridge* (1996; page 131), an oil bar on canvas scroll, stands nearly six feet tall. It is one of those pieces that simply enthralls the viewer. Sinewy tree trunks shoot from a newly thawed river bottom. Bits of snow peek from the mossy bottom. The dark forest lurks beyond, pulling the eye to a foreboding place. It is a painting that seems to exist outside of time, with no hint of early morning or dusk. The winding, still bare willows tipped with their russet branches crouch in the foreground. DeWeese's instinct for the portrayal of that private place, a place that speaks to the personal in a way that also reflects the universality of not only nature but human nature, is underlined here. It is a perspective that can come only from someone who knows the grounds, who has walked that path, with the full knowledge of the landscape both physically and artistically. She said in an interview for her 1996 retrospective at the Missoula Art Museum that, when she was deciding what to paint, the subject had to make her say, "Wow…I don't consciously do it a certain way, I just put down what I see." She added that she retained a sense of color and discarded the unnecessary elements.

In a departure from the lush landscapes DeWeese was usually drawn to, with *Clear Cut* (1990; page 126), DeWeese's voice deepens through the patterned stumps set against the dreary, cloud-darkened horizon. The complete devastation depicted here speaks to her non-objective style in a way that substantiates the overtones of the piece. The distance instilled by repetition feels almost cautionary, like protective armor. DeWeese portrays a place invaded, violated—a place no longer imbued with purpose. Upon considering the land as "mother nature," the expanse of defilement rings with the voices of women, of betrayal, and loss.

In 1989 DeWeese curated the show *Women's Work*. The show traveled around museums in Montana from 1989 to 1991. The show's purpose was to create a collection of the work of women artists from around the state to celebrate the Montana Centennial. At the onset of the project, she thought it would be difficult to find enough women artists to fill the show, but,

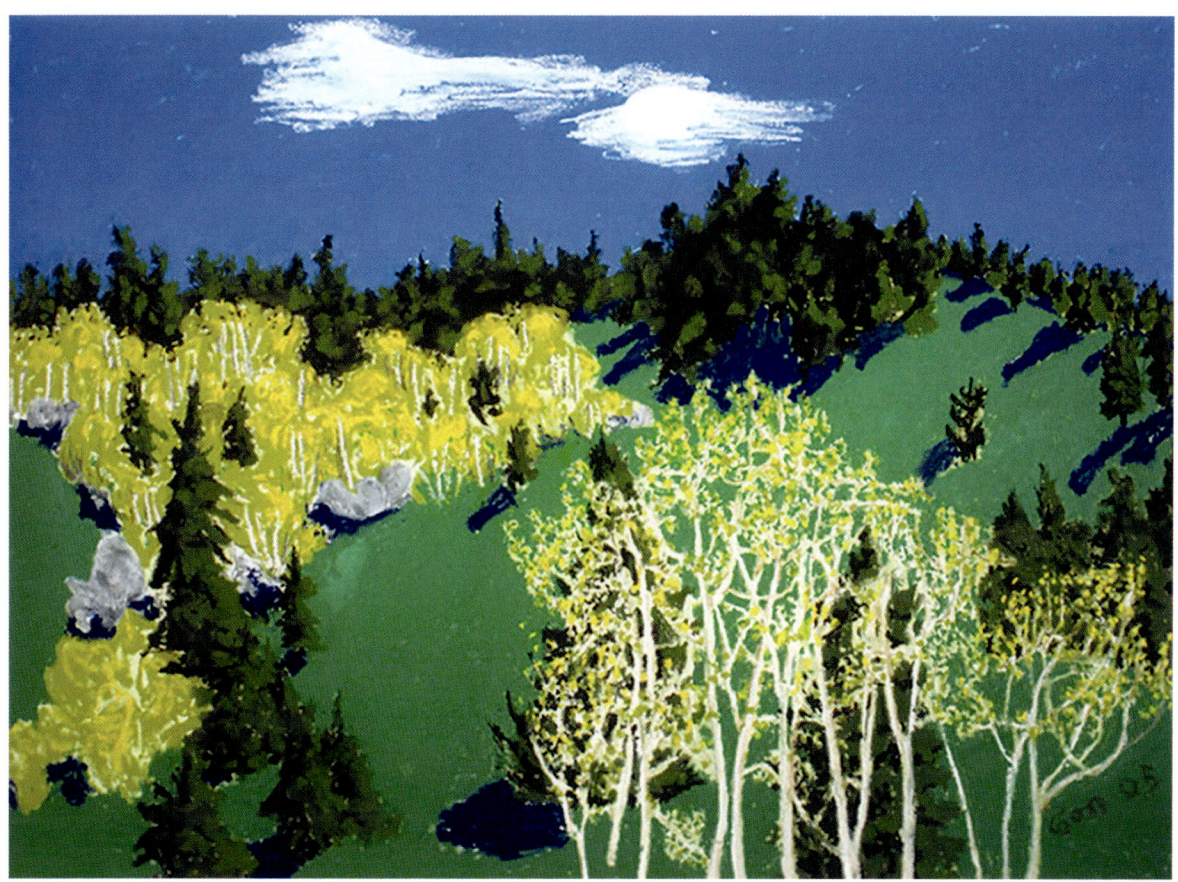

Gennie DeWeese, *Springtime in the Rockies*, 2005, scroll, oil bar on canvas, 60 x 86.5 inches. Courtesy of the DeWeese Family.

as she said in her curator's statement, "After several phone calls…I found myself inundated with lists of names and consequently the difficult task of selecting."[106] This show, *Women's Work: The Montana Women's Centennial Art Survey Exhibition*, while revealing how many women artists were working at that time, also exposed how lit-

tle recognition they had received. When the call went out, DeWeese said she found a "remarkable" number of women who stayed in Montana and remained productive. In 1990 DeWeese thought she was well-aware of most artists, so how was it possible for so many women to have stayed under the radar? Of course the idea that women often

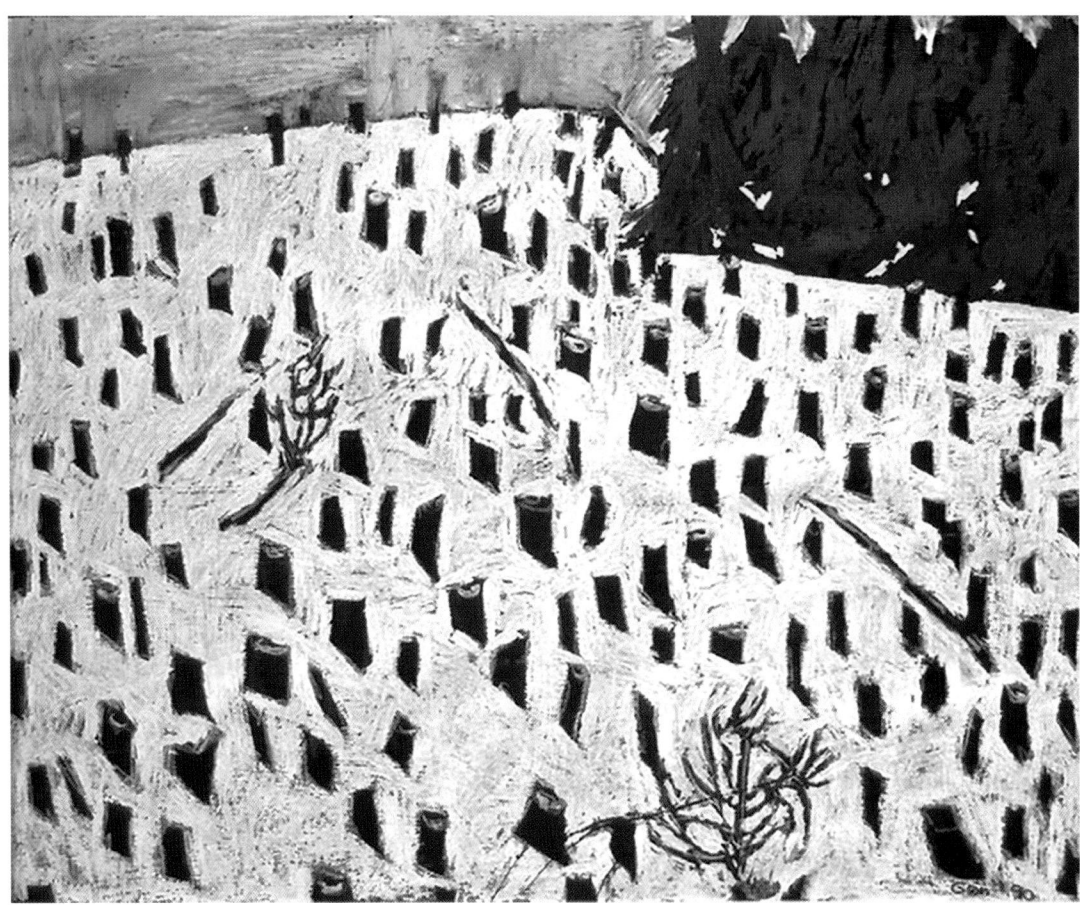

Gennie DeWeese, *Clear Cut*, 1990, paint stick on paper, 39 x 47.5. Courtesy of the Missoula Art Museum.

went unheard and unseen was nothing new to her. She had spent her life creating her own voice while raising five children. However, the question instilled a motivation to get those women's works seen by the public.

DeWeese self-identified as an artist who stood up for women. Through her paintings and through her role as the matriarch of Montana's artistic community, DeWeese pulled back the curtain on women in the arts. She wrote about the women artists who came and left, the few who stayed and raised families, and those who managed to remain in Montana:

> I can only guess that it is not only the natural beauty that surrounds us that holds [these women] here. There is a kind of camaraderie and mutual respect among the artist community that persists in spite of the vast distances that prevent frequent contact. And, of course, there is a kind of isolation that allows time for observation and reflection not so easily attainable in the major art centers.[107]

DeWeese included Isabelle Johnson in the show and noted that Westerners needed exposure to Modernism. Besides work by Frances Senska, Jessie Wilber, sculptor Deborah Butterfield, ceramic artist Beth Lo, and painter/sculptor Lela Autio, DeWeese included the artist Helen McAuslan (1895–1970). For DeWeese, McAuslan offered something that no one else did. McAuslan, nearly twenty-five years older than she was, had seen the world. She had studied in New York City, Paris, and Mexico. McAuslan traveled internationally as often as

she could, bought and sold a ranch in Springdale, Montana, built a cabin in McLeod, Montana, and built a Modernist house in Bozeman. McAuslan, independently wealthy, politically active, and prolifically creative, became someone DeWeese respected and considered a friend and fellow Modernist. McAuslan's success in the art world did not dissuade her from living in Montana. Perhaps that attitude and her unabashedly political perspective attracted DeWeese as well.

A reviewer of a McAuslan show in 1985 at the Beall Art Center in Bozeman remarked, "Much of McAuslan's best work here, including the abstractions, is a testament to the high quality available to artists who develop an awareness of Cezanne's ordering of perception."[108] The reviewer went on to say that the strongest works in the show were the paintings she did in 1970 after the Kent State riots, showing the slain bodies of protesters. "This painting is one of McAuslan's strongest, a vivid response to an unexpected political intrusion."[109] Art professor and art historian Rafael Chacon stated of the Kent State paintings:

> They have a sense of moral outrage and indignation and depth of content...Painted in a dark palette, these paintings are both horrifying and somber. The recumbent figures are not casual models lounging in a studio, but rather fallen innocents clutching their breasts, uttering their final pleas, and pouring out their blood like rivers across the canvas. They not only represent her mature, modernist style, but also reveal the ideas of freedom and civility that she most valued in life.[110]

In an essay McAuslan wrote for the *Montana Institute of the Arts* magazine in 1955, she explained:

> Painting is an attempt to create forms and colors on the canvas with a life and relationship of their own, without reference to the material world; to divest the picture of anecdote or illustration to the point where the emotions of the spectator will be wholly aesthetic, as when listening to music. Since I have lived in Montana, I have an enriched awareness of space and time—caused by the mountains, the space, the great distances around us. This quality I attempt to indicate in my paintings and sculpture.[111]

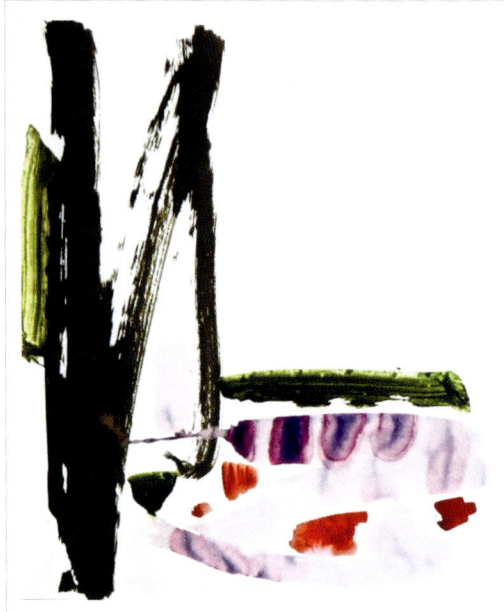

Gennie DeWeese, *Aniline Dye Brush Drawing*, ca 1960s, aniline dye on paper, 22 x 17 inches. Courtesy of Royce Smith.

She concluded the article with the idea that artists must use their inner eye, rather than their outer eye, or they will return to the pre-Modernist mimetic art. "With this vision we may then see that the present-day artist is searching for an order and faith in life, and perhaps expresses as an individual that for which the collective human mind is also searching."[112]

After McAuslan's death, Helen Conrad, whose husband directed the art department at MSC, worked tirelessly to convince the Museum of the Rockies, Bozeman, Montana, to pursue the accession of all of McAuslan's paintings, sketches, and art collection, consisting of over 545 pieces. As a memorial to her, a group of friends, including the DeWeeses, published a portfolio of her drawings covering forty years. The seventy-four cardstock drawings were accompanied by a short biography, a note from a cousin, and a free-form poem by Gennie DeWeese evoking imagery indicative of McAuslan's life. It starts:

> Slow, unhurried movements, sparse conversation, sketch book and inks, red-visored hat to ward off the sun, comfortable walking shoes, well-worn wool plaid shirt and loose-fitting pants...The cabin on the Boulder River. Shelves of books with the newest ones on the table in the process of being read.[113]

The herculean effort Gennie DeWeese put forth to keep McAuslan's legacy alive and to intermittently curate shows of her work speaks not only to the significance of McAuslan's friendship with DeWeese but also to DeWeese herself and her continual fight for women artists to be recognized. For Gennie DeWeese a woman's place was in the studio and in the galleries. She came to art at a time when women were scarcely heard. Museums and galleries routinely dismissed female artists. It became vital to break the "glass frame," so to speak. Not only did she curate the traveling show *Women's Work*, but, in 1995, she served on a panel for the National Museum of Women's Art. DeWeese showed extensively in the Northwest and, just as importantly for her, she championed young artists whenever and however she could. The art community she was instrumental in forming not only sustained her but also became her legacy.

The DeWeeses built a community based on their experiences in art school, where they enjoyed deeply connected friendships, long days in the studio, and long nights talking about art. They kept up those friendships through frequent correspondence over many years. In Montana they sought out that type of camaraderie and found it in an environment filled with young men and women just out of the military, going to college on the G.I. Bill, and looking for new ways to see themselves in a world constantly in flux.

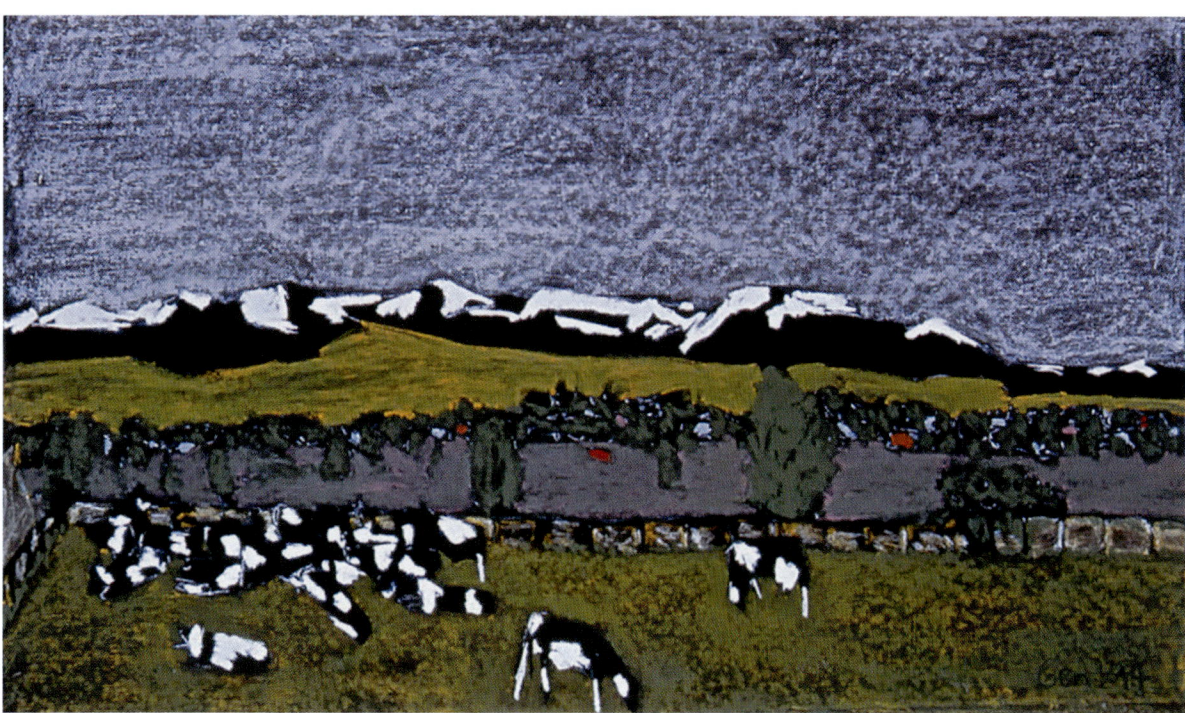

Gennie DeWeese, *June Patterns*, 1994, oil bar on canvas scroll, 40 x 70 inches. Courtesy of the DeWeese Family.

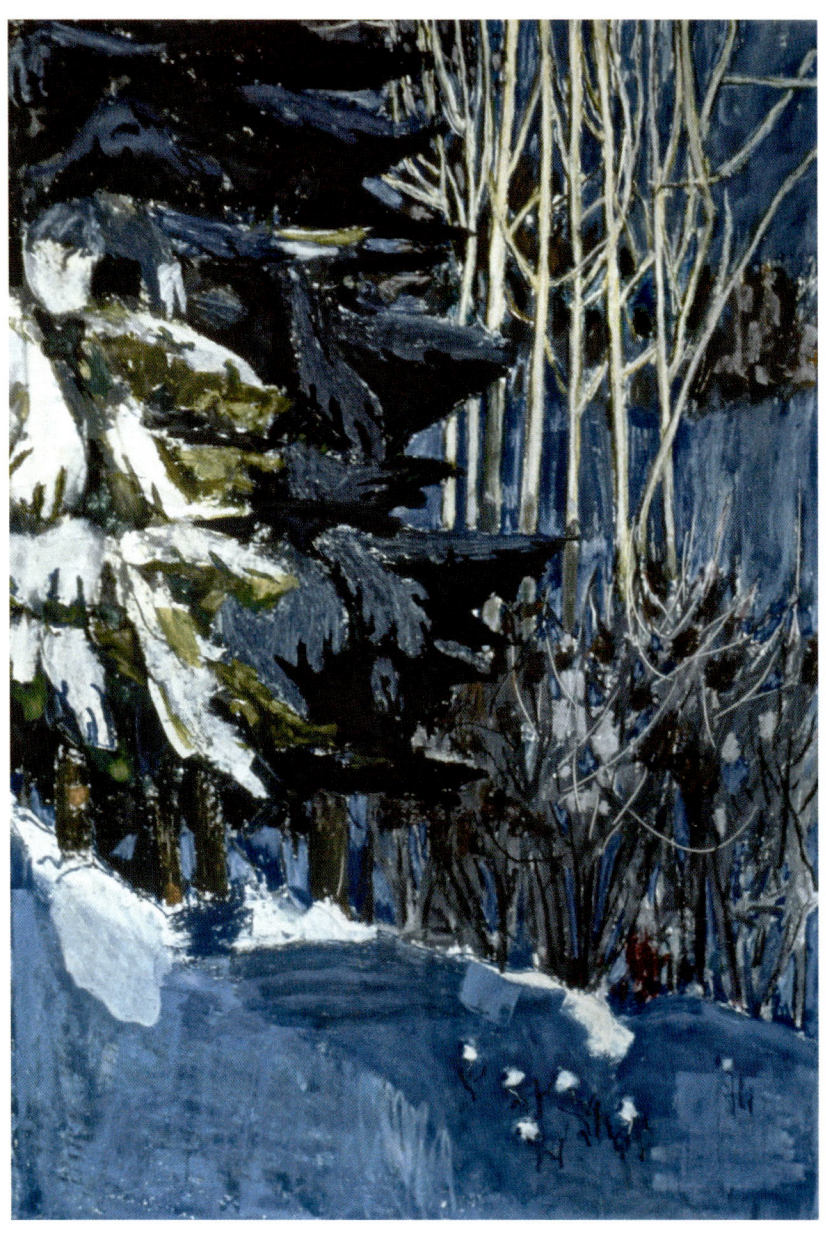

Gennie DeWeese, *Winter Morning*, 1984,
cattle marker on milk carton paper 60.75 x 43 inches.
Courtesy of the DeWeese Family.

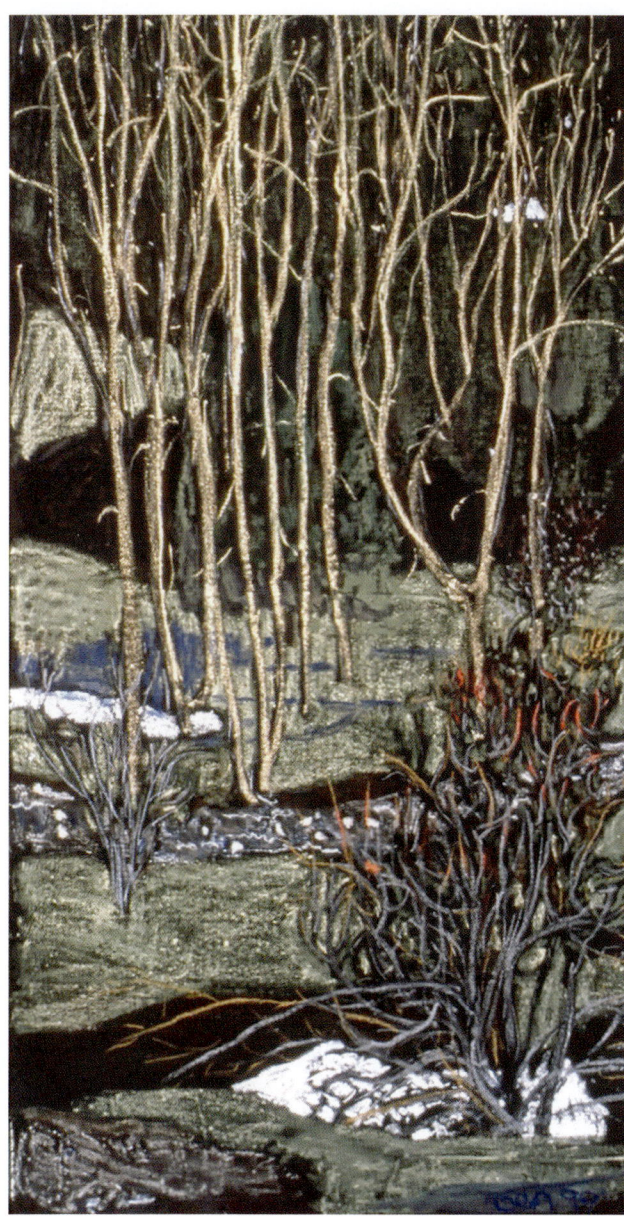

Gennie DeWeese, *Spring by Karl's Bridge*, 1996,
oil bar on canvas scroll, 55 x 39 inches.
Courtesy of Kim Reineking.

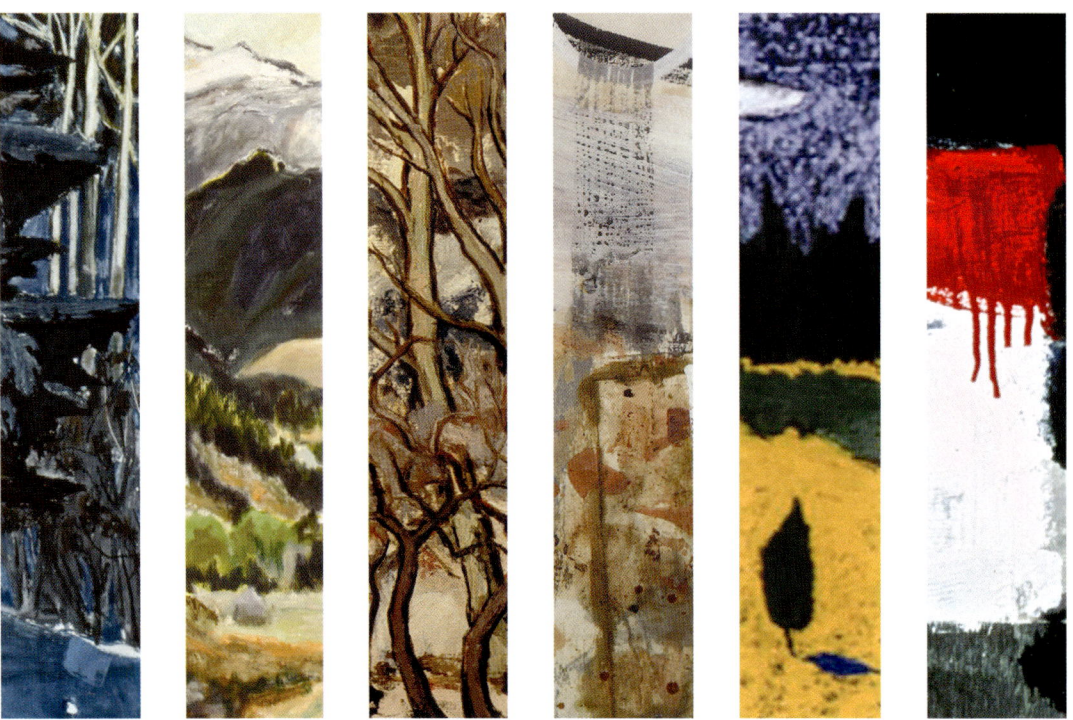

CONCLUSION

REDEFINING WESTERN ART IN MONTANA

Modernism in postwar Montana, by its very definition, implied a forward motion, a new direction, an innovative perspective on contemporary ideas, a new way of seeing. Modern art focused on the present as compared to the prior art in Montana, which focused on the past. As art historian Philip DeLoria noted, "Modernism is the slippery kind of object that one makes sense of by surrounding it on all sides."[1] Making sense of Modernism in Montana is exactly that—to see it from all sides: the mountains, the gullies, the rivers, the pastures, the soft hillsides, an increasing population, the newly built highways, and the backyards. The Montana Modernists painted, sculpted, and printed. They taught, shared, and joined together as a community. By reframing Western art in Montana, they offered a new way for Montanans to view themselves, and they revealed a broader perspective that engaged the viewer with the common aspects of daily life.

To fully understand the significance of Isabelle Johnson, Bill Stockton, Jessie Wilber, Frances Senska, Robert DeWeese, and Gennie DeWeese is to appreciate the lack of Modern art in the state prior to their presence and their vision. These six artists persisted in challenging themselves and their students to overcome the status quo and to adhere to their individual principles, their training, and their unique perspective. The Montana Modernists lifted Montanans out

of the past and introduced a new vocabulary as read through the language of art, and through that, an alternate lens for understanding. Mimetic portraits of mountains and the nostalgic illustrative work of the pre-war era no longer spoke to all Montanans. Modernism reflected the drastic changes of a postwar America and, in particular, a state that was outgrowing its own mythology.

Through the exploration of place, artistic lineage, and community, the Montana Modernists developed a deep-seated aesthetic that felt true to themselves and true to Montana. They set forth a new paradigm by which artists could feel the density and full range of human expression without having to resort to historical tropes.

The sense of place put forth by these six artists included the articulation of Modernism, but also encompassed the landscape, which made their work more accessible to those unfamiliar with the art world outside of Montana. They understood place as a source of sustenance and production, of home and hearth.

Of the six artists discussed here, four were women who used their role as teachers and artists to shine a light on what it meant to be a woman in Montana. They challenged gender roles in Montana through their art and through their lived lives. Senska used clay from the land itself to create her pots and glazes. She expressed an independence and identity directly through the

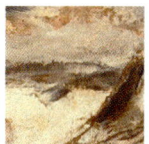
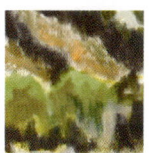
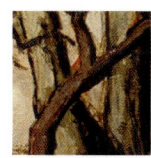
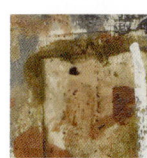
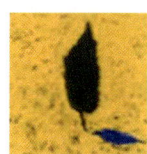

Modernistic imagery she used in her work. Translated into words, her work says "Not everything is as it seems": a bottle may become a partridge, and a wine set may be portrayed as a chicken. She also added the language of the "primitive power" of sgraffito scratched into dark glazes. Johnson told the world that she could do what she wanted, however she wanted, without regard for expectations. She stepped out of the role of a traditional rancher-woman and became an independent artist who also ranched. Wilber took the simple step of disregarding the "lady-hobbyist" reputation of women artists in Montana and modeled the value of professionalism, elevating the role of teacher to art professor. Gennie DeWeese, although a mother of five children, carved out her own space and, by doing so, established her voice. By brushing off the traditional view of a college professor's wife, she instead showed Montanans the power women could have when they committed themselves to their art, without distraction.

Robert DeWeese made social and political comments on postwar America, most strongly through his tie constructions and collages. He asked what it meant to be a man in a commodity-driven society. He blasted print media and television's intrusion into people's lives through the form of advertising. Bill Stockton also spoke to the mistrust of the mainstream art world through his life lived in Grass Range, rather than close to the art markets of New York or Denver, although he could have taken part in them.

All of these artists took the further step of expanding the parameters of Montanans, leading by example. Embedded in the lexicon of the land, they translated and transformed the understanding of the Western landscape into something more than an advertisement for dude ranches. For Johnson and Stockton their direct relationship to the land they worked, as expressed through visual language, moved beyond the landscape format produced in the 1800s. They painted with a tenderness and, at times, conveyed the hardness of what it meant to find frozen livestock in the dead of winter and the struggle to survive in lean times. Through their use of color, line, and form, they revealed the richness offered by living off the land.

Although not ranchers, Jessie Wilber and Frances Senska adopted Montana as their lifelong home. Senska connected to the land in a visceral way through the raw materials she utilized and through her excursions into the field to collect clay with her students in tow. Wilber's references to nature through her prints about her garden, the magpies she watched in winter, and her cats as they sunned themselves outdoors brought the Modernist aesthetic of the personal into her classroom and into her studio. Like Wilber, Gennie DeWeese portrayed the landscape through her deeply personal experience of nature. Her daughter, Tina DeWeese noted:

> Even from her early years at Pentwater, Michigan, where she spent a great deal of time with her sisters on the beach, she was connected to nature. In Montana, there were many years of camping every summer at Flathead Lake with the Autios, and later at Cliff Lake with their circle of friends, and many trips to the West Coast.[2]

Tina added that Cottonwood Canyon became a personal excursion into the heart of the mountain woods, down at the creek, "and through the seasons on the land where she had her tipi. [Gennie DeWeese] did not live in her tipi but it was her stake in the ground of having made her way to nature."[3] This sentiment harkens back to the letters she wrote to Bob pining for a life close to the land. Tina said, "The studio was where she made the paintings, but she gathered sensual information from all of these spaces in the heart of nature."[4] Tina, who also knew Senska and Wilber very well, noted that they had nature in "their blood and bones and heart and soul. Nature was the source of so much inspiration for all of their work. In this way life and art were not separate."[5]

Stockton and Robert DeWeese devised a visual shorthand while concerning themselves with the formal aspects that defined Modernism. Each one confronted the truth through the limitations of a flat surface, the conveyance of line, and the overall balancing/unbalancing/rebalancing of composition and color. They brought their mentors with them, from Johnson's time at Skowhegan School of Painting and Sculpture in Maine, to Stockton's semesters at Montmartre, from Gennie DeWeese's adherence to non-objective abstraction, to Senska's experience in the Bauhaus, and they made it their own. The lessons of Hans Hofmann, the forms of Paul Cezanne, the Fauvist colors of Henri Matisse, and the energy of Willem de Kooning can be perceived beneath their work like a pentimento.

After World War II colleges served as a springboard for a new zeitgeist, a kind of collective consciousness that spread from newly formed and invigorated art departments. In Montana, art professors found themselves teaching their peers, as many of their students were of the same age and had served in the war as well. These veterans returning to civilian life began to question the notion of their American identity, which contrasted with a view of themselves before the war. Big questions about the power of the atom bomb, the role of America in the world, the pros and cons of a capitalistic society versus a socialist society, the failure of Communism as a worker's utopia, the onset of McCarthyism, and the Cold War against the Soviet Union all led to many intellectuals and artists debating not only the fate of the world, but the role of the artist within that world. In Montana this questioning could not be answered with the art of the past, with the language of C. M. Russell or Edgar S. Paxton. It needed to be rethought, reframed, and redefined.

This herculean rethinking of what it meant to make art in Montana fell to the art teachers as they allowed their students to experiment, to break into the studios afterhours in order to pursue answers to their questions. They threw away the old master/apprentice pedagogy and equalized the classroom, creating validation for young artists. The process of lifting students from pupils into peers helped them to find a footing in Modernism, and beyond.

Modernism in Montana became possible through the unequaled, lifelong friendships and ties to a community they created, much of which germinated at the DeWeese home. As Rudy Autio pointed out in his memoir, *It Comes around Again*, the DeWeeses were like a "truth farm and everybody in Bozeman gathered there." Autio summed up the experience of the DeWeese salon-like atmosphere as, "Everyone was welcome and felt at home. People from all walks of life came to visit. Art was constantly in the air being discussed and made and talked about."[6]

Montana presented both a challenge and an opportunity in its vastness. The population during these postwar, formative years was sparse in most areas but burgeoned in college towns. The challenges included connecting one community to the next. Through sheer willpower, facing bad roads on long journeys in old cars, the rewards of connecting Bozeman to Helena to Billings to Great Falls (and later Missoula) enabled the strengthening of and building upon artistic ideals. A small group in the right place could make an indelible mark. The landscape of Montana, as the backdrop for artists and a common undercurrent, became a language comprehensible to nearly everyone.

The task of reframing art in Montana fell on their shoulders as artists and as art teachers. By redefining the language of art in Montana, they also answered the lingering question of what it meant to be a Montanan: By changing the palette of art, they began the journey of addressing a new identity—of what it meant to live and work and create art in a state clinging to nostalgia. To come away with a critical understanding of the Montana Modernists is to acknowledge the cultural rift between tradition and change in the form of artistic expression. The Old West was represented by illustrative paintings and tall-tale narratives, while the Montana Modernists presented a new way to see the West. The first Montana Modernists fought hard to get their art in front of people other than each other. (Senska made a point of pricing her work at affordable rates so anyone could buy her pots.) It took time, but many museums and private collectors today display the work of these artists.

Identity is strongly tied to storytelling. Personal narratives, the bombastic style of advertising, media, and historical factors often morph into mythologies. The Montana Modernists began to deconstruct that mythology, which they encountered all around them. It is only by providing a broader context for establishing a narrative that people can begin to understand their place within that story. The Montana Modernists did that through their art, by providing a fresh canvas on which all Montanans could see themselves portrayed. To re-envision the Montana identity, they needed to open up the conversation about the nature of art in the state.

The tension between commercially viable art and artistically independent art still exists. The question of whether to furnish the market with redundant iconography or to create art that speaks to the experience of understanding place—from white-out January nights to summer-glorious, star-drenched skies—still preoccupies studios and galleries all over the state. What is the role of the artist in contemporary Montana? This was the question the Montana Modernists asked themselves and their students. Their answer—to offer up alternatives to the status quo, to break the rules, and peel away the old narrative—laid a sturdy foundation for current artists and for artists to come.

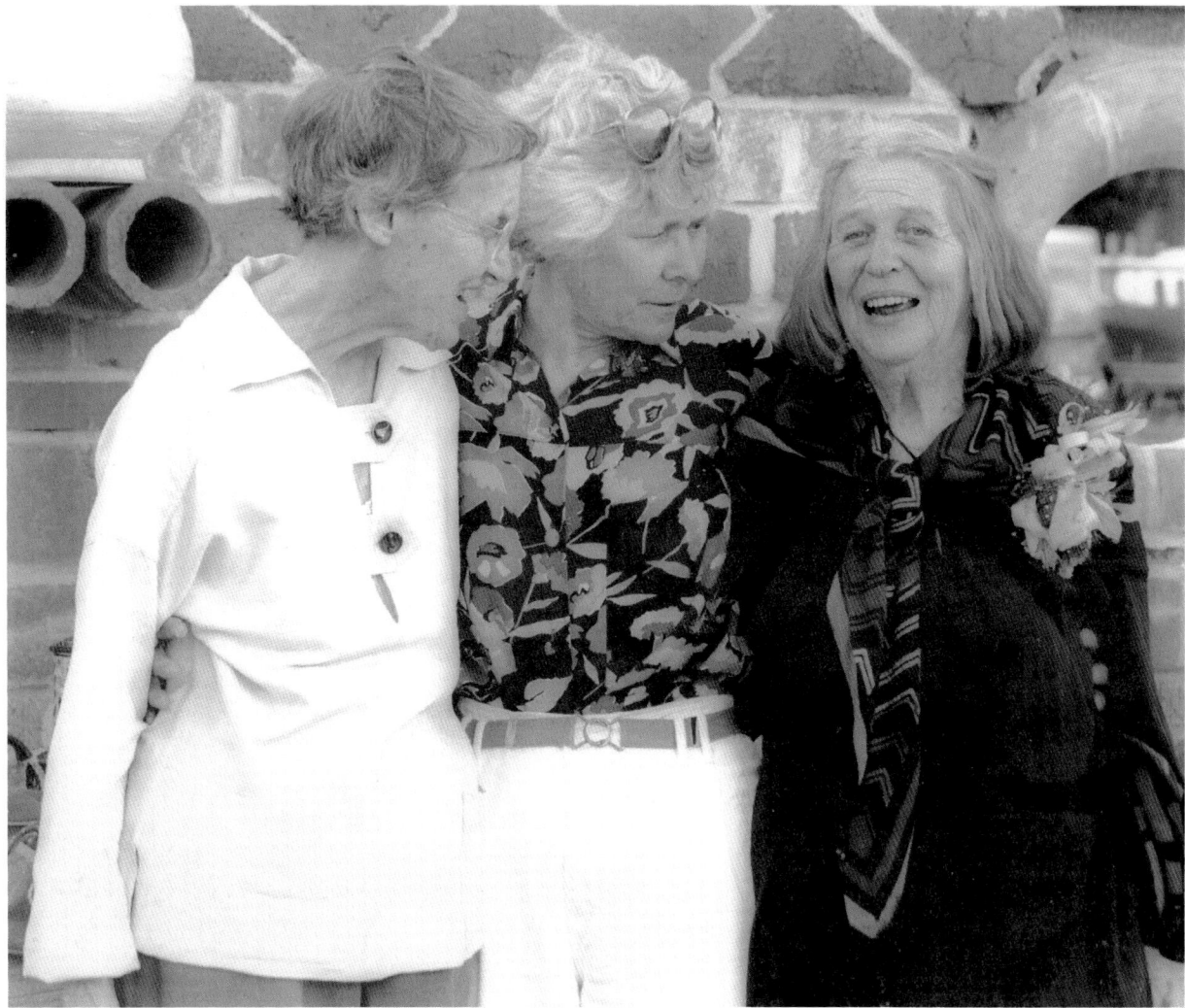

Francis Selska (left), Leila Autio (center), and Gennie DeWeese (right) at the Archie Bray Foundation, Helena, MT, 1993.

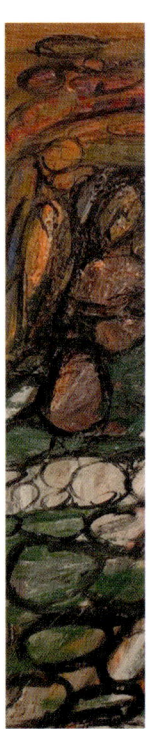
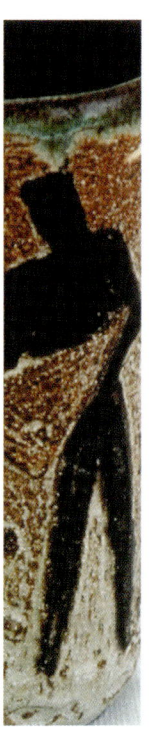
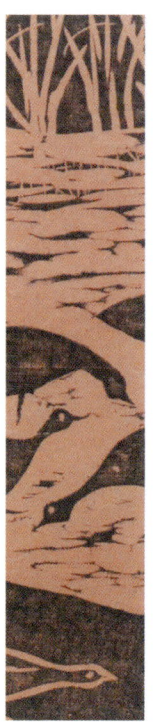
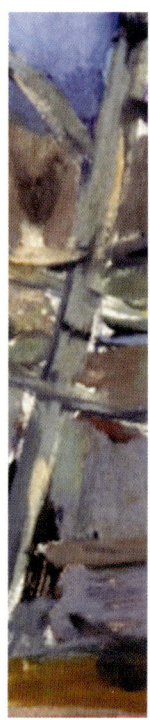
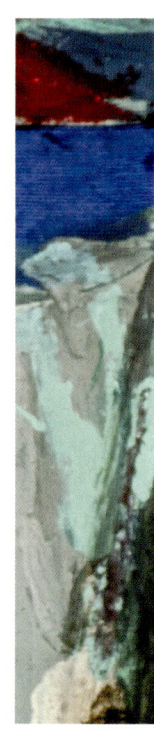
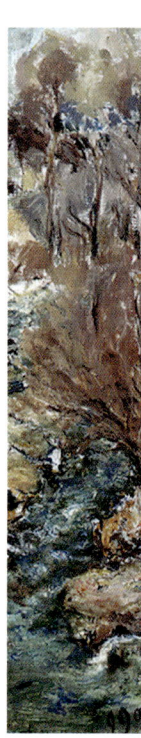

NOTES

INTRODUCTION

1. Gordon McConnell, phone interview by author, March 21, 2019; transcript in possession of author.

2. Clement Greenberg, "Modernist Painting," in *Clement Greenberg: The Collected Essays and Criticism, Volume 4: Modernism with a Vengeance, 1957–1969* (Chicago: University of Chicago Press, 1993), 86.

3. Kirk Varnedoe, *Jackson Pollock: New Approaches* (New York: Museum of Modern Art, 1999), 329–331.

4. Meyer Schapiro, *Modern Art:19th and 20th Centuries* (New York: George Braziller, Inc., 2011), 213–232.

5. Walter Benjamin, *The Work of Art in the Age of Mechanical Reproduction* (New York: Harcourt Brace Janovich, 1968), 217–242.

6. John Berger, *Ways of Seeing* (London: Penguin Books, 1972), 19.

7. Berger, *Ways of Seeing*, 20.

8. Bill Stockton, interview by Gordon McConnell, Yellowstone Art Museum Archives, n.d.; conducted after Johnson's death in 1992.

9. Robert DeWeese, in *Spirit of Modernism* (Kalispell, MT: Paris Gibson Museum, 1987), n.p., http://www.deweeseart.com/new-page-25.

10. While not all regions experienced a similar art movement, some—like New Mexico, Texas, California, and the Pacific Northwest—had their own shifts in art styles.

11. Yi-Fu Tuan, *Space and Place: The Perspective of Experience* (Minneapolis: University of Minnesota Press, 2011), 184.

12. Ray Campeau, interview by author, June 6, 2016; transcript of interview in possession of author.

13. Butte Public Library, *Montana's Art and Her Artists* (Butte: Butte Public Library, 1940), 39.

14. Brian Dippie, *Charles M. Russell: Word Painter, Letters 1887–1926* (Fort Worth: Amon Carter Museum, 1993), 3.

15. *C.M. Russell and the American West*, directed by Gus Chambers (Missoula, MT: Montana PBS, 2017), DVD.

16. Michael P. Malone, Richard B. Roeder, and William Lang, *Montana: A History of Two Centuries* (Seattle: University of Washington Press, 1976), 322.

17. US Department of Commerce, *1950 Census of Population by Counties*, Preliminary Counts, July 31, 1950. https://www2.census.gov/library/publications/decennial/1950/pc-02/pc-2-03.pdf.

18. Dude ranches provided a place for well-off Easterners to experience riding horses, living in bunk houses, and trying on the lifestyle of cowboys and cowgirls. Meals, activities, and often transportation were provided.

19. Malone, Roeder, and Lang, *Montana*, 340.

20. Associated Press News Service, "Record Season for Tourists in State Seen This Summer," *Bozeman Daily Chronicle*, March 14, 1946, 1.

21. However, that did not keep Modernist painter Helen McAuslan from becoming seduced by ranch life, as she stayed at a dude ranch in McLeod, Montana, in 1932, and moved to a ranch of her own in 1947.

SECTION ONE

1. Wendell Berry, "A Vision," in *Selected Poems by Wendell Berry* (Washington, D.C.: Counterpoint, 1998), 102.

2. Edward S. Casey, *Getting Back into Place* (Bloomington: Indiana University Press, 1993), 21.

3. Casey, *Getting Back*, 23.

4. Edmunds Valdemars Bunkse, "Feeling is Believing, or Landscape as a Way of Being in the World," *Geografiska Annaler, Series B, Juman Geography* 89, no. 3 (2007): 219–231, http://www.jstor.org/stable/4621582.

5. Karl Benediktsson, "'Scenophobia': Geography and the Aesthetic Politics of Landscape," *Geografiska Annaler* 89 no. 3 (2007): 203–217, http://www.jstor.org/stable/4621581.

6. Donna Forbes, interview by author, October 7, 2017; transcript in possession of author.

7. Bill Stockton, essay in *Isabelle Johnson: A Retrospective* (Billings: Yellowstone Art Museum, 1986), n.p.

8. Isabelle Johnson, Drew Bennett, Robyn G. Peterson, Bob Durden, et al., *A Lonely Business* (Billings: Yellowstone Art Museum, 2015), 23.

9. Once retired, she dedicated time to researching and writing the history of Stillwater County.

10. Addison Bragg, "Western? Who—Me?" *Billings Gazette*, December 5, 1971.

11. Isabelle Johnson, interview by Terry Melton for Montana Media Productions, n.d.; transcript in Yellowstone Art Museum archives.

12. Johnson, interview by Melton.

13. Johnson, interview by Melton.

14. Karl Zerbe was a German American Expressionist painter noted for his revival of encaustic paint.

15. Johnson, interview by Melton.

16. Johnson, interview by Melton.

17. Gordon McConnell, *The Montana Collection* (Billings: Yellowstone Art Collection, 1998), 28.

18. Bragg, "Western? Who—Me?"

19. Johnson, Bennett, Peterson, Durden, et al., *A Lonely Business*, 40–41.

20. Theodore Waddell, interview by author, January 5, 2019; transcript in possession of author.

21. George Santayana, *Reason in Art* (New York: C. Scribner's Sons, 1905), 66.

22. Isabelle Johnson, *For What Is the Amateur Painter Working?* (Missoula, MT: Montana Institute of the Arts, 1952), 170–172.

23. Terry Melton, Interview with Isabelle Johnson, *Montana Portraits* (Montana Media Productions, Yellowstone Art Museum, n.d.).

24. Terry Melton, essay in *Isabelle Johnson: A Retrospective*, n.p.

25. Melton, *Isabelle Johnson: A Retrospective*, n.p.

26. Melton, *Isabelle Johnson: A Retrospective*, n.p.

27. Terry Melton, personal correspondence with author, March 29, 2019.

28. Terry Melton, correspondence with Dennis Gould, 1971, Yellowstone Art Museum archives.

29. Terry Melton, personal correspondence with author, March 29, 2019.

30. Donna Forbes, essay in *Isabelle Johnson: A Retrospective*, n.p.

31. Gordon McConnell, *Making Connections* (Billings: Yellowstone Art Museum, 2005), 20.

32. Meyer Schapiro, *Modern Art: 19th and 20th Centuries* (New York: George Braziller, 1979), 19.

33. Gordon McConnell, *Isabelle Johnson: Life and Legacy* (Billings: Yellowstone Art Museum, n.d.), n.p.

34. Yellowstone Art Museum, *Theodore Waddell: Into the Horizon* (Seattle: University of Washington Press, 2001), 18.

35. Melton, Interview with Isabelle Johnson, *Montana Portraits*.

36. Melton, Interview with Isabelle Johnson, *Montana Portraits*.

37. Melton, Interview with Isabelle Johnson, *Montana Portraits*.

38. Melton, Interview with Isabelle Johnson, *Montana Portraits*.

39. Forbes, *Isabelle Johnson: A Retrospective*, n.p.

40. Forbes, *Isabelle Johnson: A Retrospective*, n.p.

41. Forbes, *Isabelle Johnson: A Retrospective*, n.p.

42. Beginning in 1969 the C.M. Russell Museum began its annual Auction of Original Western Art. Many artists from around the state attended the auction.

43. Isabelle Johnson, personal correspondence with Terry Melton, 1971, Yellowstone Art Museum archives.

44. *Johnson, personal correspondence with Terry Melton.*

45. Bill Stockton, in *Montana Impressions* (Missoula, MT: University of Montana, 1999), n.p.

46. Stockton, in *Montana Impressions*, n.p.

47. Gordon McConnell, interview by author, March 21, 2019; transcript in possession of author.

48. McConnell, *The Montana Collection*, 27.

49. A farm accident as a teenager broke Stockton's jaw, and, even after reconstructive surgery in Minneapolis, his crooked jaw stayed with him throughout his life.

50. Gilles Stockton, interview by author, July 2, 2019; transcript in possession of author.

51. Terry Karson, "Oral History with Bill Stockton, 1994"; interview recordings in possession of Gilles Stockton.

52. Karson, "Oral History with Bill Stockton."

53. Seena B. Kohl, "Oral History with Elvia Stockton," Montana Historical Society, 2001.

54. Karson, "Oral History with Bill Stockton."

55. Stockton, in *Montana Impressions*, n.p.

56. Karson, "Oral History with Bill Stockton."

57. Gilles Stockton, interview by author.

58. Gilles Stockton, interview by author.

59. Kohl, "Oral History with Elvia Stockton."

60. Kohl, "Oral History with Elvia Stockton."

61. Marie-Laure Pellose, *Bill Stockton*, video available through the Stockton Family Archive, 2017.

62. Karson, "Oral History with Bill Stockton."

63. Karson, "Oral History with Bill Stockton."

64. Bill Stockton, *Today I Baled Some Hay to Feed the Sheep the Coyotes Eat* (Helena: Sky House Publisher, 1983), 41.

65. US Department of Commerce, *United States Census*, 2010, https://www.census.gov/programs-surveys/decennial-census/decade.2010.html.

66. Karson, "Oral History with Bill Stockton."

67. Bill Stockton, personal correspondence with Isabelle Johnson, October 10, 1966, Yellowstone Art Museum archives.

68. Kohl, "Oral History with Elvia Stockton."

69. Kohl, "Oral History with Elvia Stockton."

70. Terry Melton, notes from his unpublished memoir, e-mailed to author, March, 2019.

71. Melton, notes.

72. Karson, "Oral History with Bill Stockton."

73. McConnell, interview by author.

74. Gordon McConnell, *The Rural Avant-Garde* (Clearmount, WY: Ucross Foundation Art Gallery, 2002).

75. Pelosse, *Bill Stockton*.

76. Waddell, interview by author.

77. Bill Stockton, *Paris 1948—the End of an Era* (Missoula, MT: The Arts in Montana, 1961), 8.

78. McConnell, interview by author.

79. Karson, "Oral History with Bill Stockton."

80. Kohl, "Oral History with Elvia Stockton."

81. Kohl, "Oral History with Elvia Stockton."

82. Kohl, "Oral History with Elvia Stockton."

83. Montana Arts Council, Governor's Awards for the Arts, 2003.

84. Forbes, interview by author.

85. Forbes, interview by author.

SECTION TWO

1. Hans Hofmann, *Search for The Real and Other Essays* (New York: Addison Gallery, 1948), 64.

2. The Bauhaus Movement started in Germany in the 1920s and combined fine arts with arts and crafts. It moved to America during World War II.

3. László Maholy-Nagy, *Vision in Motion* (Chicago: Chicago Institute of Design, 1947), 64.

4. Maholy-Nagy, *Vision in Motion*, 68.

5. Maholy-Nagy, *Vision in Motion*, 113.

6. Maholy-Nagy, *Vision in Motion,* 113–116.

7. Maholy-Nagy, *Vision in Motion*, 116.

8. Frances Senska, interview by Chere Juisto and Rick Newby, Bozeman, June 9, 1998, the Archie Bray Foundation Archived Interviews.

9. Michael Schreyach, "Re-created Flatness: Hans Hofmann's Concept of the Picture Plane as a Medium of Expression," *The Aesthetic Journal* 49, no. 1 (2015): 44–67.

10. Hofmann, *Search for the Real*, 60–74.

11. Tina Dickey, *Color Creates Light* (Salt Spring Island, BC: Trillistar Books, 2011), 30.

12. Dickey, *Color Creates Light*, 31.

13. Dickey, *Color Creates Light*, 275.

14. Hans Hofmann, *Search for the Real*, 62.

15. A few years later, the artist Roy Lichtenstein attended Ohio State University. Years later he donated the money needed to keep the lab open due to the influence it had had on his work.

16. Hoyt Sherman, *Drawing by Seeing* (New York: Hinds, Hayden & Eldridge, 1947), 9.

17. Sherman, *Drawing by Seeing*, 9.

18. Sherman, *Drawing by Seeing*, 10.

19. Sherman, *Drawing by Seeing*, 75–76.

20. Sherman, *Drawing by Seeing*, 75–76.

21. Sherman, *Drawing by Seeing*, 75–76.

22. Jenni Sorkin, *Live Form* (Chicago: University of Chicago Press, 2016), 73–85.

23. Marguerite Wildenhain, *Pottery: Form and Expression* (Palo Alto: Pacific Books, 1959), 9.

24. Wildenhain, *Pottery: Form and Expression*, 50.

25. Wildenhain, *Pottery: Form and Expression*, 58.

26. "Wilber Exhibits Art Works," *Montana Exponent*, April 14, 1949, 5.

27. In 1936 the Broadmoor Art Academy rebranded itself and became the Fine Arts Center in Colorado Springs.

28. Jerry Bywaters, "Otis Dozier: Growth and Maturity of a Texas Artist," *Southwest Review* 42, no. 1 (Winter 1957): 35. http://www.jstor.org/stable/43464260.

29. Schapiro, *Modern Art: 19th and 20th Centuries*, 39–42.

30. Isabelle Johnson, *The Wonderful World of Color* (Missoula, MT: Montana Institute for the Arts, 1963), n.p.

31. Rick Newby, *Theodore Waddell: My Montana* (Helena: Drumlummon Institute, 2016), 40.

32. Johnson, Bennett, Peterson, Durden, et al., *A Lonely Business*, 3.

33. Gennie DeWeese taught at all levels of education and served as an adjunct at MSC as needed.

34. John Dewey, *Art as Experience* (New York: Penguin Group, 1934), 11.

35. Neil Jussila, interview by author, June 23, 2016; transcript in possession of author.

36. Bill Neff, *Art All the Time*, KUSM-TV, 1997.

37. Neff, *Art All the Time*

38. Neff, *Art All the Time*.

39. The printing studio working environment is similar to the ceramic studio in its sharing of equipment.

40. Campeau, interview by author.

41. Jessie Wilber, *Jessie Wilber: Retrospective* (Bozeman: Montana State University, 1983), n.p.

42. The Yellowstone Art Center would later become the Yellowstone Art Museum.

43. Half of the collection consists of paintings, and the rest comprises works on paper.

44. Ben Mitchell, *The Most Difficult Journey* (Billings: Yellowstone Art Museum, 2002), 15–32.

45. Mitchell, *Most Difficult Journey*, 16

46. Jussila, interview by author.

47. Jussila, interview by author.

48. Jussila, interview by author.

49. Jerry Rankin, interview by author, August 19, 2017; transcript in possession of author.

50. Robert DeWeese, "On Painting," in David Dragonfly, Wes Mills, Neil Parsons, Jerry Rankin, et al., *DeWeese's Legacy*, n.p. (Holter Museum of Art, Helena, 2006).

51. Rankin, interview by author.

52. Al Tennant attended Montana State College from 1966 through 1969.

53. Al Tennant, interview by author, June 11, 2016; transcript in possession of author.

54. Tennant, interview by author.

55. Tennant, interview by author.

56. Tennant, interview by author.

57. Tennant, interview by author.

58. Tennant, interview by author.

59. Dewey, *Art as Experience*, 18.

60. She was teaching students how to pull a bottle on the wheel and, when she was done, she pinched the top.

61. Neff, *Art All the Time*.

62. US Interior, National Register of Historic Places (February 27, 1989), https://www.kshs.org/resource/national_register/mps/kansas_post_offices_artwork_mps.pdf.

63. Wilber, *Jessie Wilber: Retrospective*.

64. Stinchfield studied with Andre Lhote and O. Friesz in Paris.

65. Wilber, *Jessie Wilber: Retrospective*.

66. Montana State College is now Montana State University. Founded in 1893 as a land-grant college, it was named the Agricultural College of the State of Montana. In the 1920s, it was renamed Montana State College, and, on July 1, 1965, it was again renamed Montana State University in recognition of its science and humanistic research.

67. Jessie Wilber, interview by Dr. William Walter, October 24, 1985, Session 03001, Box 8—transcript, Montana State University Special Collections.

68. Olga Ross Hannon (1890–1947) was chair of the MSC art department from 1921 to 1947.

69. Wilber, interview by Dr. William Walter.

70. J. C. Ewers, *Blackfeet Indian Tipis: Design and Legend* (Bozeman, Museum of the Rockies, 1976).

71. Ewers, *Blackfeet*; noted on p. 6, each clan's tent depicted different animals and geometric designs.

72. According to the website www.mt.gov, the Governor's Arts Awards program honors outstanding citizens and organizations in Montana whose achievements in the arts, or on behalf of the arts, benefit all Montanans.

73. Transcribed from Mark Rothko's papers at the Smithsonian Museum's Archives of American Art.

74. Woodblock printing was used by the Chinese and Japanese and was later reinvigorated by the Impressionists as well as the German Expressionists.

75. Frances Senska, *Jessie Wilber* (Missoula, MT: The Arts in Montana, 1977), 110.

76. A local rumor tells of a rancher walking into a Bureau of Reclamation office with a box of dynamite assuring those in the office he would not hesitate to use the contents of the box on any dam built on the Yellowstone.

77. Greenberg, "Modernist Painting," 85.

78. Wilber, interview by Dr. William Walter.

79. Tina DeWeese, e-mail correspondence with author, September 23, 2019.

80. McConnell, *The Montana Collection.*

81. Connie Lange, Annotated List of Prints, *Jessie Wilber: Retrospective*, 1991, n.p.

82. In 1929 she moved to Iowa City, Iowa, when her parents were transferred back to the States. She attended the University of Iowa for both her undergraduate and master's degrees. Her masters' degree was in tailoring.

83. Frances Senska, Interview by Donna Forbes, *Oral History*, Smithsonian Archives of American Art, April 16, 2001.

84. Senska, Interview by Donna Forbes, *Oral History.*

85. Brandon Reintjes, essay in *Frances Senska: A Life in Art* (Helena: Holter Museum of Art, 2004), n.p.

86. Steve Jackson, "Frances Senska: A Biography," in *Frances Senska: A Life in Art*, n.p.

87. Tim Schwab, Frances Senska, and Nanette L. Laitman, *Evolving Forms.* Documentation Project for Craft Decorative Arts in America (Bozeman: Montana State University, 1978).

88. Greenberg, "Modernist Painting," 85.

89. Nyame Akuma, "The Ceramic and Society Project," *The Society of Africanist Archaeologists* 46 (December 1996): 11–17.

90. H. W. Wilson, "11 Montana Potters," *Studio Potter* 8, no. 1 (1979): 33–46.

91. Silvia Forni, "Containers of Life: Pottery and Social Relations in the Grassfields (Cameroon)," in "Ceramic Arts in Africa," special issue, *African Arts* 40, no. 1 (Spring 2007): 42–53.

92. Charles Harrison and Paul Wood, *Art in Theory, 1900–2000: An Anthology of Changing Ideas.* 2nd ed. (Malden, MA: Blackwell Publishing, 2003), 311.

93. Harrison and Wood, *Art in Theory*, 311.

94. Dean and Geraldine Schwarz, *Marguerite Wildenhain and the Bauhaus: An Eye Witness Anthology* (Decora: South Bear Press, 2007).

95. Thomas Folk, "Frances Senska: Studio Potter," *American Ceramics* 8, no. 2 (1990): 34–39.

96. Ernest Gombrich, *Art and Illusion* (Princeton: Princeton University Press, 1960), 186.

97. Moholy-Nagy, *Vision in Motion,* 327. Senska notes this was a rhyme and made up of nonsense words.

98. Neff, *Art All the Time.*

99. Moholy-Nagy, *Vision in Motion*, 131, fig. 173 a, b.

100. Neff, *Art All the Time.*

101. Wilson, "Eleven Montana Potters," 33–46.

102. Moholy-Nagy, *Vision in Motion*, 12.

103. Schwarz, D. and G. Schwarz, *Marguerite Wildenhain and the Bauhaus.*

104. Sonoma County Museum, *Marguerite Wildenhain: Bauhaus to Pond Farm, Educator Guide* (Santa Rosa, California: Sonoma Country Museum, exhibition ran from January 20 to April 15, 2007).

105. Senska, interview by Chere Juisto and Rick Newby.

106. Senska, Interview by Donna Forbes, *Oral History.*

107. Jackson, "Frances Senska."

108. Jackson, "Frances Senska."

109. Jenni Sorkin, "Craft-in-Residence," *The Open Studio Network* (academia.edu, 2013), 25–29.

110. Marjorie Smith, "Frances Senska," *Ceramics Monthly* (September 2002): 50–53.

111. Neff, *Art All the Time.*

112. Neff, *Art All the Time.*

113. Schwab, Senska, and Laitman, *Evolving Forms.*

114. Schwab, Senska, and Laitman, *Evolving Forms.*

115. Schwab, Senska, and Laitman, *Evolving Forms.*

116. People no longer trusted a brick-built home, as the mortar crumbles under the stress of an earthquake.

117. Senska, interview by Chere Juisto and Rick Newby.

118. Rick Newby, Chere Juisto, Patricia Failing, and Janet Koplos, *A Ceramic Continuum* (Helena: Holter Museum of Art, 2001), 64.

119. Senska, Interview by Donna Forbes, *Oral History*.

120. Peter Voulkos, *Oral History of the Archie Bray Foundation*, August 7, 1978.

121. Jackson, "Frances Senska."

122. H. G. Merriam, ed., *The Arts in Montana* (Missoula, MT: Mountain Press Publishing, 1977), 68.

123. Herbert C. Anderson, *The Life, the Times, and the Art of Branson Graves Stevenson* (Great Falls: Janher Publishing, 1979).

124. Anderson, *The Life, the Times*.

125. Melton, notes, March 29, 2019.

126. Melton, notes.

127. Newby, Juisto, Failing, and Koplos, *A Ceramic Continuum*, 26–28.

128. Newby, Juisto, Failing, and Koplos, *Ceramic Continuum*, 27.

129. Merriam, ed., *Arts in Montana*, 144.

SECTION THREE

1. Anne Norton, *95 Theses on Politics, Culture & Method* (New Haven: Yale University Press, 2004), 23.

2. To be clear, the artists were being paid as teachers and professors, a position most took very seriously.

3. Joan Saab, *For the Millions: American Art and Culture between the Wars* (Philadelphia: University of Pennsylvania Press, 2004), 15.

4. Elizabeth Mentzer, "Made in Montana: Montana's Post Office Murals," *Montana: The Magazine of Western History* 53, no. 3 (2003): 44–53, http://www.jstor.org.proxybz.lib.montana.edu/stable/4520536.

5. Saab, *Millions*, 17.

6. Irving Sandler, *The Triumph of American Painting* (New York: Praeger Publishers, 1970), 7.

7. Frederick M. Logan, "Up Date '75, Growth in American Art Education," *Studies in Art Education* 17, no. 1 (1975): 7–16, DOI: 10.1080/00393541.1975.11651359.

8. *Eastern Montana College of Education Bulletin*, 1949–50.

9. New Mexico State College, *College Record*, 1949–50.

10. *Colorado Agricultural and Mechanical College, General Home Economics, Child Development, Home Management and Family Economics, Occupational Therapy and Related Art, Textiles, and Clothing Course catalog*, 1940–1950.

11. *Montana State College Course Catalogs*, 1939–41, 1941–43, 1944–45, 1946–47, 1949–50.

12. According to Martha Andrews at New Mexico State University, in correspondence with the author (November 18, 2018): "The New Mexico State University archivist suggested that art classes began quite early, but Hiram Hadley, the first NMSU president, conceived a dislike for the woman teaching them, fired her, and then later resumed them as a means of attracting female students. She indicated that the war years were quiet at NMSU, with returning students and the G.I. Bill rapidly expanding the population and curriculum at the ending [of the war]."

13. In the late 1960s, Ray Campeau and Rand Honadel opened the Ketterer Art Center in Bozeman. The center offered classes and occasionally held art shows.

14. Campeau, interview by author.

15. The MIA was founded in 1948. It issued a magazine on a quarterly basis. Both Frances Senska and Jessie Wilber served as board members.

16. Campeau, interview by author.

17. Campeau, interview by author.

18. Campeau, interview by author.

19. Campeau, interview by author.

20. Campeau, interview by author.

21. Campeau, interview by author.

22. Campeau, interview by author.

23. Jessie Wilber, letter dated July 14, 1949, DeWeese Family Archives.

24. Jessie Wilber/Robert DeWeese correspondence, July 1–14, 1949, DeWeese Family Archives.

25. Jessie Wilber/Robert DeWeese correspondence, July 1–14, 1949, DeWeese Family Archives.

26. Joel Jahnke, interview by author, June 7, 2019; transcript in possession of author.

27. Jahnke, interview by author.

28. Jahnke, interview by author.

29. Jahnke, interview by author.

30. Jahnke, interview by author.

31. Jahnke, interview by author.

32. Jahnke, interview by author.

33. Jahnke, interview by author.

34. Jahnke, interview by author.

35. Art openings in the early years were not at galleries but at the Montana Institute of the Arts shows and art fairs across the state, held in community centers and other public spaces.

36. Senska, interview by Chere Juisto and Rick Newby.

37. These nights were documented in Robert DeWeese's sketches.

38. Malone Roeder, and Lang, *Montana*, 377.

39. Merriam, *Arts in Montana,* vii.

40. Merriam, *Arts in Montana,* vii.

41. "Russell Memorial," *Bozeman Daily Chronicle*, January 16, 1949, 4.

42. Merriam, *Arts in Montana*, 160.

43. Greenberg, "Modernist Painting," 86.

44. Merriam, *Arts in Montana*, 163.

45. John Thomas McNay, *Breaking the Copper Collar: The Sale of the Anaconda Newspapers and the Professionalization of Journalism in Montana* (Master's thesis, University of Montana, Missoula, 1991).

46. Malone Roeder, and Lang, *Montana*, 380.

47. Dan Braha, Marcus A. M. De Aguiar, and Lidia Adriana Braunstein, "Voting Contagion: Modeling and Analysis of a Century of U.S. Presidential Elections," PLoS ONE 12, no. 5 (2017): E0177970.

48. Tina DeWeese, interview by author, February 7, 2019; transcript in possession of author.

49. Tina DeWeese, interview by author.

50. Page 55 for an in-depth description of the Flash Lab.

51. Aside from DeWeese, Sherman's teachings influenced many of his students, including Roy Lichtenstein.

52. Sherman, *Drawing by Seeing*.

53. Gennie Adams' letters date from 1942–1946, although many of them are not dated. DeWeese Family Archives.

54. Gennie Adams' letters date from 1942–1946. DeWeese Family Archives.

55. Gennie Adams' letters date from 1942–1946. DeWeese Family Archives.

56. Letter from Gennie Adams to Robert DeWeese, undated, DeWeese Family Archives.

57. Letter from Gennie Adams to Robert DeWeese, undated, DeWeese Family Archives.

58. Robert DeWeese letter to Gennie Adams, April 19; no year is on the letter. DeWeese Family Archives.

59. Robert DeWeese letter to Gennie Adams, April 19; no year is on the letter. DeWeese Family Archives.

60. Robert DeWeese letter to Gennie Adams, May 22, 1945, DeWeese Family Archives.

61. Gennie Adams letter to Robert DeWeese, undated, DeWeese Family Archives.

62. Terry Karson, *Gennie DeWeese Retrospective* (Missoula, MT: Art Museum of Missoula, 1996), n.p.

63. DeWeese, in *Spirit of Modernism*, n.p.

64. Ludwig Wittgenstein, *Philosophical Investigations* (West Sussex: Blackwell Publishing, 1953), 36.

65. Elizabeth Clymer Okerbloom, "Hoyt Sherman's Experimental Work in the Field of Visual Form," *College Art Journal* 3, no. 4 (1944): 143–147.

66. Sherman, *Drawing by Seeing*, 31.

67. Terry Karson, essay in *Robert DeWeese: A Retrospective* (Billings: Yellowstone Art Center, 1991), n.p.

68. Rudy Autio, "Oral History 1802" (Montana Historical Society, 1998).

69. McConnell, *Montana Collection.*

70. McConnell, *Montana Collection.*

71. Dennis O'Leary, *Robert DeWeese: Work since 1949* (Bozeman: Montana State University, 1979), n.p.

72. Terry Karson, "Curator's Statement," in Dragonfly, Mills, Parsons, Rankin, et al., *DeWeese's Legacy*, n.p.

73. Karson, "Curator's Statement," in *DeWeese's Legacy*, n.p.

74. Many Renaissance painters, like Titian, used mythology as subjects of their work.

75. Dadaism was a literary and visual art movement that preceded Surrealism. The Dadaists felt that chance played a large role in accessing the subconscious and thus a universal truth.

76. Jim Reineking, essay in Dragonfly, Mills, Parsons, Rankin, et al., *DeWeese's Legacy*, n.p.

77. D. M. Forbes, essay in Robert DeWeese, *Robert DeWeese: A Retrospective* (Yellowstone Art Center, 1991), n.p.

78. Forbes, *Robert DeWeese: A Retrospective.*

79. Elizabeth Guheen, essay in *Robert DeWeese: A Look Ahead* (Helena: Holter Museum of Art, 2006), n.p.

80. Robert DeWeese, University of Iowa notebook, 1946. DeWeese Family Archives.

81. Robert DeWeese, "On Painting," in Dragonfly, Mills, Parsons, Rankin, et al., *DeWeese's Legacy*, n.p.

82. DeWeese, "On Painting."

83. DeWeese, "On Painting."

84. Robert DeWeese, *Robert DeWeese: A Retrospective* (Billings: Yellowstone Art Center, 1991), n.p.

85. Robert DeWeese, *Robert DeWeese. A Retrospective.*

86. The DeWeese family gave me access to Robert DeWeese's University of Iowa graduate school notebooks. DeWeese Family Archives.

87. Ibid.

88. Wittgenstein, *Philosophical Investigations,* 36.

89. Robert DeWeese's University of Iowa graduate school notebooks.

90. Rudy Autio, essay in *Robert DeWeese: A Retrospective*, n.p.

91. Rudy Autio, *Robert DeWeese: A Retrospective.*

92. Mark Stevens, "Art under the Big Sky," *Newsweek*, October 31, 1983, 98–100.

93. Marjorie Smith, "A Life in Art," *Yokoi* 1, no. 3 (1991): 37–40.

94. Gennie DeWeese, radio interview with Susan DeCamp, August 1, 2001. Yellowstone Public Radio Archives. Cassette tape in author's possession.

95. Tina DeWeese, e-mail correspondence with author, November 2019.

96. Gennie DeWeese, *Gennie DeWeese: A Retrospective* (Missoula, MT: Art Museum of Missoula, 1996), n.p.

97. G. DeWeese, *Gennie DeWeese: A Retrospective.*

98. G. DeWeese, *Gennie DeWeese: A Retrospective.*

99. Tina DeWeese, e-mail correspondence with author, November 2019.

100. McConnell, *Montana Collection,* 37.

101. McConnell, *Montana Collection,* 37.

102. Dada Documentaries, *Gennie DeWeese* (Missoula, MT: Dada Documentaries, Missoula Art Museum, 2000).

103. Terry Jimmerson, dir., *I Just Paint What I See* (Missoula, MT: Dada Documentaries, Missoula Art Museum, 1996).

104. Gennie DeWeese, *Gennie DeWeese: A Retrospective.*

105. Karson, *Gennie DeWeese: A Retrospective.*

106. Gennie DeWeese, "Curator's Statement," *Women's Work* (Miles City: Custer County Art Center, 1989), n.p.

107. DeWeese, "Curator's Statement," *Women's Work.*

108. Harvey Hamburgh, "McAuslan Works Shown," *Bozeman Daily Chronicle,* April 19, 1985, A7.

109. Hamburgh, "McAuslan Works Shown."

110. Rafael Chacon, *Rediscovering Helen McAuslan: Montana Modernist* (Missoula, MT: University of Montana, 2001).

111. Merriam, *Arts in Montana,* 40–42.

112. Merriam, *Arts in Montana,* 40–42.

113. Gennie DeWeese, *Images, Memories and a Few Comments* (Bozeman: Museum of the Rockies, 1972). Exhibition catalog.

CONCLUSION

1. Philip Deloria, *Becoming Mary Sully* (Seattle: University of Washington Press, 2019), 148.

2. Tina DeWeese, e-mail to author, 2019.

3. DeWeese, e-mail to author.

4. DeWeese, e-mail to author.

5. DeWeese, e-mail to author.

6. Rudy Autio, *It Comes around Again* (Missoula, MT: Rattlesnake Valley Press, 2019), 18.

BIBLIOGRAPHY

PRIMARY SOURCES

Autio, Rudy. "Oral History 1802," November 3, 1998. Transcript through the Montana Historical Society, Helena.

DeWeese, Robert. "University of Iowa Notebooks." DeWeese Family Archives, 1946.

DeWeese, Robert, and Gennie Adams. "Correspondences." Letters from 1942–1946. DeWeese Family Archives.

DeWeese, Tina. In-person interview with author, February 7, 2019. Transcript in possession of author.

DeWeese, Tina. Personal e-mails to author, November 22, 2019.

Forbes, Donna. Interview with author, October 7, 2017. Transcript in possession of author.

Jahnke, Joel. In-person interview with author, June 7, 2019. Transcript in possession of author.

Johnson, Isabelle. Letter to Terry Melton. Absarokee, September 11, 1971. Yellowstone Art Museum Archives.

Jussila, Neil. Phone interview by author, June 23, 2016. Transcript in possession of author.

Karson, Terry. "Oral History with Bill Stockton, 1994." Interview recordings in possession of Gilles Stockton.

Kohl, Seena B. "Oral History with Elvia Stockton." July 17, 2001. Transcript available through the Montana Historical Society, Helena.

McConnell, Gordon. Telephone interview by author, March 21, 2019. Transcript in possession of author.

Melton, Terry. Letter to Dennis Gould, Director, Smithsonian Institute. Salem: Oregon Arts Commission, September 16, 1971.

Melton, Terry. Notes from his unpublished memoir. Salem, March 29, 2019.

Melton, Terry. Personal correspondence with author, March 29, 2019.

Stockton, Bill. Interview by Marie-Laure Pelosse. Family Documentary, December 4, 2017. Stockton Family Archives.

Stockton, Gilles. Telephone interview by author, July 2, 2019. Transcript in possession of author.

Tennant, Al. Telephone interview by author, June 11, 2016. Transcript in possession of author.

Waddell, Theodore. Telephone interview by author, January 5, 2019. Transcript in possession of author.

Wilber, Jessie and Robert DeWeese. Correspondence, July 1–14, 1949. DeWeese Family Archive.

SECONDARY SOURCES

Abbott, Carl. *Imagined Frontiers: Contemporary America and Beyond.* Oklahoma City: University of Oklahoma Press, 2015.

AC Comics. *Best of the West.* AC Comics (reprint), 1950s.

Adams, Henry. "The Family Tree of Mordern [sic] Art and Ad Reinhardt." Archives of American Art Journal 52, no. 3/4 (2013).

Adams, James Truslow. *The Epic of America.* New York: Blue Ribbon Books (reprinted), 1931.

Akuma, Nyame. "The Ceramic and Society Project." *Society of Africanist Archaeologists* 46 (December 1996): 11–17.

Anderson, Herbert C. *The Life, the Times, and the Art of Branson Graves Stevenson.* Raynesford: Janher Publishing, 1979.

Anderson, Nancy K., and Frederic Remington. *The Color of Night.* Princeton and Oxford: Princeton University Press, 2003.

Ashton, Dore. *A Reading of Modern Art.* New York: Harper & Row, Icon Editions, 1967.

Askey, Ruth, and Laura Brunsman, ed. *Modernism & Beyond: Women Artists of the Pacific Northwest.* New York: Midmarch Arts Press, 1993.

Autio, Rudy. *It Comes Around Again.* Missoula: Rattlesnake Valley Press, 2019.

Baxandall, Michael. *Patterns of Intension: On the Historical Explanation of Pictures.* New Haven: Yale University Press, 1985.

Bell, Clive. *Art.* London: Chatto & Windus, 1914.

Benediktsson, Karl. "Scenophobia, Geography and the Aesthetic Politics of Landscape." *Geografiska Annaler* 89, no. 3 (2007): 203–217. http://www.jstor.org/stable/4621581.

Benjamin, Walter. *Illuminations.* New York: Schocken Books, 1968.

Benjamin, Walter. *The Work of Art in the Age of Mechanical Reproduction.* New York: Harcourt Brace Janovich, 1968.

Berger, John. *Ways of Seeing.* London: Penguin Books, 1972.

Bragg, Addison. "Western? Who—me?" *Billings Gazette,* December 5, 1971.

Braha, Dan, Marcus A. M. De Aguiar, and Lidia Adriana Braunstein. "Voting Contagion: Modeling and Analysis of a Century of U.S. Presidential Elections." *PLoS ONE* 12, no. 5 (2017): E0177970.

Brandow, Todd, and William A. Ewing. *Edward Steichen: Lives in Photography.* New York: W.W. Norton, 2007.

Brown, Milton. *The Story of the Armory Show.* New York: Joseph H. Hirshhorn Foundation, 1963.

Bunkse, Edmunds Valdemars. "Feeling is Believing, or Landscape as a Way of Being in the World." *Geografiska Annaler* 89, no. 3 (2007): 219–231. http://www.jstor.org/stable/4621582.

Butler, Judith. "Performative Acts and Gender Constitution." In *The Feminism and Visual Culture Reader,* edited by Amelia Jones, 392–401. New York: Routledge, 2003.

Butte Public Library. *Montana's Art and Her Artists.* Butte: Butte Public Library, 1940.

Bywaters, Jerry. "Otis Dozier: Growth and Maturity of a Texas Artist." *Southwest Review* 42, no. 1 (1957): 33–40.

Campbell, Neil. *The Cultures of the American New West.* Edinburgh: Edinburgh University Press, 1957.

Casey, Edward S. *Getting Back into Place*. Bloomington: University of Indiana Press, 1993.

Cather, Willa. *O Pioneers!* Milwaukee: Wiseblood Books, 1913.

Chacon, Rafael. *Rediscovering Helen McAuslan: Montana Modernist*. Missoula, MT: University of Montana, 2001.

Chambers, Gus, dir. *C. M. Russell and the American West*. Missoula, MT: Montana PBS, 2017. DVD.

Cheney, Martha Candler. *Modern Art in America*. New York: McGraw-Hill, 1939.

Collingwood, Robin George. *The Principles of Art*. Oxford: Oxford University Press, 1938.

Corn, Wanda. *The Great American Thing: Modern Art and National Identity, 1915–1935*. Berkeley: University of California Press, 1999.

Council, Montana Arts. "2003 Governor's Award for the Arts." Helena: Montana Arts Council, 2003.

Cozzolino, Robert. *The Female Gaze: Women Artists Making Their World*. Philadelphia: Pennsylvania Academy of the Fine Arts, 2012.

Cronin, William. "Telling Tales on Canvas." In *Discovering Lands, Invented Pasts*, 37–87. New Haven: Yale University Press, 1992.

Dada Documentaries. *Gennie DeWeese*. Missoula, MT: Dada Documentaries, Missoula Art Museum, 2000.

Danto, Arthur. "The Artworld." *The Journal of Philosophy* 61, no. 19 (1964): 591–584.

Danto, Arthur. *What Art Is*. New Haven & London: Yale University Press, 2013.

DeCamp, Susan. Interview with Gennie DeWeese. Yellowstone Public Radio, August 1, 2001.

Deloria, Philip. *Becoming Mary Sully*. Seattle: University of Washington Press, 2019.

Dervaux, Isabelle. "The Ten: An Avant-Garde Group in the 1930s." *Archives of American Art Journal* 31, no. 2 (1991): 14–20.

DeWeese, Gennie. "Curator's Statement." *Women's Work: The Montana Women's Centennial Art Survey Exhibition 1889–1989*. Miles City: Custer County Art Center, 1989. Published in conjunction with an exhibition of the same title.

DeWeese, Gennie. *Gennie DeWeese Retrospective*. Missoula: Missoula Museum Art Museum, 1996. Published in conjunction with an exhibition of the same title.

DeWeese, Gennie. "Images, Memories and a Few Comments." In *Helen McAuslan Drawings Catalog*. Bozeman: Museum of the Rockies, 1972: 4–7. Published in conjunction with an exhibition of the same title.

DeWeese, Robert. *Robert DeWeese: A Retrospective*. Billings: Yellowstone Art Center, 1991. Published in conjunction with an exhibition of the same title.

Dewey, John. *Art as Experience*. New York: Penguin Group, 1934.

Dickey, Tina. *Color Creates Light: Studies with Hans Hofmann*. Salt Spring Island, B.C.: Trilistar Books, 2011.

Dippie, Brian. *Charles M. Russell Word Painter: Letters 1887–1926*. Fort Worth: Amon Carter Museum, 1993.

Doss, Erika. *Twentieth Century American Art*. Oxford: Oxford University Press, 2002.

Dove, Mourning. *Cogewea the Half-Blood*. Lincoln: University of Nebraska Press, 1927.

Dragonfly, David, Wes Mills, Neil Parsons, Jerry Rankin, James Reineking, and Markus Stangl. *DeWeese's Legacy*. Helena: Holter Museum of Art, 2006.

Etulain, Richard. *Reimagining the Modern American West: A Century of Fiction, History, and Art.* Tucson: University of Arizona Press, 1996.

Ewers, J. C. *Blackfeet Indian Tipis: Design and Legend.* Bozeman: Museum of the Rockies, 1976.

Falino, Jennine. *Crafting Modernism.* New York: Museum of Arts and Design, 2012.

Flores, Dan. *Visions of the Big Sky: Painting and Photographing the Northern Rocky Mountain West.* Oklahoma City: University of Oklahoma Press, 2010.

Folk, Thomas. "Frances Senska: Studio Potter," American Ceramics 8, no. 2 (1990): 34–39.

Forni, Silvia. "Containers of Life: Pottery and Social Relations in the Grassfields (Cameroon)." In "Ceramic Arts in Africa." Special issue, *African Arts* 40, no. 1 (Spring 2007): 42–53.

Foster, Hal. "The Primitive Unconscious of Modern Art." *October* 34 (Autumn 1985): 45–70.

Foster, Hal, Rosalind Krauss, Yve-Alain Bois, Benjamin H.D. Buchloh, and David Joselit. *Art Since 1900, Volume 1.* London and New York: Thames and Hudson, 2004.

Foucault, Michel. *Power/Knowledge: Selected Interviews and Other Writings, 1972–1977.* New York: Pantheon, 1980.

Gabriel, Mary. *Ninth Street Women.* New York: Little Brown, 2018.

Gibson, Ann Eden. *Abstract Expressionism, Other Politics.* New Haven: Yale University Press, 1997.

Gilligan, Carol. *In a Different Voice.* Cambridge: Harvard University Press, 1982.

Gombrich, Ernest. *Art and Illusion.* Princeton: Princeton University Press, 1960.

Goodrich, Lloyd. *Pioneers of Modern Art in America.* New York: Frederick A. Praeger, 1963.

Greenberg, Clement. "Modernist Painting." In *Clement Greenberg: The Collected Essays and Criticism, Volume 4: Modernism with a Vengeance, 1957–1969,* 85–93. Chicago: University of Chicago Press, 1993.

Guheen, Elizabeth. "Jessie Wilber Retrospective." In *Jessie Wilber.* Bozeman: Montana State University, 1991. Published in conjunction with an exhibition of the same title.

Guheen, Elizabeth. "A Look Ahead." In *Robert DeWeese: A Look Ahead.* Helena: Holter Museum of Art, 2006. Published in conjunction with an exhibition of the same title.

Guilbaut, Serge. *How New York Stole the Idea of Modern Art.* Chicago: University of Chicago Press, 1983.

Hamburgh, Harvey. "McAuslan Work Shown." *Bozeman Daily Chronicle,* April 19, 1985.

Harrison, Charles, and Paul Wood. *Art in Theory, 1900–2000: An Anthology of Changing Ideas.* 2nd ed. Malden, MA: Blackwell Publishing, 2003.

Harrison, Helen A. "Arthur G. Dove and the Origins of Abstract Expressionism." *American Art* 12, no. 1 (1998): 66–83.

Held, Peter. *A Ceramic Continuum.* Seattle: University of Washington Press, 2001.

Hess, Barbara. *Abstract Expressionism.* Cologne: Taschen, 2016.

Heydt, Stephanie Mayer. *Art of the American Frontier: From the Buffalo Bill Center of the West.* New Haven: Yale University Press, 2013.

Hofmann, Hans. *Search for the Real and other Essays.* Andover: Addison Gallery of American Art, 1948.

Holmes, Krys. *Montana: Stories of the Land.* Helena: Montana Historical Society, 2008.

Jackson, Steve. "Frances Senska: A Biography." In *Frances Senska: A Life in Art*, n.p. Helena: Holter Museum of Art, 2004. Published in conjunction with an exhibition of the same title.

Jimmerson, Terry, dir. *I Just Paint What I See.* 1996; Missoula, MT: Dada Documentaries, Missoula Art Museum.

Johnson, Dorothy. *The Hanging Tree.* Lincoln: University of Nebraska Press, 1942.

Johnson, Isabelle. *For What Is the Amateur Painter Working?* Missoula, MT: Montana Institute of the Arts, 1952.

Johnson, Isabelle. *The Wonderful World of Color* (Missoula, MT: Montana Institute for the Arts, 1963).

Johnson, Isabelle, Drew Bennett, Robyn G. Peterson, Bob Durden, Donna M Forbes, Patricia Vettel-Becker, Peter Halstead, and Theodore Waddell. *A Lonely Business: Isabelle Johnson's Montana.* Billings: Yellowstone Art Museum, 2015.

Junker, Patricia. *Modernism in the Pacific Northwest.* Seattle: Seattle Art Museum, 2014.

Karmel, Pepe, and Kirk Varnedoe. *Jackson Pollock, New Approaches.* New York: Museum of Modern Art, 1999.

Karson, Terry. *Gennie DeWeese Retrospective.* Missoula: Missoula Art Museum, 1996. Published in conjunction with an exhibition of the same title.

Karson, Terry. *Interview with Bill Stockton.* Grass Range, Montana: Dada Documentaries, 1994. Stockton Family Archives.

Katz, Vincent. *Black Mountain College: Experiment in Art.* Boston: MIT Press, 2016.

Kittredge, William, ed. *Last Best Place: A Montana Anthology.* Seattle: University of Washington Press, 1990.

Korsmeyer, Carolyn. *Aesthetics: The Big Questions.* Malden: Blackwell Publishing, 1998.

Lambert, Kirby. "Through the Artist's Eye: The Paintings and Photography of R. E. DeCamp." *Montana the Magazine of Western History* 49, no. 2 (1999): 40–49.

Laurentis, Teresa De. "Upping the Anti [Sic] in Feminist Theory." In *Figures of Resistance: Essays in Feminist Theory*, edited by Patricia White, 183–198. Chicago: University of Illinois Press, 2007.

Leja, Michael. *Looking Askance: Skepticism and American Art from Eakins to Duchamp.* Berkeley: University of California Press, 2004.

Lewthwaite, Stephanie. *A Contested Art: Modernism and Mestizaje in New Mexico.* Oklahoma City: University of Oklahoma Press, 2015.

Limerick, Patricia. *Legacy of Conquest.* Boston: W.W. Norton (reprint), 1987.

Logan, Frederick M. "Up Date '75, Growth in American Art Education." *National Art Education Association* 17, no. 1 (1975): 7–16. DOI: 10.1080/00393541.1975.11651359.

Loomis, Silvia. "Archives of American Art." http://www.aaa.si.edu/collections/interviews/oral-history-interview-with-otis-dozier-13261.

Lovoos, Janice. "The California School of Watercolor." *The American Artist* 51, no. 537 (1987): 62.

Lubin, David M. *Grand Illusions.* London and New York: Oxford University Press, 2016.

Malone, Michael P., Richard B. Roeder, and William Lang. *Montana: A History of Two Centuries.* Seattle: University of Washington Press, 1976.

Marks, Steven. "Abstract Art and the Regeneration of Mankind." *New England Review* 24, no. 1 (2003): 53–79.

Marter, Joan. *Women of Abstract Expression.* New Haven: Yale University Press, 2016.

Mavigliano, George J. "The Federal Art Project." *Art Education* 37, no. 3 (1984): 26–30.

McConnell, Gordon. *Isabelle Johnson: Life and Legacy.* Billings: Yellowstone Art Museum, n.d. Published in conjunction with an exhibition of the same title.

McConnell, Gordon. *Making Connections.* Billings: Yellowstone Art Museum, 2005.

McConnell, Gordon. *The Montana Collection.* Billings: Yellowstone Art Museum, 1998. Published in conjunction with an exhibition of the same title.

McConnell, Gordon. *The Rural Avant-Garde.* Clearmont: The Ucross Foundation, April 2002. Published in conjunction with an exhibition of the same title.

McNay, John Thomas. "Breaking the Copper Collar: The Sale of the Anconda Newspaper and the Professionalization of Journalism in Montana." Master's thesis, University of Montana, Missoula, 1991.

Melton, Terry. Interview with Isabelle Johnson (transcript). Billings: Yellowstone Art Museum, n.d.

Melton, Terry. Interview with Isabelle Johnson. In *Montana Portraits.* Montana Media Productions, Yellowstone Art Museum, n.d.

Melton, Terry, Kirk Robertson, and Ben Mitchell. *Theodore Waddell: Into the Horizon.* Seattle: University of Washington Press, 2001.

Mentzer, Elizabeth. "Made in Montana: Montana's Post Office Murals." *Montana: The Magazine of Western History* 53, no. 3 (2003): 44–53. http://www.jstor.org.proxybz.lib.montana.edu/stable/4520536.

Merriam, H. G., ed. *The Arts in Montana.* Missoula: Mountain Press Publishing, 1977.

Mitchell, Ben. *The Most Difficult Journey.* Billings: Yellowstone Art Museum, 2002.

Moholy-Nagy, Laszlo. *Vision in Motion.* Chicago: P. Theobald, 1947.

Montana Exponent. "Enrollment Hit an All-Time High." Bozeman: Montana State College, October 10, 1946.

Montana Exponent. "Wilber Exhibits Art Works." Bozeman: Montana State College, April 14, 1949.

Montana Media Productions. "Montana Portraits." Transcript of interview. Billings: Yellowstone Art Museum.

Montana Standard. "Timeline Outlines Montana Department of Transportation History." June 6, 2013.

Morgan, Edwin. "American Art at Mid-Century." *American Quarterly* 1, no. 4 (1949): 326–330.

Neff, Bill. *Art All the Time.* Bozeman, KUSM-TV, 1997.

Neff, Emily Ballew. *The Modern West: American Landscapes, 1890–2000.* Seattle: University of Washington Press, 2006.

Newby, Rick. *The Rocky Mountain Region: The Greenwood Encyclopedia of American Regional Cultures.* Westport: Greenwood Press, 2004.

Newby, Rick. *Theodore Waddell, My Montana.* Helena: Drumlummon Institute, 2017.

Newby, Rick, Chere Juisto, Patricia Failing, and Janet Koplos. *A Ceramic Continuum.* Helena: Holter Museum of Art, 2001.

Nochlin, Linda. "Why Have There Been No Great Women Artists?" In *The Feminism and Visual Culture Reader,* edited by Amelia Jones, 229–232. New York: Routledge, 2003.

Norton, Anne. *95 Theses on Politics, Culture & Method.* New Haven: Yale University Press, 2004.

O'Connor, Francis V. *WPA: Art for the Millions.* Boston: New York Graphic Society, 1973.

O'Leary, Dennis. *Robert DeWeese: Work since 1949.* Bozeman: Montana State University, 1979.

Okerbloom, Elizabeth Clymer. "Hoyt Sherman's Experimental Work in the Field of Visual Form." *College Art Journal* 3, no. 4 (1944): 143–147.

Paris Gibson Museum. *Spirit of Modernism.* Kalispell, MT: Paris Gibson Museum, 1987. Exhibition catalog. http://www.deweeseart.com/new-page-25.

Pelosse, Marie-Laure. *Bill Stockton.* Video available from Stockton Family Archives, 2017.

Platt, Susan Noyes. *Modernism in the 1920s.* Ann Arbor: UMI Research Press, 1985.

Pollock, Griselda. *Vision & Difference.* London: Routledge, 1988.

Princenthal, Nancy. *Agnes Martin: Her Life and Art.* London: Thomas and Hudson, 2015.

Prown, Jules David. *Discovered Lands Invented Pasts: Transforming Visions of the American West.* New Haven: Yale University Press, 1992.

Reintjes, Brandon, et al. *Frances Senska: A Life in Art.* Helena: Holter Museum of Art, 2004.

Rose, Barbara. *Art Since 1900.* New York: Praeger Publishers, 1975.

Rosenberg, Harold. *The Tradition of the New.* New York: New York Horizon Press, 1960.

Saab, Joan. *For the Millions: American Art and Culture between the Wars.* Philadelphia: University of Pennsylvania Press, 2004.

Sandler, Irving. *The Triumph of American Painting.* New York: Praeger Publishers, 1970.

Sandweiss, Martha A. *Print the Legend.* New Haven: Yale University Press, 2002.

Santayana, George. *Reason in Art.* New York: Scribner's Sons, 1905.

Schor, Mira. "Patrilineage." In *The Feminism and Visual Culture Reader,* edited by Amelia Jones, 249–255. New York: Routledge, 2003.

Schreyach, Michael. "Re-created Flatness: Hans Hofmann's Concept of the Picture Plan as a Medium of Expression." *The Journal of Aesthetic Education* 49, no. 1 (2015): 44–67.

Schwab, Tim, Frances Senska, and Nanette L. Laitman. *Evolving Forms.* Documentation Project for Craft Decorative Arts in America. Bozeman: Montana State University, 1978.

Schwarz, Dean, and Geraldine Schwarz. *Marguerite Wildenhain and the Bauhaus: An Eyewitness Anthology.* Decorah, Iowa: South Bear Press, 2007.

Secor, Walter. "Building Boom for Bozeman All Ready Except For Materials; 100 Cars of Lumber Needed." *Bozeman Daily Chronicle,* March 16, 1946.

Senska, Frances. Interview by Donna Forbes. *Oral History,* Smithsonian Archives of American Art, April 16, 2001.

Schapiro, Meyer. *Modern Art 19th and 20th Centuries.* New York: George Braziller, Inc., 2011.

Senska, Frances. *Jessie Wilber.* Missoula, MT: The Arts in Montana, 1977.

Sherman, Hoyt. *Drawing by Seeing.* New York: Hinds, Hayden & Eldredge, 1947.

Shipp, Steve. *American Art Colonies: 1850–1930.* Westport: Greenwood Press, 1996.

Smith, Majorie. "Frances Senska." *Ceramics Monthly* 7 (September 2002): 50–53.

Smith, Marjorie. "A Life in Art." *Yokoi* 1, no. 3 (1991): 37–40.

Sorkin, Jenni. "Craft-in-Residence." In Crafting A Continuum: Re-Thinking Contemporary Craft, edted by Peter Held and Heather Sealy Lineberry, 25–29. Tempe, AZ: Arizona State University, 2013. https://www.academia.edu/7881046/Craft_in_ Residence_The_Open_Studio_Network.

Sorkin, Jenni. *Live Form.* Chicago: University of Chicago Press, 2016.

Stevens, Mark. "Art under the Big Sky." *Newsweek,* October 31, 1983.

Stockton, Bill. "Paris 1948—the End of an Era." In *The Arts in Montana*, edited by H. G. Merriam, 2–8. Missoula: Mountain Press Publishing, 1977.

Stockton, Bill. *Today I Baled Some Hay to Feed the Sheep the Coyotes Eat.* Helena: Falcon Press, 1983.

Trachtenberg, Alan. *The Incorporation of America.* New York: Hili and Wang, 1982.

Truettner, William H. *The West as America: Reinterpreting Images of the Frontier.* Washington, D.C.: Smithsonian Institute Press, 1991.

Tuan, Yi-Fu. *Space and Place: The Perspective of Experience.* Minneapolis: University of Minnesota Press, 2011.

Udall, Sharyn. *Carr, O'Keefe, Kahlo: Places of Their Own.* New Haven: Yale University Press, 2001.

University of Montana. *Montana Impressions.* Missoula, MT: University of Montana, 1999. Exhibition catalog.

US Department of Commerce. *Bureau of the Census.* US Department of Commerce, 2010.

US Department of Commerce. *Bureau of the Census.* US Department of Commerce, 1950.

Varnedoe, Kirk. *Jackson Pollock: New Approaches.* New York: Museum of Modern Art, 1999.

Wardle, Marian. *Branding the American West, Paintings and Films, 1900–1950.* Oklahoma City: University of Oklahoma Press, 2016.

Wilber, Jessie. *Jessie Wilber: Retrospective.* Bozeman: Montana State University, 1983.

Wildenhain, Marguerite. *Pottery: Form and Expression.* Palo Alto: American Crafts Council/Pacific Books, 1959.

Wilson, H. W. "11 Montana Potters." *Studio Potter* 8, no. 1 (1979): 33–46.

Wittgenstein, Ludwig. *Philosophical Investigations.* West Sussex: Blackwell Publishing, 1953.

Yellowstone Art Museum. *Isabelle Johnson: A Retrospective.* Billings: Yellowstone Art Museum, 1986

INDEX

PAGE NUMBERS IN ITALIC REFER TO ILLUSTRATIONS.

A

About Wiley (R. DeWeese), 105
Abstract Expressionism, 3, 30, 33, 46–47, 49, 56–57, 90, 92, 117–18; definition of, 97–98
Academie de la Grande Chaumiere, xiv, 30, 41, 135
Aggressive learning, 52
Albers, Joseph, 47, 53
American Artists' Professional League, 85, 96
Amon Carter Museum of Art, 18
Anaconda Company, 98
Anaconda Standard, The, 98
Aniline Dye Brush Drawing (G. DeWeese), *128*
Archie Bray Foundation, 1, 46, 83–84, 86, 93, 96; first summer, 84–85; opening, 85
Aronson, J. Hugo, 98
Art Students League, 1, 13, 41, 48–49
Art USA, 35
Artist of the Year award, 64
Auction of Original Western Art Show, 27
Autio, Lela, 127, *137*
Autio, Rudy, 46, 56, 84–85, 105, 116, 135–36
Autumn on the Stillwater (Johnson), *26*, 27–28

B

Babessi culture, 77
Bar at the Folies Bergere, A (Manet), 64
Bare Trees (G. DeWeese), 119–20, *120*
Bauhaus Movement, xiv, 46–48, 53, 55, 73, 77–79, 83, 101, 135; ideas behind, 47, 91
Baxandall, Michael, 101
Beall Art Center, 127
Bear Canyon clay, 82
Benediktsson, Karl, 11–12
Benjamin, Walter, 3
Berger, John, 3–4
Berkeley School of Art, 96
Berman, Eugene, 65
Berry, Wendell, 11
Between Three Forks and Totem (DeWeese), 104, *106*
Billings Gazette, The, 98
Billings High School, xiv
Bill's Lil' Trees (DeWeese), 104

Birds and Trees (Wilber), 65–66, *67*
Black Boy, Cecil, 63
Black Mountain College, 53, 96
Blackfeet Reservation, 63–64
Blackfeet Tipis, 63; silkscreen series, 63–64
Bozeman High School, 46
Branch Bottle Weed Pot (Senska), 77, *78*, 81
Braque, Georges, 30, 48
Bray, Archie, 1, 83–84
Bridgeman, George, 14
Broadmoor Art Academy, 54
Bryson, Ken, 95
Bryson, Mary (Tata), 95
Buffalo Bill Center of the West, 35, 37
Bunkse, Edmunds Valdemars, 11
Burke, Kenneth, 115–16
Bush, George H. W., 107
Butte Daily Post, The, 98
Butte Public Library, 6
Butterfield, Deborah, 127
Bywaters, Jerry, 54

C

C. M. Russell Museum, 97
C.M. Russell and the American West, 7
Cage, John, 96
Calder, Alexander, 30
California Labor School, xiv, 47, 56
Calves, Winter (Johnson), 23, *24*
Cameroon, xiv, 73; Basa dialect, 80; clay, 77; dedication to functional objects, 73; pottery, 74, 77, 83
Campeau, Kay, 93
Campeau, Ray, 6, 46, 56, 92–93
Carmina Burana (Orff), 118
Casey, Edward S., 11
Cats in a Garden (Wilber), 65, *66*
Cezanne, Paul, 2, 9, 14–15, 17, 21, 27–28, 38, 46–48, 50, 52–55, 86, 117, 127, 135
Chacon, Rafael, 127–28
Charles Russell: Word Painter (Dippie), 7
Chicago Art Institute, 1
Chicken Wine Set (Senska), *76*

Circus Ties (R. DeWeese), 110–11, *112*
Clear Cut (G. DeWeese), 124–25, *126*
Clover Year (G. DeWeese), *122*, 123
Cold War, 3, 98, 135
Collages (R. DeWeese), *113*
College of Great Falls, 1, 85
Colorado Springs Fine Art Center, 14
Colorado State Teachers' College, xiv, 61
Colorado State University, 91
Columbia University, xiii, 1, 13, 25, 41, 96; School of Painting and Sculpture, xiii–xiv, 14
Communism, 3, 135
Concerning the Spiritual in Art (Kandinsky), 118
Conrad, Cyril, 94
Conrade, Helen, 128
consumerism and art, 96–98
Conversion of St. Paul, The (Stockton), 41, *43*
Conway, Dan, 6–7
Cranbrook Academy of Art, xiv, 47, 53, 56
Cubism, 17, 30, 47–48, 54–55, 61–62
Cunningham, Merce, 96

D

Dada, xiii, 107
Dallas Museum of Fine Arts School, 54
Danto, Arthur, 116
Davis, Velma, 65
Day of the Cattlemen's Picnic, The (Wilber), 61
De Kooning, Willem, 57, 111, 115, 117, 135
De Stael, Nicholas, 118
Dean, Max, 8
DeCamp, Ralph, 6
DeLoria, Philip, 133
DeNiro, Robert Sr., 57
Detroit Institute of the Arts, 101
Dew, James, 97–98
DeWeese, Gennie Adams, xiii–xv, 1, 2, 4, 8–9, 33, 49, 93–96, 105, 116–31, 133–36, *137*; birth, xv; cattle markers, xiii, 124; education, xv, 52, 99, 117; "Equal Studio Time" dictum, 117, 134; correspondences with Robert DeWeese, 100–101, 117, 135; experiments with media, 118; first meeting Robert DeWeese, 98–99; Fourth of July parties, 94–95; Governor's Award for the Arts, 117; honorary degree, xv, 117; landscapes, 49; marriage to Robert DeWeese, xv, 101; milk carton paper, 124; move to Montana, 94, 101, 117; non-objective paintings, 49, 50, *51*, 99, 117, 119–23, 135; painting, 46; paintings, 1; political involvement/feminism, 98, 126–29; scrolls, 123; studio, 96, 135; teaching, xv, 46, 55, 91–93; themes in work, 119–25, 134–35
DeWeese, Josh, 46, 81–82

DeWeese, Robert, xiii, 1, 2, 4, 33, 58, 93–94, 96, 101–17, 131, 133–36; birth, xv; collages, *102*, 103, 107, 110, *113*; correspondences with Gennie, 100–101, 117, 135; death, xv, 104, 107, 117; education, xv, 45, 52, 99, 101, 111; first meeting Gennie, 98–99; Fourth of July parties, 94–95; Governor's Award for the Arts, xv, 117; marriage to Gennie, xv, 101; military service, xv, 99–101; milk carton paper, 124; mixed media work, 107, 109; move to Montana, 94, 101; paintings, 104, 106–7, 110–15; politics, 107, 134; process, 114–15; problem-solving in art, 101, 103; "Responsibility to Respond" philosophy, 103; sketches, xiii, 103–5; studio, 110; teaching, xv, 5, 45–46, 55, 57–59, 91–92, 99, 106, 115–17; themes in work, 104–6, 110, 134; tie series, 110–11, 134
DeWeese, Tina, 71–72, 98, 117, 118–19, 134–35
DeWeese's Legacy, 106
Dewey, John, 45, 55–57, 59; pragmatic environment, 59; unified theory of education, 55–56
DeYong, Joe, 6, 7
Dickey, Tina, 50
Diebenkom, Richard, 57
Dippie, Brian, 7
"Dirty Thirties, The," 31
Dozier, Otis, 45–46, 54, 65, 72
Drawing by Seeing (Sherman), 52–53
Dusk (Stockton), *39*

E

East Fiddler's Creek (Johnson), *19*, 21
Eastern Montana College, xiv, 5, 15, 55, 91–92; Department of Fine Arts, 91; Department of Humanities, 91
Einstein, Albert, 48
"Eisenhower Equilibrium," 98
Ernst, Max, 107
Experiential color, 50
Exposition de l'Art Moderne, 73
Ewers, John C., 63

F

Faded Roses (Stockton), *36*, 38
Federal Art Project (FAP), 89–90
Figure Dancing (R. DeWeese), *104*
Figures (Meloy), 96
Fine Arts Center (Colorado Springs), 54
Fine Arts Center (Dallas), 54
Flash Lab, 52, 99, 103, 119
Flight (Red Boy) (R. DeWeese), 107, *108*, 111
Forbes, Donna, 8, 12–13, 18, 21, 25, 41–42
Franjevic, Jack, 1
Frankenthaler, Helen, 118
Freud, Sigmund, 48, 79
Fromberg High School, 13

G

G.I. Bill, 5, 30, 56, 63, 89, 91–92, 101, 131
Gazette, 27
GB DeWeese Gallery, 117
Glacier National Park, 63
Gombrich, Ernest, 79–80, 83
Gottlieb, Adolph, 64
Gould, Dennis, 18
Governor's Award for the Arts, xiv, xv, 25, 41, 64, 117
Graves, Morris, 65
Great Depression, 28, 31, 61, 84, 89, 117
Greenberg, Clement, 2, 71, 74, 98
Grinnell College, xiv, 1
Gropius, Walter, 47, 78–79
Grotell, Maija, xiv, 47, 56, 81
Guheen, Elizabeth, 110

H

Hamada, Shoji, 86
Hamm, Stacy, 64
Hannon, Olga Ross, 63, 90
Harris, Paul, 96
Heath, Edith, xiv, 47, 56
Helena Independent Record, The, 98
Herr, Gordon, 53
Herr, Jane, 53
Hoch, Hannah, 107
Hofmann, Hans, 30, 38, 45–46, 118, 135; "push-pull" color theory, 48–50, 118; teaching, 50, 52
Holter Museum of Art, 74
Home Ranch (Johnson), *22*, 23
Hungarian Partridges (Senska), *60*
Huns (Wilber), 61, *62*, 64
Huns (on a pond) (Wilber), 66, *68*

I

Illinois Institute of Technology, Institute of Design, 47–48
Impressionism, 2, 4, 15, 111, 117
Invisible Core, The (Wildenhain), 81
Iran-Contra Affair, 107
It Comes Around Again (Autio), 135

J

Jahnke, Joel, 94–95
James, Will, 6
Jessie Wilber and Frances Senska Individual Artist Award in Ceramics, 64
Johnson, Isabelle, xiii, 1, 2, 8–9, 12, 18–20, 41–42, 46, 55, 127, 133–34; birth, xiii, 12, 13; brushwork, 23; colors, use of, 17, 23, 27; community, 25, 27; death, 25, 27–28; drawing, 15; education, xiii, 4, 13–15, 25, 49, 55, 135; in Europe, 4, 13, 15, 27, 41; friendship with Bill Stockton, 12–13, 27; Governor's Award for the Arts, xiv, 25; on the role of the artist, 17; paintings, 2, 16–17, 19–24, 26–28; ranch, xiii, 12, 15, 18, 25, 27–28, 42, 134; teaching, xiv, 13–15, 17–18, 25, 45–46, 55, 92; themes in work, 12–13, 15, 17–18, 21, 23, 25, 27, 42, 134
June Patterns (G. DeWeese), 123, *129*
Jussila, Neil, 56–58

K

Kandinsky, Wassily, 46, 53, 118
Karson, Terry, 104–6, 124
Kent State shootings, 1, 127–28
Kerkam, Earl, 57
Klee, Paul, 53
Kline, Franz, 57, 117
Knight, Val, 1
Koplos, Janet, 84
Krehan, Max, 53
Kuhn, Walter, xv

L

Landschaft, 12
Lange, Connie, 72
Leach, Bernard, 86, 96
Lewiston's Art Center, 5
Life magazine, 30
Lindley, Viola, 85
Livingston Enterprise, 98
Lo, Beth, 127
Logan, Frederick M., 91
Loos, Donna, 55
Los Angeles County Museum School, xiii
Lutz, Dan, 65

M

Magpies in a Snowstorm (Wilber), *72*
Malone, Michael, 96
Malmstrom Military Base, 98
Manet, Édouard, 64
Mansfield, Mike, 98
Marcks, Gerhard, 53
Matisse, Henri, 38, 61, 64, 111, 117, 135
McAuslan, Helen, 1, 127–29; portfolio, 128–29
McCarthyism, 3, 53, 135
McConnell, Gordon, 2, 21, 25, 27, 35, 37
McCraig, Robert, 97
Meadowlark Fund, 35
Meany, Joseph, 6

Meloy, Henry, 1, 83–84, 96
Meloy, Pete, 1, 83–84
Melton, Terry, 17–18, 25, 27, 33, 85
Minneapolis School of Art, xiv, 30, 41
Missoula Sentinel, The, 98
Missoulian, The, 98
"Modern Art" (Schapiro), 3
Modernism, 1, 3, 9, 13, 28, 41, 47–49, 61–62, 89, 116–17, 127; definition of/aspects of, 2–3, 64, 71, 74, 79, 83, 96, 97, 123; California, 65; consumerism and, 96–98, 136; politics of, 96–98
Modernism, Montana, 1–9, 21, 48, 49, 55, 71–72, 86, 92, 101, 107, 133, 135–36; development of, 2–5, 91; educational lineage, 46–47; first generation of, 12, 45, 46; students, 45; teaching, 5, 55–60; venues, 93; women artists, 8–9
"Modernist Painting" (Greenberg), 71
Modigliani, Amedeo, 61
Moholy-Nagy, László, xiv, 46–47, 55–56, 61, 73, 80, 101; on painting, 47–48
Money, Claude, 117
Montana: advertising committee, 8; avant-garde, 1–9; branding, 8; community, 5–6, 92–96, 135–36; dude ranches, 7–8; earthquakes, 84; frontier nostalgia narrative, 2, 6–8, 41, 92, 96, 116–17, 136; landscape, 11–12; mining, 8; politics, 98; population, 8; postwar, 3, 4–5, 8, 92, 133; prewar, 8, 55; public funding of art, 90–92; tourism, 7–8
Montana Arts Council, 63
Montana Centennial, 126–27
Montana Dude Ranchers' Association, 8
Montana Historical Society, 57
Montana Institute of the Arts, 5–6, 64, 71, 93, 97
Montana Institute of the Arts, 5, 15, 128
Montana Museum of Modern Art, xiii
Montana Shakespeare in the Park, 95
Montana Standard, The, 98
Montana State College (MSC), Bozeman, xiv, xv, 5, 45, 54–55, 60–62, 65, 68, 70, 73, 81–84, 90–93, 99, 101, 117, 128; Art Department, 5, 9, 48, 63, 82, 91; community, 92–96; Department of Applied Art, 94; Division of Household and Industrial Arts, 91; Herrick Hall, 82; Lewis Hall, 63; Student Union Building, 57–58; Veteran's Village, 94; Women's Home Economics Department, 5, 9, 82
Montana State University, xv, 28, 46, 64, 77, 81, 105, 117; School of Art Collection, 64
Montana Writers' Project of the Public Works of Art, 63
Moose Lodge, 95
Morin, Mary Trinitas, 1, 83, 85
Murphy, Mary, 77
Museum of Modern Art, 90
Museum of the Beartooths, 28
Museum of the Plains Indian, 63

Museum of the Rockies, 128
Musicians, The (Wilber), *70*, 71

N

National Arts Education Association, 91
National Committee on Education in the Ceramic Arts, 56
National Museum of Women's Art, 129
Naturalism, 97
Nazis, 47, 53
New Bauhaus: American School of Design, 47
New Deal, 92
New Mexico College of Agriculture and Mechanical Arts, 91
New York School, 90, 92, 111–12
New York Times, 64
Newman, Barnett, 64
Newsweek, 116
Nine Ties, Seven Chains (R. DeWeese), 110, *111*
Non-Objective Painting (G. DeWeese), 50, *51*, *119*
Norton, Anne, 89
Notes (Meloy), 96

O

O'Connell, Jerry, 90
Ohio State College, 85
Ohio State University, xv, 52, 99; Art Club, 99; Art Honorary, 99
Okerbloom, Elizabeth Clymer, 103
O'Leary, Dennis, 105
Olson, Charles, 96
"On Painting" (R. DeWeese), 112–13
Oregon Arts Commission, 18
Orff, Carl, 118
Otis Art Institute, xiii, 13–14, 46
Overlie, Mary, 46
Owls (Wilber), *69*, 71

P

passive/inattentive seeing, 52
Patterns of Intention (Baxandall), 101
Paxson, Edgar S., 6, 21, 98, 135
Payne, Charlie, 95
PBS, 7
Perceptual Unity, 52, 99, 119
photography, 2–4, 113; invention of the camera, 3; mechanical reproduction of art through, 3–4
Picasso, Pablo, 30, 47–48, 61, 111
Plains Sunset, 113, *114*
Plato, 117
plein-air painting, 2, 120
Poindexter, Everton Gentry "George," 57–58
Poindexter Collection, 57–58

Pollock, Jackson, 3, 30–31, 57, 117
Pond Farm, 47, 53, 81
Poor, Henry Vanum, xiv, 14–15
portable paint tubes, 2
Portland (R. DeWeese), 104, *105*
Portraits (Meloy), 96
Post–Impressionism, 2, 4, 21, 38, 46, 54–55, 117
Post-Modernists, 15
post office murals, xiv, 61–62, 90
Pound, Ezra, 3
problem-solving in art, 48, 80, 101
public art, 90–92
Public Works of Art Project (PWAP), xiv, 61–62
Pullman, Bill, 95

R

Rankin, Jerry, 46, 58
Rauschenberg, Robert, 96
Reagan, Ronald, 107
Realism, 97, 111
Red Willows in Winter Landscape (Johnson), *16*, 17
Reineking, James, 46, 110
Reintjes, Brandon, 73
Rembrandt, 38
Ring Necked Bottle (Senska), *75*, 76
Renoir, Pierre-Auguste, 117
River (Don't Dam It!), The (Wilber), 68, *69*, 98
River Rocks (Stockton), 37–38
Robert DeWeese: Work since 1949, 105
Robinson, Boardman, 54
Rock Formation (Stockton), *42*
Rocky Mountain College, 13
Rocky Mountain Fever Lab, 63
Rocky Mountain Spotted Fever Mural (Wilber), 63
Roosevelt, Franklin D., 89
Rothko, Mark, 64
Russell, Charles M., 6, 7, 15, 18, 21, 55, 97, 98, 112, 135; museum, 97
Russell, Nancy, 7

S

Saab, Joan, 90
Sample, Joe, 35
Sample, Miriam, 35, 37
Sandler, Irving, 90
Santayana, George, 15
Saxony Oil Company, 96
Schapiro, Meyer, 3, 21, 54
School of Arts and Crafts, 96
Schreyach, Michael, 49

Seltzer, O. C., 6
Senska, Frances, xiii, 1, 2, 4, 8, 84–85, *87*, 93–96, 127, 133, 135–37; in Africa, 73–74, 77, 83; birth, xiv; ceramics, xiii, 59–61, 73–80, 86, 105, 133–34; childhood in Cameroon, 73, 77, 83, 86; clay used in pots, 77, 82, 105, 133–34; collage work, 80; death, 64; education, xiv, 45, 47–48, 53, 56, 81, 135; in Europe, 73; gardening, 71–72; gifted pots, 77; glazes, 82–83, 133–34; Governor's Award for the Arts, xiv; lithographs, 73; military service, xiv, 9, 47, 56; move to Montana, 9, 81–82; parents, 73; printmaking, 74; process, 79–80, 82–83, 105–6; sgraffito technique, 73–74, 134; slips, 77; teaching, xiv, 2, 9, 45–46, 55–60, 73, 80–83, 91–92, 134; themes in work, 73, 76–77, 79–80, 83, 134
Servicemen's Readjustment Act of 1944, 5. *See also* G.I. Bill
sgraffito, 73–74, 134
Sheets, Millard, 65
Sherman, Hoyt, xv, 45–46, 55, 100, 103, 119; teaching, 52–53, 99, 118
Skowhegan School of Painting and Sculpture, xiv, 14, 41, 55, 135
Smithsonian Institute, 18
Snow Formation (Stockton), *32*
Socony Vacuum Oil Company, 85
Spring by Karl's Bridge (G. DeWeese), 124, *131*
Springtime in the Rockies (G. DeWeese), 123–24, *125*
Start of Spring (Stockton), 33, *34*, 35
Stevenson, Branson, 1, 83–86, 96
Stinchfield, Estelle, 61–62, 72
Stockton, Bill, xiii, xiv, 1, 2, 4, 12, 25, 27, 46, 49, 95, 98, 133–35; art shows, 35; artist statements, 29, 32; birth, xiv, 28; brushstrokes, 32; childhood, 28–29; color, use of, 38–39; creative process, 38–39, 41; death, xiv, 41; drawings, *36*, 39–41; education, xiv, 28–30, 135; in Europe, 13, 29–30, 41, 135; on Isabelle Johnson, 12–13, 18, 21, 27; Governor's Award for the Arts, xiv, 41; letters to Isabelle Johnson, 32–33; military service, xiv, 29–30; paintings, 29–35, 37–39; parents and siblings, 28, 38; ranch, xiii, xiv, 28, 30, 32, 41, 134; sculptures, 41, *43*; sign painting, xiv, 29–30; teaching, 5, 46–47; themes in work, 12–13, 28, 31–33, 35, 38, 40–42, 134
Stockton, Elvia Cirefice, xiv, 29, 30, 32–33
Stockton, Gilles, 28–30
Sun Dance ceremonies, 63
Surf Fishers (Senska), *79*, 80
Surrealism, 65, 111

T

Tall Footed Vase (Wildenhain), 80, *81*
Tennant, Al, 58–59
Texas Technological College, Lubbock, xv, 94
They Gazed on the Beartooths (Montana Memory Project), 28
Third Paris World's Fair, 2
Three Necked Vase (Wildenhain), *81*
Three Penny Opera, 95, 110

Time magazine, 86
Today I Baled Some Hay to Feed the Sheep the Coyotes Eat (Stockton), 31
Tone, Ben, 95
Trail Creek Glaze, 82
Trees, Winter (Johnson), *20*, 21
Tuan, Yi-Fu, 5, 12
Twain, Mark, 3
Tworkov, Jack, 57

U

unified theory of education, 55–56
United States Army, xiv–xv; Air Force Band, xv, 99, 101
United States Navy, xiv, 47
United States Treasury Section of Fine Arts, 90
University of California, Berkely, 46
University of Great Falls, 1
University High School, xiv
University of Iowa, xiv–xv, 101, 111
University of Michigan, xv, 99
University of Montana, xiii, 13, 46, 97
University of Southern California, xiii, 13

V

Varnedoe, Kirk, 3
VFW, 95
VFW Studio Wall (R. DeWeese), 107, *109*
Village in Winter (Stockton), 40–41
Vision in Motion (Moholy-Nagy), 80
Voulkos, Peter, 45–46, 56, 60, 82, 84–85, 96, 105

W

Waddell, Theodore, 15, 25, 35, 45–46, 55
Waiting for a Chinook (Russell), 7
Walden, Sage (Sigerson), 64
Western Painting (R. DeWeese), *102*, 103
Wilber, Jessie Spaulding, xiii, xiv, 2, 4, 8, 61–62, 83, 85, *87*, 92–96, 127, 133–35; in Africa, 74; Artist of the Year award, 64; birth, xiv; color, use of, 64; education, xiv, 45, 54, 61, 72; gardening, 71–72; Governor's Award for the Arts, xiv, 64; move to Montana, 9, 92; paintings, 60–62, 86; portrait of DeWeese family, 93; prints, xiii, 60, 63–72, 74, 86, 98; PWAP commission, xiv, 61–62; teaching, xiv, 2, 9, 45–46, 55–57, 59–62, 65, 72–73, 92, 94, 134; themes in work, 64–66, 71–73, 98, 134
Wildenhain, Marguerite, xiv, 46, 47, 55, 73, 80–81, 83; Master Potter certification, 53; teaching, 53–54, 56, 59, 81
Wilder, Mitch, 18
Wiley, Bill, 105
Willows and Mountains (Poor), 15
Winter Morning (G. DeWeese), 124, *130*

Winter Willow Grove (G. DeWeese), *121*, 123
Wittgenstein, Ludwig, 116
Wolny's Hill (One Cloud) (R. DeWeese), *115*
Woman (de Kooning), 57
Women's Work: The Montana Women's Centennial Art Survey Exhibition, 126–27, 129
Works Progress Administration, 89, 90
World War II, xiv, xv, 1, 3–6, 8, 11, 28–30, 55–56, 62, 84, 89, 91, 99, 100–101, 135; Battle of the Bulge, 29
World's Fair, 93

Y

YaBaBo pots (Senska), 73, *74*, 76–77
Yanagi, Hamada, 96
Yanagi, Soetsu, 86
Yellowstone Art Center, 8, 17, 25, 32–33, 57
Yellowstone Art Museum, 8, *12*, 13, 17, 21, 25, 27, 35, 85; Montana Collection, 37
Yellowstone National Park, 8, 29
Yellowstone River community, 71

Z

Zentz, Pat, 46
Zerbe, Karl, 14

ABOUT THE AUTHOR

Michele Corriel is an award-winning freelance art writer contributing to *Big Sky Journal, Western Art & Architecture*, and other art and culture publications in the West. She is the curatorial director for the Paul Harris and Marguerite Kirk Gallery and works with galleries and museums consulting in the area of Modern art and its effects on contemporary work. Michele holds a master's degree in art history and a PhD in American art. She is an assistant teaching professor at Montana State University.

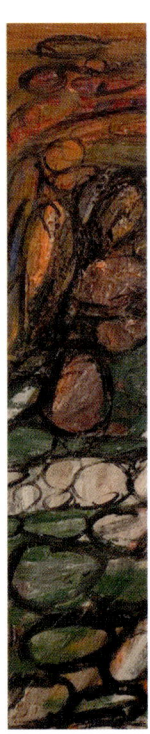
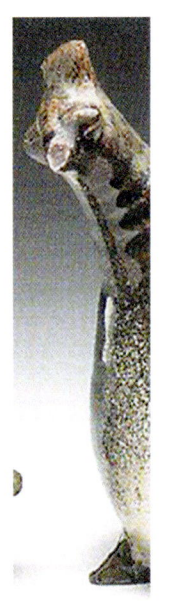
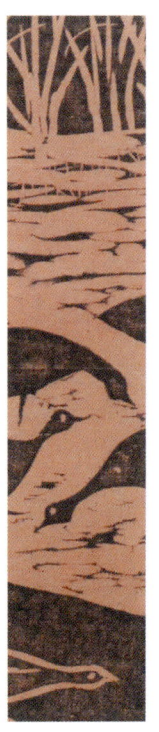
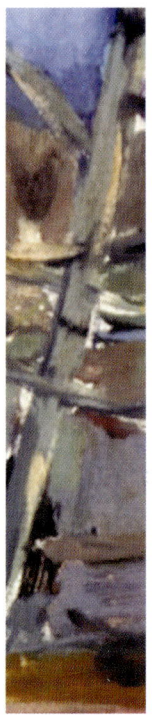
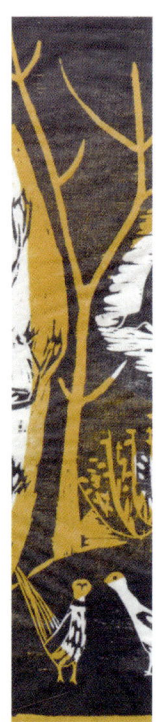
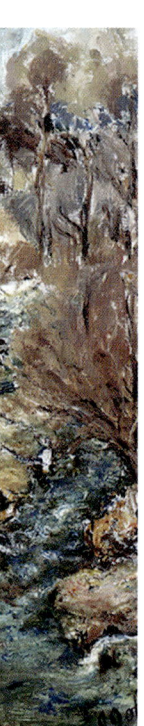